Praise for *Writing That Gets*

"This generous and wise book on writing and getting published is the culmination of Estelle Erasmus's vast experience as a writer, editor, mentor, and teacher. The advice, techniques, astute observations, and essay analysis will benefit all writers, whether novice or expert. If you want to stand out in a crowd of writers, read this book and gain Estelle's competitive edge."

— **William Dameron**, author of *The Lie* and *The Way Life Should Be*

"Estelle Erasmus has written a valuable resource with creative tips for veteran authors and aspiring writers alike. Inspiring and easy to follow, this book will get your ideas flowing and help your work get the audience it deserves."

— **Jen Maxfield**, Emmy Award–winning reporter and author of
*More After the Break: A Reporter Returns to
Ten Unforgettable News Stories*

"As a data scientist and former executive editor at Gallup, I truly appreciated the tips and commentary about the importance of data in a writer's research. *Writing That Gets Noticed* is essential beyond data, however, as I enjoyed the 'Estelle's Edge' tips throughout the book, pithy aphorisms that are illuminating."

— **Art Swift**, professor of political communications at American
University and host of *The Nexus with Art Swift* podcast

"Whether you're an aspiring writer wondering how to break in or a seasoned pro looking to up your game, *Writing That Gets Noticed* is a great guide to the world of writing and publishing from someone who's been there, done that, and taught others to do it as well. Filled with actual examples of articles, essays, and pitches that worked (and a few that didn't), this is a great tool to help you launch a successful writing career."

— **Minda Zetlin**, author *Career Self-Care:
Find Your Happiness, Success, and Fulfillment at Work,*
contributing editor of *Inc.*, and former president of the
American Society of Journalists and Authors

"The prolific, indefatigable, and astonishingly generous Estelle Erasmus has written the quintessential bible for aspiring writers. Not only is this book a must-have guide through the trials and tribulations, joys and elations of the publishing process, it is an intimate, highly entertaining exemplar of great storytelling and a gift to writers and readers alike."
— **Jenny McPhee**, author of *The Center of Things* and translator of *Family Lexicon* by Natalia Ginzburg

"Whether you're just launching your freelance writing career or years into it, this is an invaluable guide to everything you need to know about the craft and business of getting your work seen. It's quickly become my new go-to reference."
— **Wendi Aarons**, author of *I'm Wearing Tunics Now*

"This clear, user-friendly guide is filled with concrete, easy-to-follow advice. Estelle Erasmus demystifies the writing, pitching, and publishing process like a wise friend in your corner."
— **Dawn Raffel**, developmental editor, fiction editor at *Northwest Review*, and author of *Boundless as the Sky*

"Estelle Erasmus has spent years in the writing and editing trenches, and now she's surfaced to share all her best secrets. From practical exercises and checklists to insider information you won't find anywhere else, *Writing That Gets Noticed* is full of invaluable tips and tricks that won't just get you results — they'll get you published."
— **Noah Michelson**, editorial director of *HuffPost Personal* and host of the *D Is for Desire* podcast

"*Writing That Gets Noticed* is a must-read for writers, especially members of Gen Z, who want to break through the noise in today's fast-paced world of publishing and content creation."
— **Ava McDonald**, founder and CEO of Zfluence

"*Writing That Gets Noticed* is a tour de force in storytelling. Estelle Erasmus is a generous teacher with the spark that comes from having her own time on the stage. Readers will give this book a standing ovation."

— **Ken Fakler**, Emmy, Olivier, and three-time Tony Award winner and coproducer of *Dear Evan Hansen, Beautiful, Piano Lesson, Funny Girl,* and *Some Like It Hot*

"Upbeat and wise, *Writing That Gets Noticed* by Estelle Erasmus is an essential guide for nonfiction writers. From inspiration to publication and beyond, Estelle helps writers navigate the landscape, generously sharing from her deep well of experience."

— **Vanessa Hua**, author of *Forbidden City*

"Estelle Erasmus's *Writing That Gets Noticed* is the book I would hand to every new writer eager to make an impact and get their stories into publications that matter. Packed with actionable advice on landing pitches and stories at national outlets, it's also an essential guide to understanding what makes a good idea in the first place and building on your own storytelling strengths before you commit words to the page."

— **Alan Henry**, special projects editor at *Wired* and author of *Seen, Heard, and Paid: The New Work Rules for the Marginalized*

"This book is brilliant — exactly what every writer needs to stand out from the pack, navigate through the bumps and bruises of publishing, and thrive."

— **Michele Borba**, EdD, educational psychologist and bestselling author of *Thrivers: The Surprising Reasons Why Some Kids Struggle and Others Shine*

"If you want to invest in yourself as a writer, no matter what age or stage you're in, this book is the ticket to growth. Estelle Erasmus shares savvy strategies and a plan to give you an edge in publishing."

— **Bobbi Rebell**, CFP®, founder of Financial Wellness Strategies and author of *Launching Financial Grownups: Live Your Richest Life by Helping Your (Almost) Adult Kids Become Everyday Money Smart*

WRITING
THAT GETS
Noticed

WRITING THAT GETS Noticed

Find Your Voice, Become a Better Storyteller, Get Published

Estelle Erasmus

New World Library
Novato, California

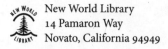
New World Library
14 Pamaron Way
Novato, California 94949

Text design by Tona Pearce Myers

Library of Congress Cataloging-in-Publication Data

Names: Erasmus, Estelle, author.
Title: Writing that gets noticed : find your voice, become a better storyteller, get published / Estelle Erasmus.
Description: Novato, California : New World Library, 2023. | Includes bibliographical references and index. | Summary: "An experienced magazine editor and writing instructor shows aspiring writers of nonfiction how to get published. Topics include generating ideas, finding a personal voice, building a narrative, editing one's own work, and pitching editors. Includes real-life examples of successful essays and pitches, along with advice from acquiring editors"-- Provided by publisher.
Identifiers: LCCN 2023009364 (print) | LCCN 2023009365 (ebook) | ISBN 9781608688364 (paperback) | ISBN 9781608688371 (epub) Subjects: LCSH: Authorship--Vocational guidance. Classification: LCC PN153 .E77 2023 (print) | LCC PN153 (ebook) | DDC 808.02--dc23/eng/20230302
LC record available at https://lccn.loc.gov/2023009364
LC ebook record available at https://lccn.loc.gov/2023009365

First printing, June 2023
ISBN 978-1-60868-836-4
Ebook ISBN 978-1-60868-837-1
Printed in Canada on 100% postconsumer-waste recycled paper

New World Library is proud to be a Gold Certified Environmentally Responsible Publisher. Publisher certification awarded by Green Press Initiative.

10   9   8   7   6   5   4   3   2   1

For my husband, Werner, and daughter, Crystal.
You complete me.

Contents

Part 4: All about the Expert

Part 5: All about Editors and Editing

Part 6: Protecting Your Psyche

Part 7: Words of Wisdom

Introduction

I write entirely to find out what I'm thinking,
what I'm looking at, what I see and what it means.

— JOAN DIDION

Writing That Gets Noticed is the guidebook I wish I'd had when I was getting back into the spotlight as a freelance writer after a career as a magazine editor. I wanted to get my writing recognized and published, but it took trial and error for me to get where I wanted to be.

I want you to learn from my mistakes.

I want to save you those steps so you can be successful.

Throughout these pages you will find examples, strategies, creative exercises, resources, and my best pro tips, which I call "Estelle's Edge." I include advice from editors, the science behind why a piece of advice works, and stories from my life of editing magazines and developing writers' voices. I also share examples of my own essays and pitches and some from my students.

From the late 1990s until 2005, I was the editor in chief for a succession of national glossy consumer magazines and a beauty editor at *Woman's World*. I also wrote freelance articles about health, beauty, fitness, and relationships for hundreds of print publications and websites. I was briefly a stringer for *People* magazine and taught writing for magazines at New York University. Then I stepped out of the spotlight with life changes: marriage, infertility, and the birth of my daughter in midlife. I had a long stint of working in medical education. When I re-emerged in 2009, after my daughter, Crystal, was born, I was a newbie in a publishing field I no longer recognized — and which no longer recognized me.

To get back into the spotlight, I had to develop a strategy for getting published, getting noticed, showcasing my voice, and creating a social media profile. So I focused my creative energy on carving out my new identity. I started blogging and joined the mom influencer community. Although I never expected I would want to write for free, the thought of writing only what I wanted to write was empowering. My blog was called Musings on Motherhood and Midlife, and the subhead was "A Journalist's Transformative Journey." The blog covered parenting, humor, lifestyle, travel, fashion, beauty, and social good. I had a unique perspective: the wisdom of midlife coupled with the challenges of early motherhood. Mom bloggers formed a close-knit community, and I was proud to be part of it.

I was thrilled when I was offered a *Mom's Talk* column in my town Patch, a local news and information online platform, after reaching out to an editor when it was acquired by its former owner, AOL, in 2009. Despite my background as a magazine editor, I don't believe I would have been considered if I hadn't already been blogging about motherhood. For the column, I wrote about binkies, breastfeeding, and my quest for baby-free time, and I loved interviewing experts on parenting. I also became a contributing writer to *Easy Solutions*, a former A&P store publication, while editing for a publishing company.

In 2012 I ended up back in the spotlight, reading an essay I'd written about Crystal, as a cast member in the show *Listen to Your Mother*. I also won the first of my three BlogHer Voice of the Year Awards that year for an op-ed advocating for women's and mothers' rights, and my piece was selected to be in *The BlogHer '12 Voices of the Year* anthology, the first of many anthologies I would contribute to. I call my daughter my muse, because she inspired me to get back to what I truly love, writing.

In 2014 I moved back into mainstream markets with a personal essay in *Marie Claire* about a crazy former roommate. Since then, I have placed my essays and articles in hundreds of publications. In 2015, because I was so prolific, people wanted to know how I did it, so I became a writing coach, using my no-nonsense style and savvy strategies to help writers of all levels of experience find their voice, get noticed, and get published.

As my daughter grew, she continued to be my inspiration. After a trip to Vermont when she was hard to handle, I wrote a piece titled "My Child Is Out of Control" for the *Washington Post*. The piece was syndicated all over the world and discussed on ABC's *The View*. The editor, Amy Joyce, asked me to write a follow-up a year later, which was titled "My Child Is Still Out of Control." After a new babysitter contacted her male friend and introduced him to my pajama-clad daughter via FaceTime, I wrote about the new rules for babysitting and social media for the *Washington Post*. (My rule was "Nobody comes into the home, and that includes on social media.") In another piece of many I wrote for the *Washington Post*, I shared why it was positive for our marriage that we did not let our daughter sleep in our bed.

As Crystal became more social and neared her tweens, I focused on providing her with a resilience-building emotional toolkit. I wrote for the *Week* about powerful phrases every parent needs, like "No one is the judge and jury of your self-worth" and "I'm proud of you, but you should be proud of yourself." After researching the scientific benefits of getting a pet for *Your Teen*, and appearing on *Fox 5 News with Ernie Anastos* to discuss the findings in my article, we added a spirited Havanese puppy, Rose, to our family, joining our senior orange cat, Percy. In 2019, I once again became an adjunct instructor at New York University.

In 2019 I wrote "How to Bullyproof Your Child" for the *New York Times*. Attracting more than five hundred comments and trending as a top story for several weeks, it led to an appearance on *Good Morning America*, hundreds of letters, and an award from the American Society of Journalists and Authors (ASJA). I was even the focus of the newspaper's *Well* newsletter. I've since contributed several articles and essays to the *New York Times*.

I've stopped writing about my daughter as she is now a teenager, and I'm more focused on storytelling — and helping my students get published.

In 2020 I pitched an idea for a column to *Writer's Digest*'s editor in chief, Amy Jones, that I'd wanted to write for years. She loved it, so in 2021 I started writing *All About the Pitch*, a column in which I interviewed editors and analyzed pitches from freelance writers to show what works (and what doesn't), and why. I wrote the column for two years and loved the emails from readers saying how much they learned.

In response to the demand for more publishing wisdom, I launched the *Freelance Writing Direct* podcast, with a cohost, covering the craft and business of writing, strategies to give writers a leg up in the marketplace, and informative interviews with authors and writers.

From my years working in medical education, I learned to love scientific studies, and I draw on plenty of them in this book. Cognitive studies show that the brain understands and remembers best when facts and skills are embedded in memory through experiential learning. That's one reason why my continuing education courses at NYU for adults, and my journalism courses there for high school students, incorporate a lot of real-life activities, such as demonstrations, editor interviews, exercises, pairing up for interviews, journaling, virtual and in-person field trips, and class readings of student work. I also wrote an article for *Wired* about how to keep kids engaged in school — with games.

Words Are Like Music

I studied opera as a child, and I am a trained mezzo-soprano. I love opera and its clearly defined beginning, middle, and end — its narrative arc.

Words, with their rhythm and cadence, are just as powerful as music, and they have the power to create stories that mesmerize and enchant us. I want you to come away from this book with the belief that words can change lives and the understanding of how that alchemy works, so you can do it yourself.

That proverb "Give a man a fish, and you feed him for a day; teach him how to fish and you feed him for a lifetime" is one I live and teach by.

Just as my clients and students keep me in their back pocket, ready to help them find their voice and get published, like a literary fairy godmother, my wish is for this book to be viewed and used as a source of inspiration and encouragement to readers and writers.

PART ONE

Generation Station

CHAPTER ONE

Creative Alchemy

Mining Your Life for Ideas

As you start to walk on the way, the way appears.
— JALĀL AL-DĪN MUHAMMAD RŪMĪ

I have had many fallow periods in my life where the creativity just wouldn't come. After the birth of my daughter, I struggled to write anything. And how could I? I'd put all my energy and motivation into dealing with painful, invasive infertility treatments and becoming a mother in my forties. So I forgave myself. I decided to treat myself well and hope my creative voice would come back.

I wrote in a blog post:

Kids are work. Important work; but I want my words back.

During the first year of motherhood, my creative output was extremely low. The words that had always flowed just wouldn't. And I didn't know how to bring them forth.

That is why it was such a surprise when I woke up the day after taking my daughter to the library for a reading group and wrote about the experience. Suddenly, the words flowed again.

Estelle's Edge: Every writer has fallow periods, but your words will come back, just as mine did and always do. Trust in the process.

Many writers want to write and have lots of ideas, but they just can't get them out. The adage about sticking your butt in the chair and writing sounds inspirational, but it's not that simple. When that feeling of futility strikes (and it does for everyone), I reassure them it's part of the process and suggest remedies for getting unstuck. If the muse just won't manifest, here are a few ways supported by scientific evidence to knock down those roadblocks so you can build something lasting with your words and achieve your goals.

Thirteen Ways to Find Your Best Ideas

1. Repetitive action relaxes. So let your creative energy flow while doing something over and over again, such as folding laundry, mailing out batches of holiday cards, vacuuming, coloring a complex geometric design (your own or from a coloring book), or doing dishes. According to a study done at the University of Oregon, rote activity allows the mind to wander, making it easier to tap into our creativity.
2. Still at a loss for words? Get those endorphins pumping. To generate creativity, try working out on a treadmill, going for a bike ride, or running outside. Research demonstrates that aerobic exercise allows the growth of new cells in the hippocampus, the part of the brain involved with memory, idea generation, and imagination.
3. Music helps you access the creative, expressive part of the brain and get yourself into a relaxed state. Some writers use classical music to kickstart their writing because it has no distracting lyrics.
4. For a change of pace, head to a local coffee shop or library to write. Research shows that being around people working on their own creative projects encourages you to copy

them — infusing you with a shared work ethic, concentration, and productivity.

5. Can't seem to get started? Change the format. Turn your essay into a poem or letter. Or try a different font. I change my font from Times New Roman to Garamond or Comic Sans when I'm stuck. I also try writing essays in the form of a poem or letter to inspire my creativity. Changing the mode or format of your writing breaks up established patterns of thinking and encourages your brain to make new connections.

6. Water can wash your blocks away. Many writers find their best creative ideas or solutions while taking a shower. The more relaxed and disengaged you are — like when you're showering or bathing — the more dopamine your brain releases, spurring creativity, insights, and ideas. (Dopamine is a neurotransmitter that communicates messages between nerve cells in your brain and body and works as a feel-good reward center.)

7. Try taking a stroll. A slow twenty-minute walk can help you break through a creative slump. Researchers at Stanford University found that walking increases a person's creative output by 60 percent, compared with sitting. That's because walking offers the same boost to your endorphins and serotonin — hormones that help improve mood, cognition, and concentration — as an aerobic workout.

8. Engage in new experiences. Try a new restaurant, take a vacation (or a staycation), or see a new movie to disrupt thought patterns that keep you stuck. If I feel stymied, sometimes I stretch my brain by researching odd topics (best chocolate cake recipes, or why camels spit), or the topic I'm writing about. Our brains process familiar information quickly, but they are slower to organize and synthesize new information, which makes the experience more memorable and pleasurable. This state encourages creativity.

9. When you are blocked, try blocking your social media, too. Multitasking — in this case, switching between your writing and checking social media sites — overstimulates your brain,

causing inefficient and scrambled thinking. Try making a deal with yourself to write for an hour or two without checking or posting. Apps and extensions like StayFocused and Block Site allow you to block distracting websites or set daily time limits for each site.

10. Go ahead and have a mental margarita. Take a break from writing for an hour, a day, or a weekend. The mind needs downtime to think, ponder, incubate, and create. A study from the Netherlands found that even when we take a break from a project, our unconscious mind continues to process it. When I veg out, I spend time with family, watch TV (I love to binge on *Real Housewives*), or read a novel. I always come back refueled because my brain has been working in the background to crystallize my ideas.

11. Try writing in free flow. In *Bird by Bird*, her influential guide to writing, Anne Lamott says, "Write shitty first drafts." This advice is empowering. Many of my students edit as they write, which is a mistake. Your first draft is not the time to parse or refine your words; that will come later. Sit down and write as much as you can, without worrying about grammar, spelling, word count, structure, or phrasing.

12. Give yourself a deadline — a short one, about fifteen minutes. Some people set a timer. See how much you can write without thinking about what you are writing, or second-guessing yourself during that time span. When the timer sounds, give yourself a five-minute reward, like a cup of tea or a small piece of dark chocolate, and then do it again. A short deadline reduces the pressure on you because you know it will be over soon, so all you need to do is get to work. You might feel compelled to keep writing, even after the buzzer sounds, and that's okay. You can continue, or you can stop, give yourself a break and a reward, and then do it again for an even longer time, perhaps twenty minutes or more.

13. As I write my first draft, when I am at a loss for a word, a phrase, or a quote, I don't stop writing. I simply write the word *SOMETHING* in caps (you can choose your own term, like

BLANK, FILL IN, or *WORD*). The point of doing this is to keep the words coming without censoring yourself. You will find it easy to fill them in once you get to the editing step.

My goal is always the same: to get to a flow state, a positive mental state in which you are so completely absorbed in a task that you lose your sense of time and place. It's a destination that isn't easy to reach, but getting there is worth the wait. So trust in the process, and you will find your words once again.

CHAPTER TWO

Incubating Ideas

Everybody walks past a thousand story ideas every day.
The good writers are the ones who see five or six of them.
Most people don't see any.

— ORSON SCOTT CARD

When I was a magazine editor in the mid-1990s, I took a business assessment quiz to find out my strengths (and weaknesses). I discovered that I specialize in quick starts, launching concepts, and presenting them (through teaching and speaking). The quiz identified me as intuitive and visionary, with a knack for finding alternatives and discovering original ways to get work done.

My ability to synthesize ideas has led me in unexpected directions. When I was senior editor at *American Woman* magazine, we focused on single and divorced women and created our own dating column, called *Dial-a-Dreamdate*. I used my new expertise to generate a side career for myself as the Dating Diva and taught relationship classes at the Learning Annex and Seminar Center such as "Power Dating, or How to Marry the Man of Your Dreams." I also spoke as a dating expert on TV talk shows. When I appeared on *Rolanda*, I was surrounded by six single women dressed in bridal gowns (not my idea), all desperate to get married.

My experiences created fodder for a column in a short-lived magazine for singles, as well as articles on dating, mating, and relating that I pitched to major magazines. I also got my own *Love Coach* column in one of the magazines I edited. But when I decided to settle down with Werner, now my husband, I decided I didn't want to be a dating expert anymore, and I put the kibosh on a dating-advice book proposal my agent had been shopping around to publishers.

While I thrive with short-term projects, such as teaching classes and coaching students, to complete a project that stretches over several months, I must break the task down into smaller units with multiple deadlines and fool my brain into thinking it is a short-term undertaking.

Coming Up with Ideas

One of the questions I'm often asked is "How can I come up with ideas?" Even if you are creative, that can be challenging. One way to start is to consider what you talk about at brunch with your friends. What problems or issues are they dealing with or solving? What are other people talking about that you might overhear while at a restaurant, shopping, or people watching? What books, articles, or essays have you read, and what do they make you think about? What have you seen on television or in the movies? What is important to you?

Mining your life for writing ideas is a productive way of brainstorming. But professional writers also need to understand how to find ideas in the zeitgeist that will appeal to an editor (your first reader) and how to package those ideas to make them timely, relevant, and interesting or provocative.

Mapping Template: Defining Yourself and Your Interests

Creating a visual map of who you are, what you care about, and what's going on in the world that's related to your sense of self is a great way to generate writing ideas. Once you've set up the template as described below, allow five to fifteen minutes every day to look at it and add to it. You'll be surprised at how well it works.

Creating Your Template

Take a piece of paper and separate it into four sections or a four-slice pie chart. If you run out of space, just add more sections.

If brainstorming on paper is not your speed, you can use an online tool like Google Jamboard (which lets you add photos and gives the option for you to journal with others) or another interactive journaling format app like Padlet. You can also do an online search for interactive journals.

Step 1: Focus on You

In this section, note everything that defines you and all your experiences. After all, you are going to write an essay or article that only you can write. So who are you? What makes you stand out? Are you an adoptive parent? An empty nester? Did you climb Mount Kilimanjaro? Start running races in midlife? Or perhaps you are an expat? Did you get married early in life? Does someone in your family suffer from an unusual medical condition? Do you have a deadbeat dad? Whatever your situation or experience, write it down. The more passionate or obsessed you are about it, the better. Include the communities you are part of.

My list includes the following: I got married and had my daughter in midlife; I am klutzy; I have pivoted many times in my career; I had a devastating ectopic pregnancy; I have worked as a magazine editor in chief; and I had an abusive therapist as a teen. I write about it all. Add to your list every day as new situations emerge in your life.

Step 2: Spotlight News Items

Every morning, check the news on TV (CNN, Fox, ABC, PBS, local stations) and check online and in newspapers for stories that tie in with your interests or experiences. Look at popular movies or TV shows and social media to put a timely spin on your ideas. List interesting items in a second section of your map, next to the one about you. The idea is to connect the news items with your own experience. If you are an avid bowler and a new study shows that bowling increases intelligence, add that. If a celebrity is in the news for experiences like yours, such as adopting a child from a developing country or dealing with a deadbeat dad, write it down. Is an expat starting up a new website for women who followed their partners abroad? You get the picture. You've now added the element (also sometimes called the *peg*) that shows why the reader or editor should care about your topic.

> *Estelle's Edge*: Many editors reach out to people on social media if they see a post that could become a story. It's always helpful if you can peg a personal essay to a celebrity event, a news story, or something provocative that makes an editor take notice.

Step 3: Accentuate Assistance from Alerts, Journals, and Newsletters

To connect your story to current events, you need to know what's going on. Sign up for online alerts (with Google and news platforms) using keywords related to the ideas and subjects that interest you. Authors researching a nonfiction book often set up alerts on their topic so they learn about new information or studies as soon as they come out. Add pertinent information from alerts into the third section of your chart.

Longer, more specific search strings get better-targeted results: for example, enter "new studies on health and happiness in women in midlife" rather than "health in women in midlife" or "studies on midlife women's health."

Sign up for email newsletters from organizations or associations related to topics that interest you. These organizations often publish useful fact sheets, press releases, or reports online (check the "Media" or "Press" section of the site).

These associations' websites are especially useful if you write about health. Every major health association publishes a journal (some are pricey, but you can write them off your taxes as a cost of doing business), and many offer free email newsletters summarizing the latest research. If you are interested in psychology, sign up to receive weekly notifications tailored to your interests on the latest psychological research in APA PsycInfo, from the American Psychological Association. If you want to write about your struggle with type 2 diabetes, look for recent research on the website of the American Diabetes Association.

Other sources to scan for interesting studies and research include Medpage Today for medical news, ScienceDaily, newsletters from SmartBrief, and theSkimm, a curated news feed that you can tailor to your interests. You can also sign up for EurekAlert from the American Association for the Advancement of Science. Wherever you sign up, save links to interesting studies, and each time you find a trend that has possibilities, add it to your template.

Step 4: Title Your Ideas As If You Were Pitching Them

Pick a few ideas based on your mapping template and quickly draft catchy titles for them. Play with alliteration, vary the length (between five and ten words), and try for wording that will excite, engage, or enrage the reader, or sound a call to action. If you know the publication you want to publish in, try modeling your title on their titles.

> *Estelle's Edge*: Part of your "sell" is the title. Often an editor will offer an article assignment to a writer based on a compelling headline, even if the pitch isn't fully fleshed out. I always tell my students to come up with a tantalizing or provocative title that tells the story of their essay or proposed article. I pitched "How to Bullyproof Your Child" with that title to the *New York Times*, and I submitted another essay with the title "The Doula Who Saved Me from Depression," which became "The Doula Who Saved My Life," to the *Washington Post*.

Remember, your experience and viewpoint (aka spin), plus relevant data, expert interviews and quotes, or a connection to current events, make publishing gold. I've mined my experiences of having a child in midlife, getting married later to someone not of my culture, and working with millennials. You have your own life to draw on.

The Six-Word Memoir

Another exercise to get your creative juices flowing is the six-word memoir — using a few words to hone the idea of who you are. One of my six-word memoirs is "Midlife mom finds self writing/teaching." According to legend, Ernest Hemingway placed a bet with his friends that he could write a short story in six words. They took the bet, and he quickly wrote down six words on a napkin and passed it around. They were "For sale, baby shoes, never worn." This is maybe the best narrative arc (beginning, middle, and end) anybody has ever seen.

Journal Your Way to Your Story

If you don't already keep a journal, you might want to start. Many writers swear by their morning notes. I like to call them "life notes." Mine include dreams, memories, musings, and bits of dialogue, plus jottings on people's characters, situations, and observances.

There are benefits to writing your journal in longhand. A study published in *Frontiers in Psychology* found that the regions of the brain associated with learning and creativity were more active when subjects completed a writing task by hand instead of on a keyboard. Apparently the act of forming letters by hand involves parts of the brain that deal with emotion. The study also discovered that writing by hand promoted "deep encoding," so you are more likely to retain what you write. Typing does not produce the same results.

Not everyone wants to write by hand, despite the research. If typing is easier for you, use a word-processing app on your computer or tablet. But you can also get creative with electronic journaling. Some journaling apps allow you to use audio and pictures as well as text. Free apps solely for voice journaling include Murmur, Journify, and Voice Diary. Search online for other options. You can also use the voice memo app on your phone and write up your entries later.

Effective Journaling Elements

If you want your journal to help you tell stories that engage readers' attention and stir their emotions, it needs to be more than a rote accounting of your activities. Think of your diary from your teen years: "I went here and did this, and he said that." The result is a catalog of events without any insight. As Vivian Gornick points out in *The Situation and the Story*, a good essay needs to show both the outer (the situation) and the inner emotional underpinnings (the story). It has to be more than a chance to vent or indulge your revenge fantasies.

When I wrote "The Doula Who Saved My Life" for the *Washington Post*, I wrote about my emotional state of mind when I was pregnant.

> Then the night terrors started. In between crying jags, anxiety, sadness and a feeling of impending doom, nobody — including me — realized that I was dealing with antepartum depression.

And I shared the evolution of my faith in the doula.

> As I echoed her chants and affirmations, my fears began to dissipate, along with my distrust of the birth process.

Imagine you are writing a scene from a movie. Use all your senses to fill in the details of the scene (smell, feel, taste, etc.). After I had an ectopic miscarriage, I used my journal to capture the sterile environment where I got an injection from the nurse, the sunglasses I wore day and night to hide my tears from my three-year-old daughter, and my husband's stoic demeanor. That allowed me to access those emotions and details when I wrote an essay about it years later.

So write down bits of dialogue in your journal that are provocative — forget the pedestrian snippets of dialogue ("Hi, how are you?" "I'm fine"), and go with the more explicit "You made me miss my exit," or the way your partner always says, "I've got this."

Estelle's Edge: As with writing stories, start with the inciting incident — the point when something happened — or the most provocative moment in the dialogue. Sometimes starting in the middle is what will make your journal most useful when you want to mine it for an essay or article years later.

IDEA GENERATION CHECKLIST

❏ What are people talking about in your circles or in conversations you overhear?

❏ What is trending on social media and blogs?

❏ Are you filling out your mapping template every day?

❏ Are you signed up for newsletters on topics that interest you?

❏ What events in the news are connected to your personal situation?

❏ Are there cultural events, TV shows, books, movies, or podcasts that you connect with and want to write about?

❏ Are you collecting research, studies, polls, and statistics to use?

❏ Are you keeping a folder of ideas?

❏ Is there a national holiday coming up that you can connect to your own experience?

❏ Have you written your own six-word-memoir?

❏ Are you keeping a journal?

CHAPTER THREE

Finding and Honing Your Voice

There is no greater agony than bearing an untold story inside you.
— MAYA ANGELOU

It took me a long time to find my voice. Not my singing voice — my writer's voice. Yes, I was a magazine editor and wrote columns and articles for the magazines I worked for, as well as other publications, but mostly I approached my work in a journalistic way, keeping my own voice out of my writing.

After 9/11, the work I had done launching publications for other publishers dried up, and I pivoted into the field of medical education. I learned valuable skills in interpreting medical studies, speaking to physicians, and leading teams that created continuing medical education programs for physicians.

As my daughter became an active toddler, I found myself focusing on women's issues. After being active in my local chapter of Mothers & More, I was invited to join the board of directors for the nonprofit organization, which focused on having society and government recognize and value the invisible, unpaid work of mothering — the constant responsibilities of cooking, cleaning, chauffeuring, making appointments, planning, and managing. Because that was a goal I felt strongly about, I became an accidental activist in my goal of separating the role of mother from the work of mothering.

Two years later, I learned about *Listen to Your Mother*, a nationwide series of readings created by Ann Imig, in which authors, writers, bloggers, and performers read their original essays celebrating motherhood in all its complexity, diversity, and humor. The producers wanted original stories that "displayed something that's totally you — your feelings about motherhood."

Of all the journalistic pieces I had written during my career, none of them had showcased my own voice. But I had written an essay about my daughter when she was eighteen months old, taking center stage at a Mommy-and-me reading group at the library. Defying the dictates of sitting and being quiet, she stood up and danced. I expected her performance to make people feel angry, but her joyful dancing captivated them, making me ponder my own possibilities and wishing I could feel as unconcerned about my effect on others.

Although I'd made numerous TV and radio appearances when I was a magazine editor, I was nervous about reading my piece for the audition because I'd been out of the spotlight for so long, and this was *my* voice, my personality, my expression of hopes and dreams and fears for my daughter. I didn't want to hide behind my impartial journalist's mask — and I couldn't. In a way I'd never done before, I expressed my frustration and emotions about parenting my daughter. That was when I discovered my voice, which is hopeful, enthusiastic, and a little funny, while looking back on the wisdom I've achieved just living my life — my midlife wisdom.

For the first time, I wrote without thinking of a reader or an audience. I wrote just for myself.

A week later, I was invited to join the show. We had two months to rehearse. Everyone in the show was a mother, and everybody was supportive. That experience melded my passions of writing, performing, and storytelling.

Here is a passage from my essay "And She Danced," which showed my voice for the first time and gave life to my emotions.

I watched my daughter spin around the floor in reckless abandon, her feet moving in a wild motion, to some music in her mind. The music first carried her toward the other mothers and children and then away; I felt her palpable joy. I worried that the other moms would resent my child's insistence on taking center stage, but I saw smiles on their faces instead of the disapproving frowns I feared. I marveled at the wonder that is my daughter as she moved. She acted so clearly in the moment. No worries, fears or thoughts for the future interfered with her actions.

I found my voice, and you can find yours, too.

A Voice Is Like a Song

The key to getting your writing noticed is to develop your voice. Like the voice of a great singer, a writer's voice has its own character and energy. Think about it: you can always tell when Rhianna, Kelly Clarkson, or Barbra Streisand is singing just from listening to the first few notes. A writer's voice is like music, too. It creates mood and gets attention. And like a fingerprint, it is yours only. It shows your personality, your wit, your idiosyncrasies, and your way with words. It reflects the way you view the world, offering the reader a combo platter of your experiences, attitude, approach, and favorite phrases.

Your tone can also be revealing: it can be funny, dramatic, skeptical, grandstanding, snarky, or all-knowing. But while tone can change from project to project, your voice remains constant. Your voice is what engages an editor, and eventually, a reader. It makes them feel connected to you and curious about you.

Your voice is revealed by the tense of your verbs and the expressions you choose. Are you writing that a sunset looks like a kaleidoscope of color, or like runny eggs thrown against a skyline? Whatever phrasing you choose, your voice is distinct. It is what makes you, well, you.

The way to get someone to forget you is to write in a boring manner, with lots of esoteric thoughts, musings, and meanderings that go nowhere. A good voice can enhance and elevate any story, whether it's about an abortion, a long marriage, coming out, a work catastrophe, or a celebrity. It can come through even in impersonal reported pieces. Think of Pulitzer Prize–winning stories you've read with riveting narrative arcs.

> *Estelle's Edge*: When writing your essay, write it for yourself, without focusing on an audience or publication. That will allow your words to flow, and your voice to emerge.

You want your voice to make an impact, to make the editor and reader want to follow your story.

Here are some of the elements that help create a writer's voice.

Giving Attitude

Are you funny, silly, outrageous, willing to break the rules to get attention?

Ivy Eisenberg showed her voice in a piece she wrote for Narratively, which I edited, on how she came up with the idea of a custom corporate fortune-cookie business focused on Yiddish sayings, called Work Favors the Fortune-ate, to escape the corporate drudgery of working in IT. The fortunes had IT-related sayings on the front and Yiddish sayings on the back. Her voice comes through as she describes a mandatory "team-meeting-slash-luncheon-slash-dessert-swap" in the week before the December holidays, comparing her coworkers' creations to her fortune cookies.

Amy, who's missed all of her work deliverables all year, has turned out 100 chocolate snowballs with perfectly crisp outsides, covered in powdered sugar snow. Sandy, who works so hard in the office I never imagined she would set foot in a kitchen, has fashioned perfect miniature green wreaths out of Corn Flakes and Red Hots, with bright green icing. Janet shows up with sleighs made of Christmas candies. She has driven through three states to get here, yet her sleighs are fastened by melted peppermints, with such expert engineering precision they could tackle a sleigh ride in a blizzard. And Joey produces his "remarkable" chocolate pecan cookies. He's been touting their re-markability all fall, but there isn't actually anything remarkable about them. They're just cookies (no humor or education or brilliance in *his* cookies). In the middle of this fabulous buffet is my Rubbermaid con-tainer with the stupid, cloaking tea towel.

At dessert time, I whip off the tea towel and declare: "Time for dessert." Everyone is filling their plates with the other desserts, but no one is taking a fortune cookie. I walk around with the bin to each person and say, "Here, take one." Everyone politely takes one. They work for me. They have no choice. But no one is eating them.

I walk over to Joey.

"Joey, open yours. Read it."

He obliges. "May you have more bugs in your code than you have in this cookie."

No one smiles. "Read the back," I command.

Joey struggles. "Chaz — a — ray...Chaz a?"

"CHAZERAI!" I correct him. [In Yiddish, *chazerai* is garbage or junk, or food that is awful.] Joey's from Canada. He can't speak Yiddish.

Finding Your Rhythm and Syntax

How do you write your sentences? Are you like Hemingway, short, staccato, and to the point? Short sentences can connote urgency, anger, annoyance, or a feeling of being rushed. Do you prefer a flowing style of writing, with long, legato sentences letting the reader bask in the discoveries you are illuminating? Or do you combine these styles? Do you use repetition as a literary device and underscore your points by repeating words, phrases, or cadences? Do you write in asides (as I often do)? Do you use parentheses and em dashes? (Really — who doesn't?) Do you use alliteration? I love alliteration and use it a lot. In a story for Yahoo I started a sentence by saying I was deeply in love with my "conservative Cupid."

For a story I wrote for Romper about the time when a fake Uber driver tried to pick up me and my daughter, I tried to convey urgency with short sentences. I wrote:

I looked at the license plate and then checked it against the profile to confirm it matched. I'd taken many Ubers before, and it always matched. This time it didn't.

Surprised, I checked again. No match. Then the man who had driven up got out of the car (why he did this confused me because we didn't have luggage).

"Hi. Let's go," he said jovially striding over to where I stood with my daughter and mother. As he did this, I saw his visage matched the tiny photo of his scruffy face.

"No," I said. "We're not getting in. Your license plate doesn't match the license on your profile." I motioned to my daughter to move farther away next to where my mother was standing.

"I was in a snowstorm and had to make a change," the man argued with me, moving closer. "Get in the car. It's OK."

No it wasn't.

"We're not getting in. Please cancel the ride," I said loudly.

He continued to argue with me, as I gathered my family and walked back into the security of the building.

In contrast, when I wrote about the early days of motherhood for Parenting.com, I used a more languorous, poetic style.

As the doctor checked her vitals and my husband counted her 10 perfect fingers and toes, I realized I had achieved what no amount of clips or professional accolades could ever duplicate: my body had produced a miracle.

Choosing Your Words

Do you have favorite words or pet phrases? Do you stick in unusual words to get attention? I keep an eye out for new or interesting words that I want to use. I put them in a list and refer to it later in the editing process, so I can try out the words that I've collected. For example, in a piece for *Salon*, about dealing with the challenges of my aging parents at the same time I was navigating the burgeoning independence of my toddler, I used the word *detritus*, which I'd been saving to try out.

I watched as my parents methodically divested themselves of the detritus of their lives. In record time, they sold their co-op of 40 years, held a furniture fire sale — including heirloom pieces I had no place to store — and brought their leased car back to the dealership.

I once fell in love with the word *unspooled* and used it in an essay about my dad for the *New York Times*:

> On our last call, I told Dad how much I loved those carefree times from childhood. "I'm sorry, Estelle, I don't remember," he said, his voice cracking. "I forget a lot of things." "That's OK, Dad." I was upset, too, that a memory so dear to me had unspooled from Dad's mind. But I knew how to bring him back. "Want to hear a song?" "Sure," he replied.

Sharing Your Philosophy of Life

Are you an optimist, or do you think of the world as a scary place? Do you see intrigue at every turn? Are you competitive? Are you sugar sweet (even to your enemies)? Are you action-oriented or more passive? Yes, all these traits come through in your writing.

For a piece I wrote for *Good Housekeeping* about fighting with my husband, you can tell my philosophy on fighting:

> I joke to my friends that when my hubby and I fight it's like the *Clash of the Titans*. I think it's no secret that when two strong personalities get together they release a phalanx of emotions — resulting in conflict.

After saying that bickering is like a sport, even a form of stress relief, I take it even further:

> We could be Olympic medalists, although we'd probably argue about who rightfully won the gold. I am a stay-at-home writer and mom, and I love to do my jousting with words. He is a businessman, stoic, able to calmly find the holes in my passionate championing of an idea or action.

In a piece I wrote for Yahoo about meeting my husband's mother for the first time when I had a broken foot and was strung out on Percocet, I showed how I act when I feel threatened:

"So, are you treating my boy right? Do you cook for him?" his mother asked in a rolling accent, startling me out of my drug-induced stupor. Her perfectly applied lipstick, carefully coiffed hair, and subtly sophisticated blouse and slacks contrasted with my slovenly, sweat-stained appearance. Historically, when challenged I have a bad habit of becoming grandiose. Squaring my hunched shoulders I haughtily replied. "No, I don't cook. I don't need to. And even if I wanted to, I'm hardly able to stand on my feet these days." She stared at me and shook her head.

Being Vulnerable, Not Pitiful

You want to show your humanity in your writing without projecting "Woe is me." The willingness to be vulnerable (without dumping on the reader by oversharing every detail of your life) is key to succeeding and thriving as a writer. Your vulnerability should move the story forward, not stop it in its tracks.

During a class I taught at NYU, Salina Jivani wrote about moving into a haunted house when her family first emigrated from Kuwait. The story was published in *HuffPost Personal*.

At first, they didn't want to accept that we were dealing with a ghost. We continued to look for other logical explanations for the activity we were experiencing, but there were none.

One day, my mom gathered her confidence and, using her fractured English to string enough words together, asked our neighbor if she knew anything about the history of our home. The woman leaned in conspiratorially and whispered that the previous owner had passed away inside of it. The house had apparently been her pride and joy, and she'd been particularly obsessed with organizing her kitchen a specific way. We were officially spooked.

My mom began to pray every night after that. She would extract her rosary beads from a wooden tissue holder, roll out a red rug, and squeeze her eyes shut as she swayed back and forth in deep concentration. The musky scent of incense sticks burning from our kitchen wafted beyond the front door to the street. She believed that no evil would befall a house filled with prayers and praise for God. Because we were poor, moving simply wasn't an option, and my parents tried to face the situation with as much grace as they could, determined to make the best out of a circumstance we couldn't escape.

The reader understands that the family is poor, but because Salina is describing vividly how her mom relied on her religious background and prayed for her family, the reader becomes invested in the story and the family instead of just pitying them.

I wrote about my Holocaust-surviving Grandma Genia in an essay for *Brain, Child* magazine:

"I luff you, because you're sveet like a piece of chocolate," my Grandma Genia crooned in her thick, Yiddish accent, handing me a hunk of a Hershey bar. No exotic fare like Godiva for Grandma — she eschewed exports, even though she herself was one.

First, I personalize my grandmother through dialogue and her distinctive accent, so the reader can relate to her love of her granddaughter. Then I share the horrors:

Grandma had suffered bitterness in her life. When the Nazis first invaded Poland, my grandfather wanted to stay and fight. She convinced him to take their family — including baby Miriam, my mother, and flee. Escaping into the forest, they made their way to Russia. Their siblings and cousins couldn't get out, and perished in the Warsaw Ghetto uprising.

Then we go back to the joy, which leaves no room for pity:

Perhaps because she had thwarted death, Grandma treated life like an adventure. I rode horsey on her back for hours. After I threw Jell-O on the wall in the midst of a toddler tantrum, Grandma celebrated as if I were a budding Picasso. At a Bat Mitzvah, she joined me on the floor, scooping up chocolates showered from a piñata, even though the Holocaust had long since transformed her into an avowed atheist. "Family is de only ting dat matters," she would say.

I strove to portray Grandma Genia as a loving, complicated, and complete person. After she died, when I was consumed with fears about my pregnancy and guilt about forsaking my heritage by marrying someone outside my faith, she gave me a sign that all would be okay. I ended the essay with these words:

> Grandma Genia's love had left a permanent hug on my soul — and that of my unborn child. And when my daughter was born, while my parents beamed from the bema, we gave her the Hebrew name Gavira ("powerful ruler") to honor the woman who had fled a war-torn country to save her family, which ultimately gave me the freedom to choose mine.

In a piece I wrote for the anthology *Mothering through the Darkness*, I wrote about postpartum depression. Because of my family history, I knew I was at high risk for the condition, and I carefully prepared to stave it off. I vowed to my husband that for me, genetics would not be destiny. Then I was caught unawares as a malevolent melancholy manifested itself smack in the midst of my pregnancy. (I told you I love alliteration.)

> Nothing about my pregnancy went according to plan.
>
> With a bill of good health from my doctor, I was supposed to glowingly bask in nine months of bliss, while devouring bonbons and spreading bonhomie, much like the pregnant midlife celebrities we regularly see smiling on the covers of *People* magazine.
>
> Instead, severe, palm-sweating nausea presided over my days, making me dizzy and forcing me to feverishly suck on lemon ice pops — a panacea against fainting and throwing up. I never fainted, but I did vomit copiously before and after dinner each night like clockwork.
>
> Oddly, by the beginning of my third trimester I had gained seventy pounds while subsisting on a diet of pizza, watermelon, and fruit juice.

The reader might start out feeling sorry for me, but as I recount my funny and perhaps familiar travails, they also get to know me, and maybe see themselves in me, too.

To Discover Your Voice...

Phone a Friend

Ask a friend or partner to describe several strengths of your personality. Make sure you imbue your writing with those characteristics. Then have them read your story and ask them if it is exciting or boring. Ask them what makes them want to know more.

See a Show

Attend spoken-word performances, like *The Moth* and *Listen to Your Mother*, where writers read stories they have written. You will learn so much about voice by listening to them and will understand more about your own rhythms and cadences.

Read Aloud

Read aloud essays by writers whose voices you admire. Think about how you can showcase your voice by adding humor or metaphors to your writing.

Elevate Your Word Game

In TV, every word counts. That's how you need to approach your writing. Watch television with the captions on. Reading and listening simultaneously helps solidify the experience and gets you thinking in sound bites. Characters on TV express themselves through dialogue, so listen to how they speak. Jot down what they say, their phrasing and their tone (sad, happy, snarky, funny). Imagine how you would speak and act in the same situation, and use that reaction in your writing.

Deploy Dialogue

Starting with dialogue is a way of getting the reader into the story immediately, and it can work as an inciting incident, as long as the dialogue moves the story forward. For her essay on her struggle with infertility and the pressure to be a mother for AARP's *The Girlfriend*, a digital publication for women forty and over, my NYU student Tess Clarkson opened with a conversation with her partner that got to the heart of the matter:

> My future husband sat beside me on a Manhattan bench. "What's wrong? Where are you going?" Steve asked, aware of my coping mechanism of detaching.
>
> I felt flooded from a conversation I'd just had with my mentor, who drilled me about Steve, asked about my fertility and told me I'd get bored in the Midwest and should have a kid. At 43, I was a former Riverdancer turned Wall Street lawyer and unexpectedly had met Steve, a divorced father of three in Missouri, when I was in our home state caring for my father.
>
> "I shouldn't have let her ask such personal questions. My fertility doctor said I could have a baby for several more years." I began shaking. "I have more time to figure this out. We have more time."

Heidi Borst worked on a pitch in my NYU class for a story about bolstering her son's self-esteem. When it appeared in the *Washington Post*, her son's question served as an entrée into the piece:

> Rays of pride beamed from my 7-year-old's cherubic face as he held his drawing up for my assessment. "Ten out of ten?" he asked. Though I wanted to be honest (this artwork was far from his best attempt), my fear of triggering his harsh inner critic took over, and I nodded in approval.
>
> When providing feedback that might bruise my son's self-esteem, I'm ultra-careful. A borderline perfectionist, he's hard on himself and extremely sensitive to criticism. Still, I worried whether praising my son for a subpar effort was the right move. It felt good in the moment, but experts say that loading kids with validation, a common parenting perspective in the '90s, does more harm than good in the long run.

And in a piece for *Salon*, about an inappropriate therapist I went to as a teen, my opening line revealed the man's manipulative words:

"Do you think of me when you masturbate?" the man asked. The lights in the room had been switched off, the shades drawn. I couldn't see him, but I could sense him licking his lips in anticipation of my answer, like some old-time villain in a film noir.

"Yuck, no. That's gross," 16-year-old me replied, disgusted at the thought.

His name was Ron. He was my married, 45-year-old child psychologist. This mode of questioning was par for the course during our weekly therapy sessions.

"Come on. Don't I turn you on?" he cajoled.

"No. You don't."

My answer never changed, though he campaigned constantly as if one day it could.

"Why not?" he whined in the hurt tone of a hormonal teenager, which I found ironic because I was supposed to be the only hormonal teenager in the room.

Write Like No One Is Looking

Try writing up a dream you had, or note what you say when you talk back to the news, or to your pet when no one is around. That's how you'll get to hear your true voice.

EXERCISE: TAPE YOUR TALK

Dictate your story into an audio recorder, as if you were telling it to a friend, even before you write it down. Give it a narrative arc — a beginning and a middle, with an end that shows some sort of change or transformation. Then, before you write it down, listen to how you sound. It should help you capture the nuances of your personality. Then write the story up as a draft. Finally, edit out all the non sequiturs and sentence fragments in the oral version (they work for literary writing but not for consumer writing), and you will be telling your story in your voice.

Adding Voice to Reported Articles

Reported articles, by their nature, create distance between the writer and the reader because the journalist's natural voice is the third person. That can make it difficult for your personality to shine through. I've helped many students develop their voice in reported pieces with a simple strategy: add voice to your pieces by personalizing the beginning of the piece. It doesn't have to be long, just a few sentences. Then add another personal slant at the end.

Here is an example from my former student Cheryl Maguire's *New York Times* article "How to Stop Thinking Your Teen Is Pushing Your Buttons":

> My 14-year-old daughter constantly abandons her coat on the floor and leaves half-eaten food in the living room and crumpled papers in the hall. I end up cleaning after her, which I've repeatedly told her makes me upset.

After quoting several experts and providing tips for parents, she ends on a personal note:

> I can accept that she will never be the next Marie Kondo, but I've seen progress for both of us. Now, when I see a coat on the floor, I try to remind myself to see only a coat, not an affront to my authority.
>
> My daughter has a sense of humor about it, too. When I told her I was writing about this, she announced with a smile: "I left my jacket at tennis practice, so it's not on the floor today."

Now, imagine if the writer had just launched into the article with an impersonal observation, something like this:

> At some point, most parents feel as if their teenager is acting in ways to intentionally make them angry. But experts say that the interaction is often more about how the parent responds than about the teenager's behavior.

This opening is informative, but it reads as impersonal and dry. The personal opening provides a nice segue into the more journalistic part of the piece. And that's what gives it voice.

CHECKLIST FOR FINDING YOUR VOICE

❏ Did you watch television with the captions on to hear and see examples of characters' voices, jotting down dialogue that resonated with you?

❏ Did you read your story aloud and record it to discover your natural rhythm, cadences, and pauses?

❏ Did you write your piece as if no one was looking?

❏ If you have a story with sad elements, are you showing your vulnerability without allowing the reader to pity you, by sharing specific details illuminating your character?

❏ When you read your work out loud, do you sound like yourself, with your usual turns of phrases and quirky words?

❏ Did you read your writing to a friend or family member and ask them if it sounds like you?

CHAPTER FOUR

At Your Readers' Service

The message behind the words is the voice of the heart.
— JALĀL AL-DĪN MUHAMMAD RŪMĪ

When I was studying communications at Boston University, my class was assigned the project of creating a new magazine with an interesting concept. Nearly everyone chose to do a men's or women's magazine, or a fashion magazine. I went in a different direction.

My magazine was a fashion and beauty magazine for female prostitutes, called *Bu$iness Beauty*, complete with ads for feminine and beauty products, like makeup, hair color, and depilatories for the bikini area; luxury products like watches, perfume, jewelry, and fur coats; plus pregnancy tests, lingerie, and breast-enhancing devices. My cover lines were: "Violence and the Single Woman," "Herpes," "The New Contraception," "Sexual Confidence," "Sex Survey," "You!" "Looking Great," and "Two Jobs … At Once." The articles were intended to be service-oriented and empowering. They covered the beauty, health, practical, and erotic aspects of sex work and being on your feet. My makeup article covered doing the perfect makeup in three minutes flat; my medical article covered bunions; my money article talked about being scared to apply for credit; the fashion spread featured outfits for seduction; and the cover art featured a group of strong woman decked out in gold lamé dresses facing, but not looking at, a man with his back to the camera. One woman looked directly at the camera, in the style of *Cosmopolitan*'s covers. While it wasn't a candidate for publication according to the mores of the time, my teacher appreciated the thought and creativity behind it, and I received an A. I think it amused him and got his attention, but my project was mainly about sharing information in a reader-friendly way for my audience — prostitutes. That was my risqué entry into service journalism.

So what is service journalism? It provides information that helps the reader. That's it. Can someone who reads your work get a better deal, save money, take better care of themselves, or improve their relationships and parenting through the information and advice you have shared?

I cut my teeth on the concept while working as a beauty editor for *Woman's World*, traveling around the country with a team of hair and makeup people and stylists in a Winnebago doing makeovers for readers, but also speaking to experts, reading their books, and scouring them for tips I could include in my stories and columns.

The key is to package advice in a way that makes it appear fresh and new. What can you offer that is interesting and surprising? Once you determine that, you can craft your piece around the tips.

Early in my career I focused on writing how-to stories, sharing tips, expert advice, and experience. To break up the copy on the page and make it easier to read, I used subheads and sidebars — strategies that I use in my writing to this day. The "Estelle's Edge" tips in this book are a form of service journalism. In fact, this entire book is service oriented.

An editor once told me content can be divided into three categories: informational/utility (providing information people are searching for), supportive (helping readers with issues), and heartwarming (offering stories that are relatable). Each of those categories has a service element.

Now, I'm going to be honest: you won't get noticed from writing a ton of how-to articles without somehow getting your own story in there, but service journalism is the heart of most writing today. Every time I write a hybrid reported essay with tips and advice from experts, I am writing a service piece. And some of those service pieces have gone viral.

There are several ways to incorporate service into your writing.

Let Ledes Work for You

The lede is the first few sentences that identifies what the story is about. It should get readers' attention, make them want to read on, or pose a question that needs to be answered.

For service pieces the lede needs to get to the point of what the article is about so the reader knows that help for their problem or dilemma is on the way. Service journalism is never just straight reporting: it focuses on showing the reader why they will benefit from the information and creating a sense of urgency. Ledes I have written over the years include strong statements and compelling questions:

> Feeling a little under the weather? Give yourself an instant "quick fix" using acupressure, yoga moves, or specific foods. Best of all, these cures can be done anywhere.

> It is unanimous: All the experts agree that poor health habits take a devastating toll on your body, mood and appearance, leaving behind uncomfortable reminders of their nasty little visits. Premature wrinkles, irritated skin, muscle aches and general lethargy are just some of the side effects left by these hit and run habits. Arrest the beauty burglars — catch 'em in the act — before they make a clean getaway.

> OK — the honeymoon's over, and it's been over for a while. You're feeling less than connected with your significant other. It seems that all you do is watch TV and go to the movies. And you hardly ever talk anymore. What should you do?

> When you think of Cinco de Mayo celebrations, one thing probably comes to mind, for better or worse: tequila. In other words, parties that can sometimes render kids personae non gratae. But with a few tweaks to the usual party, you can throw a Cinco de Mayo that's decidedly kid friendly. And here's how.

Here is a longer lede from a story I wrote for *Your Teen* about scientific reasons to get a pet, which also included a quote from an expert:

Every parent with a tween or teen child has had that moment when your child begs you to get a pet. You may have considered it, but now there are more reasons than ever to make that leap into pet ownership. In my experience, though we have a cat who is attached to me, I am seriously thinking about getting my 10-year-old a dog to give her an "emotional support" of her own. It turns out my timing is right.

"If you are thinking of getting your child a pet, the best time is that tween time, around 11 years old," says Dr. Sheryl Ziegler, a Denver-based therapist specializing in anxiety and stress and author of *Mommy Burnout.* "The younger you get the pet before the massive challenges of being a tween, the better."

Here are some scientific reasons it makes sense to add a pet to your family — joining the 80 million U.S. households who have one — and the emotional, mental and social benefits to making that choice.

Here is a longer lede from my NYU student Cheryl Maguire for a piece that ran in the *Washington Post* on the importance of building social capital (the ability to obtain resources, favors, information, and goodwill through personal connections) when you have ADHD:

A group of medical school friends nominated Sasha Hamdani to create a memory book for their pregnant classmate. Hamdani worked hard on the task for several weeks. She printed pictures, gathered mementos and listened to stories about their friend. The book — meant to be a group gift for their classmate's baby shower — was more than 100 pages long, with items such as anatomy class doodles and fabric from a white medical coat.

On the flight to the baby shower from Kansas, Hamdani realized when she was searching in her bag for her headphones that she had left the memory book behind. She felt awful. "I'm sure that half of the people here thought I never even made anything," she recalled thinking.

Hamdani, now 35, was diagnosed with attention-deficit/ hyperactivity disorder at age 9. She frequently misplaces important items, runs late or struggles with a disorganized purse — all symptoms of ADHD. She has been labeled a "flake" because she forgets social engagements or to reply to texts. People have often told her, "If it was important to you, you'd remember."

The repercussions of such missteps are an important yet underdiscussed issue for children and adults diagnosed with ADHD.

Here's a much shorter lede from my article in the *New York Times* that went viral:

When my 10-year-old daughter was shunned by her friends a few years ago, we tried a surprisingly effective anti-bullying strategy.

And a lede with a straightforward approach to service from an article for *Your Teen*:

Parents of LGBTQ teens have difficulty discussing dating, sex and sex education with their kids (and may avoid the subject), according to a study by Northwestern University. Why?

My student Kimberly Nagy used this lede for a piece she pitched to *Your Teen* after a *Writer's Digest* pitching class with me:

It was the third night my 15-year-old daughter had fallen asleep on top of her books during what theatre kids call tech week — and I was concerned.

My NYU student Jessica Fleming pitched and wrote this longer lede for a hybrid piece for the *Washington Post* on why roughhousing is good for kids and how to keep it safe:

My 5-year-old launches himself from the couch, landing precariously close to his 7-year-old brother on the floor. The boys form a wild ball of limbs, rolling on our living room carpet. Multiple times a day, their energetic play drives me to the brink, and I shout, "STOP WRESTLING!"

But maybe I should encourage their horseplay instead? According to experts, the answer is yes.

Probing questions, direct statements, quotes from experts, and the promise of expert advice make the reader want to read on. Here are some basic service setups.

How-To Articles

The how-to format works best for technical topics (how to get your stylist to give you the perfect haircut for your face shape, cook lemon chicken, change a tire, or apply makeup on super-dry skin). It also works well for simple articles on parenting (e.g., how to swaddle a baby), health (how to avoid the common cold), and money management advice (how to save on your grocery bill). When I started out, I wrote beauty guides for *Teen* magazine, such as the "Beat the Heat Summer Beauty Guide," with how-to tips on every page. For example, in the section titled "No More Makeup Meltdown," I added the subhead "No-Fade Foundation," followed by this copy:

> To help foundation stay on your skin, smooth a lightweight, oil-free moisturizer onto clean, damp skin, then wait three minutes before applying foundation. Foundation will also cling better if you whisk an oil-blotting lotion over the T-zone (the forehead, nose and chin).

Many editors like how-to stories that cover how a writer got through a situation and all the accompanying emotions, and those stories are far more likely to get your writing noticed. I wrote a story for Yahoo titled "Can Honey Cure Rosacea? One Beauty Editor Says Yes" about my struggle with the skin disorder, and "How I Fell in Love with Growing Older" for *Redbook*. My student Salina Jivani wrote a story for *Wired* that was titled "These Apps Saved My Sanity (and Probably My Marriage)" about the smartphone apps that got her family organized.

Framing Structures Stories

Although I wrote a lot of straightforward how-to articles earlier in my career, today I find that framing offers a better way to explain a concept. Framing involves sharing bite-sized bits of information in an interesting and helpful way. It works for any topic: beauty, health, finance, business, money, parenting, or psychology.

Ask yourself how you can present pieces of information in a way that breaks up the copy and shows a lot of white space, so the reader doesn't get deluged with information. You can be as creative as you like, as long as the framework you use serves the reader.

Giving a Grade

One example of framing is using a report-card format, as I did for my *Washington Post* story "My Child Is Still Out of Control," a follow-up to my viral story "My Child Is Out of Control." I used a pithy subhead, then wrote up the content in the form of a report card. I used humor and my own voice to connect with the reader, most likely a fellow frustrated parent.

This is what I wrote in a section titled "Give Myself a Moratorium on Meltdowns":

> Although I still stew when getting cut-off at drop-off, I have managed to maintain my composure. I think that's especially due to witnessing a frightening, almost-come-to-hair-pulling melee between two frustrated moms at my girl's school. I have tapered off on the road rage, and have kept other grievances to myself. For example, when the phone company put me on hold, instead of screaming, I turned on the speakerphone while I addressed holiday cards. My daughter has been modeling my behavior and appears to be more emotionally resilient than last year. She does have her moments, though, because, well, she's a child. But please tell me why she gets annoyed when I refuse to carry her "heavy" book bag for her, which contains all of a snack, a folder, and a pair of gloves?
> My Grade: A
> Her Grade: A–

I carried this concept throughout the entire article, using varying grades.

The Psychology Typology

For a story I wrote for *Good Housekeeping* called "What Should I Do about My Tween's Toxic Friend?," I didn't want to include my daughter in the story. Instead I interviewed other moms and used a framework of different types of friends, followed by advice from experts:

Friend Type 1: If You Have Nothing Nice to Say, Say It Anyway

"Look at her shoes — they are so ugly," one child whispers to a friend. "Don't you think so?"

Friend Type 2: If I Don't Get My Way, I'll Ruin Your Day

Some friends want everything their way, including the spotlight all the time

Friend Type 3: Let's Just Forget about It

This kid pits other friends against yours by using an "us vs. them" scenario that includes a kernel of truth, like "We don't wear pink anymore, but you do."

I followed each heading with expert advice under the subhead "How to Deal."

Problem and Solution

I learned this way to frame a piece when I wrote beauty and health articles. Start with a problem (such as dry hair), follow it with a solution (use a hair mask), and then give varying examples of how to implement it (at home, apply coconut oil; if you need outside help, get a professional hair treatment), and with products ranging in price: homemade, cheap, or high-end. You can also pick a general issue, like how to avoid looking bad when you have a cold, and then identify specific examples, such as "flaky, dry skin," "pasty face," "red nose," and "puffy eyes," offering a solution for each.

For a story about healing yourself, I created subheads for several health issues, like insomnia, colds, and menstrual cramps. Under each subhead I offered a selection of remedies: an acupressure move, a yoga pose, and diet remedies.

Tinkering with Timing

You can organize service stories by timeline: a story I wrote about appearing on the soap opera *Guiding Light* took the reader through my day on the set, hour by hour, so they could see behind the scenes and get my perspective on what it is like to film a popular television show. It's a good format because it breaks details down into easily digestible bits. You can also organize information by the length of time a problem takes to fix — immediately, a few weeks, or a longer time frame — or by using a calendar format — week, month, or year. This structure would work well for a money piece discussing deposits, investments, or purchases that are best made at certain times of the year.

For a humorous piece for the *Independent*, talking about the differences in celebrating Passover before and during the pandemic, I used the concept of time, contrasting my past and present observances.

We Wash Our Hands

Tradition: Not only do we wash our hands at the beginning of the seder; we also wash them before we eat. Because, hygiene.

This year: We will wash our hands before, during, during, during, during, after, while singing Happy Passover to you, Happy Passover to You. Happy Passover, Happy Passover, Happy Passover to you. And…repeat till our hands are as dry and as flaky as a piece of matzah — the unleavened bread that the Jews carried with them when they fled, because they didn't have time to allow the dough to rise for actual bread.

Eliyahu's Blessing

Tradition: Eliyahu Hanavi (Elijah the prophet) comes to your door and takes a sip from the wine glass you have filled at the table while you sing.

This year: Due to an abundance of caution with the coronavirus, Eliyahu will be practicing social distancing. He will, however, be available for a Zoom toast.

Break It Up with Subheads

Service stories can overwhelm the reader with information. That's why they need to be broken up with devices such as subheads, bullet points, and numbered lists. This approach has the additional benefit of making stories easy to read on a small screen. Subheads themselves can be numbered, as in a piece I wrote about healthy eating habits:

(1) Eat Breakfast

(2) Go for the Greens

(3) Cut Back on Cold Cuts

(4) Add Olive Oil

When I was the editor in chief of a beauty magazine called *Esthétique*, I named a column *News You Can Use*, covering developments in cosmetic dentistry, health, beauty, plastic surgery, and makeup. I loved writing subheads such as "Get Stoned" for a piece about a desert stone massage at a spa, and "Decay-Free Developments to Chew On" for an article on dental products, including chewing gum that heals early tooth decay.

For a story in the *New York Times* titled "When Your Tween Is Bored," I used these subheads: "Lend Perspective without a Lecture," "Go with the Flow," "Try Something New for a Better Mood," "Create a Non-perfect Present Moment." For another *New York Times* piece, "When Your Tween Acts Up on Lockdown," I used these subheads: "Take Your E's," "Family Meals Heal," " Meditation and Meaning," "Create a Chore Jar," "Take Away Special Play," and "Commiserate Compassionately." See how you can tell the flow of the piece from the subheads? The only one that needed clarifying was "Take Your E's," which referred to advice from the expert I interviewed, Dr. Justin Coulson: explore, explain, and empower.

Using subheads in your copy is a time-tested and effective device to keep a reader on the page. Editors love them because they break up the text on the page and work as beacons guiding the reader through the article.

Sidebars Serve the Reader

Sidebars — blocks of copy set apart from the rest of the copy in boxes or at the side of the page — can be used to add a service element to any subject. In sidebars you can offer nuggets of advice, quizzes, and resources such as helpline numbers. They're useful devices because the information in sidebars doesn't interfere with the flow of the main story or essay. I would often use them for my articles or columns. For example, for a piece I wrote for *Vegetarian Times* about how to ease eye irritation, I included a sidebar with bullet points on eye-soothing natural skin-care products, creams, and lotions. For a story on aromatherapy for *Energy Times*, I included a sidebar on essential oils. And for a winter exercise story in my mind/body column for *First for Women*, I included a list of places to purchase weather-appropriate workout wear.

When I was a magazine editor at *American Woman* and *Woman's Own* and *The American Breast Cancer Guide*, part of my job was putting together sidebars for articles on domestic violence or divorce, party planning, the latest surgery for ovarian cancer, or an excerpt from a new book. Examples included "Ten Ways to Spot an Abuser before Tying the Knot," "The Dirty Dozen: Dangerous Activities for Couples," "How to Crash a Bash with Panache," and "Weighing Your Risks," using expert advice from books or interviews. For the serious pieces, we usually ended with a call to action — for example, urging readers experiencing violence to contact a domestic violence hotline, organization, or safe space, or a list of places readers could contact for more information about breast cancer. Sometimes we had more than one sidebar in an article.

Today, magazine editors rarely have time to do research or compile information, so they will expect you to provide the content for service-oriented sidebars, and that expectation should be included in your assignment (see chapter 12 on publishing agreements).

Estelle's Edge: I don't recommend writing listicles — articles consisting of a series of items presented in the form of a list — or other round-ups. I swore them off early in my career because they just don't get you recognition, except as someone who is good at gathering information. Writing listicles doesn't showcase your insight, opinion, or experience, so it won't help you get your writing noticed.

CHECKLIST FOR SERVICE JOURNALISM

❑ Is your lede focused on telling readers what they will learn?
❑ Does the lede use a direct statement or compelling questions?
❑ Did you break up the copy with bullet points or numbers?
❑ Did you use consistently phrased subheads throughout the article, setting off each piece of information?
❑ Did you use a framing device to structure the service information?
❑ Did you use sidebars?
❑ Is the content you shared going to empower readers and help them make better decisions?

PART TWO

All about

Essays

CHAPTER FIVE

Essay Formats

I do not overintellectualize the production process.
I try to keep it simple: Tell the damned story.

— TOM CLANCY

When I started out as a writer, I just wanted to write. I had a summer job working for a guy who sold Canadian stocks. I knew nothing about the stock market, but he would ask me to write up vivid descriptions of the stocks and allowed me to be creative (which is probably what his business was, too).

After that summer, I continued to write, first in a public relations position, and later as a magazine editor, columnist, and freelance writer. I wrote brochures, book jacket copy, beauty booklets, the editorial part of a fifty-page beauty advertorial for *Glamour* magazine, and a newsletter for a vitamin supplement company. I also helped people with their publicity and book proposals. I wasn't picky. If it was a writing job, I took it.

When I became senior editor at *American Woman*, I wrote columns, selected book excerpts, wrote features, hired writers, did first line edits for all our features, read galleys, coordinated photo shoots, worked with the art and production departments, and helped come up with cover lines. During that time, I started freelancing for *New Body*. I also started writing for the magazines *New Woman*, *The Beauty Handbook*, *Energy Times*, *Let's Live*, and *Longevity*.

Eventually, I homed in on the kind of writing I like to do: articles, op-eds, personal essays, hybrid essays and micro memoirs, and writing about writing, as in the column I wrote for *Writer's Digest*, called *All About the Pitch*.

Choosing the right format for your essay can help showcase your voice and your story. This chapter covers the most common formats. The next chapter presents ways to become a better storyteller.

Narrative or First-Person Essays

A narrative essay tells a story, usually about a personal experience. These can be short nonfiction pieces (from 600 to 1,500 words, with a sweet spot of 800 to 1,000 words) or longform pieces (2,000 words and up). In a narrative essay the writer tells a story about a personal experience in a vivid way. The essay builds a bridge between the personal story and larger issues, situations, or conversations, and it often contains an element of cultural analysis to provide deeper insight, assess the experience, or answer a question.

> *Estelle's Edge*: Most editors prefer to see finished essays before they decide to run them. "Writing on spec" (speculation) means that you write a complete piece and submit it. If the editor wants it, they will work with you on revisions. What makes a good essay is the execution and the voice. You can't convey those qualities through a pitch.

Developing a Narrative Arc

A narrative arc is an essay structure with a clear beginning, middle, and end, along with a final catharsis or transformation. For example, you may have a funny story about how you ate a peanut butter, marmalade, and olive sandwich as a child and then threw it up later at school, but it's not a real personal essay until you share an insight with the reader. Apart from the obvious point that this combination of foods is gross, what is the point of the story? Did you learn the extent of your stoic dad's caring for you when he came to pick you up, or later that night? What was the transformation that happened? What made an impression on you and why?

> *Estelle's Edge*: People are always painting pictures in their minds. You need to do this for the reader. When writing an essay, think in detailed scenes. Include anecdotes that make scenes. Take the personal and add your insight and thoughts and analysis about what happened and how it changed you to give it broad appeal. In a way, you need to show the reader the unusual in the usual.

Reported Essays

When I first started teaching about hybrid essays, also known as re-ported essays — articles framed around a personal experience, with reported elements — they were little known. Today most editors I've spoken to say they are more interested in hybrid essays than regular personal essays because they allow the writer to include timely infor-mation, such as a new study, trends from social media, a poll, or a statistic that illustrates the topic's relevance to the reader.

As a writer, you need to convince the editor that the situation or the event you're describing is important. You can do this by including information that shows how your experience is meaningful to others.

What can you find in the news or the culture that you can connect with in your life?

> *Estelle's Edge*: Adding reported elements (studies, quotes from experts, polls) to your personal essays gives them greater traction. The best hybrid articles work with a framework: Start with a personal situation and then move to the service or information-sharing aspect of the article. Another tactic is to peg your experience to that of a celebrity: for example,

"I'm no [public figure currently in the news], but I had a similar experience." The implication is that your story will be just as interesting.

A piece I wrote for the *Washington Post* on helping seniors avoid falls in the home was framed around my own experience of observing the changes in my aging parents' lives. I wrote:

My parents lived together their whole lives, first in their suburban home, later in an apartment and even later in an independent-living apartment in a senior community. But last year, when my dad, suffering from Alzheimer's disease, had to be placed in memory care, my octogenarian mom had to live by herself for the first time in her life.

She is not alone in facing a change in living situation in her older years. For the millions of seniors in the United States (predicted to grow from around 58 million to around 88 million by 2050), life transitions such as experiencing widowhood, having a partner with dementia, or downsizing after decades in the same home can be a huge challenge. One way to ease the adjustment is to ensure that any new home is comfortable, safe, and adaptable to physical limitations.

After that intro, I shared quotes from the first of several experts I spoke to.

Jocelyn Cox, a former competitive figure skater, wanted to write an essay about feeling worried about the pain of childbirth when she was pregnant with her son, after her experience of being injured all the time. I suggested she frame her piece around the upcoming Olympic figure skating competition, and *Insider* snapped it up.

She wrote:

When I get paper cuts, I freak out. If I get blisters on my feet, I can't help but limp.

I wasn't born with low pain tolerance. I developed it by getting hurt often as a child.

I was a competitive figure skater for 11 years, from ages 8 to 19. While I love watching the Olympics, cheering on American skaters like Mariah Bell and Nathan Chen, I'm more than just a fan because I know the toll this sport can take.

My expertise was pair skating and ice dance, where the woman gets tossed around like salad — and sometimes gets dropped. I got injured so many times that it made me terrified of getting hurt or feeling pain during everyday activities. That became even more of an issue when I was set to give birth to my son.

With hybrid essays, there are many ways to connect your story to something in the news or zeitgeist.

What to Add to Your Stories to Hook an Editor

If you are framing a reported piece around a personal story, include research, news hooks, science-based studies, and digital and cultural trends. In a piece I wrote for *Wired* with the title "*Friends*, Fleetwood Mac, and the Viral Comfort of Nostalgia," I mentioned that Atari, the pioneer video game manufacturer, was getting in on the nostalgia boom by planning a chain of video-game themed hotels, including the latest in virtual reality and augmented reality.

Reported Features

Most feature articles are strictly reported, which means that the writer is sharing information in search of the truth. Good features tell a story using plot, characters, and dialogue. They may or may not be connected to breaking news.

> *Estelle's Edge*: Study prize-winning feature articles to see the art and arc of good feature writing. Many features with strong narrative arcs and characters are turned into movies. The movie *Saturday Night Fever* was based on a feature, and a feature on the fake German heiress Anna Sorokin (also known as Anna Delvey) by the journalist Jessica Pressler led to a Netflix miniseries and a book deal.

Micro Memoir

A micro memoir is a short autobiographical piece, up to two hundred words. It's a great format for writing about life experiences that might be dark in a way that usually ends with some sort of resolution. I love using it as a device to get my students in touch with their stories.

This style of writing has come into vogue in recent years, mainly because of the *New York Times* column *Tiny Love Stories*, where I have published, along with many of my students. Writers are asked to craft a story in one hundred words or less. Submissions need to show momentum through dialogue or action.

> *Estelle's Edge*: Micro memoirs are complete stories opening up a window into the past. They can cover a single moment that encapsulates a person's life, opening with a piece of information, a question, or a provocative statement or a bit of dialogue. They work best when they include snippets of scenes, short descriptive sentences using sensory language (evoking sight, smell, sound, taste, and touch), spare but potent dialogue, texts, phone messages, conversations, memories, and reflections or observations. They have a conflict, resolution, and transformation or catharsis, just like a full-length essay.

If you are struggling to come up with a micro memoir story, try listing events in your life that have had the biggest transformative effect on you, or identify a pivotal moment. Write it down and then ask yourself why it was so important. You might end up with something like this:

> When I was twelve years old, my parents had boarders stay in our home, because my dad lost his job and we had to make the mortgage payment. While some kept to themselves, one woman became my de facto parent while my parents went to work. She was a survivor of ethnic cleansing in Bosnia and taught me about the value of family and the importance of staying true to yourself.

That could be the start to a micro memoir. However, you may want to dig deeper by figuring out the catalyzing events, the challenge you rose to (or fell down on), or a poignant conversation. Keep writing those scenes.

This is my tiny love story for the *New York Times*. It was accompanied by a photo of me in an ad for one of my Power Dating classes at the Learning Annex.

Maybe More Than Slightly

"Why can't you find someone?" my parents asked when I was 26. "He's not here yet," I said. "He's in Africa." (I've always been slightly psychic; my parents have always been slightly skeptical.) As the "Dating Diva" at Manhattan's Learning Annex, I felt confident in my ability to help myself and others "find a mate or just a date." In my 40s, I still felt confident, but relied less on my "dating tricks." One rainy night, I bumped into a tall man who rolled his R's. Today, my South African husband says he loves me and our daughter in Afrikaans.

This essay works because it starts with a provocative question, followed by an equally provocative answer. Then it goes into my history as the Dating Diva and how I evolved from a person employing "dating tricks" to someone feeling and projecting true confidence. Instead of saying I met a man from South Africa right away, I describe his height and the way he spoke. I end with a compelling statement that confirms my husband is South African and we have a daughter together. It's a complete story in under one hundred words.

This is my student Jennie Burke's contribution to *Tiny Love Stories*:

My Bright, Freckle-Faced Little Brother

My joyful, bright, freckle-faced younger brother was voted "Joe High School" in his yearbook. Less affable, more opinionated, I was voted "Most Likely to be Heard." But decades later, no noise could stop the addiction Matt developed to prescription OxyContin. I pushed him to rehab; he said he hated me. After his fatal overdose in May 2020, I begged him for a sign that he didn't hate me. On his birthday, I found the message he'd written in his yearbook: "Jen…thank you for believing in me…I love you." When I cried out for my brother, I know he heard me.

This essay starts with a vivid description. The words "Joe High School" connote an All-American kid. The opening also shows the writer's personality: less popular, but forceful. In a few sentences, it covers her brother's descent into prescription drug addiction, rehab, relapse, and overdose. Finally, grieving for her brother, the writer finds a message in an old yearbook that expresses his love, making her feel that he had answered her. We, the readers, feel her pain and her sense of consolation.

Here is a longer micro memoir that my friend Linda Lowen, a writing instructor, published in *The Writer* magazine:

Pat the Bunny

In the dance recital photograph I'm beaming. Rag curls, plump cheeks, four years old. Satin bustier, jaunty rabbit-eared headband, wrists and ankles cuffed in soft, downy fur. Earlier that year the fifteenth Playboy Club had opened in Atlanta, and my dance teacher had an idea: Wouldn't it be cute if the little ones were Bunnies?

Afterwards, back at the apartment, my parents threw a party. Daddy carried me in on his shoulder. Everybody clapped, but I cried until he put me down. Too much noise. Too many grownups.

Ted, our upstairs neighbor, squatted down to my level. He had two little boys. A beautiful wife. He offered me his hand and I held on tightly as he led me down the long hallway to the bathroom.

Inside, he turned on the water in the tub. I was confused. Am I taking a bath?

Through the lens of forty years I'm back in that room. A roar like a chorus of cautionary voices reverberates off porcelain tile. I rock back and forth in my therapist's office, remembering that hand guiding my head, the other stroking long white ears.

In less than two hundred words, Linda tells her traumatic story of child abuse. She describes what she looked like as a child and mentions the dance teacher's perverse notion of dressing up small girls like miniature Playboy Bunnies. Instead of explicitly describing what the neighbor, Ted, did to her, she evokes it through the language of sound and touch. Then she jumps to the scene forty years later in her thera-pist's office. The reader knows exactly what happened to her all those years ago, and how the bunny ears (once so innocent in a little girl's mind) played a role in the depravity.

> *Estelle's Edge*: If you feel your memory is failing you when writing about key events, try listing the events, actions, settings, and sensory experiences that you remember to anchor the story. For example, you can write: "Trip to Paris in 2010: Walking down the Champs-Élysées, the smell of baguettes, kissing Jake by the Eiffel Tower, a perfect honeymoon, attaching 'love locks' to the Pont des Arts, our first fight, watching the perfect moonlit night reflected on the Seine." Sometimes looking at photos can help stir lost memories. Keep going with that list until you have enough material to write the scenario.

In addition to the essay formats I've just described, there are two literary essay formats that I want to mention. They are covered in more depth in *Tell It Slant* by Brenda Miller and Suzanne Paola, and Brenda Miller's *A Braided Heart*.

Hermit Crab Essays

Like a hermit crab taking refuge in a borrowed shell, a hermit crab essay houses the vulnerable, revealing material of the essay in a more rigid structure, like a list, quiz, rejection letter, recipe book, prayer book, guidebook, report card, license plate, note from a teacher, or multiple-choice test. These devices allow the writer to go deep and share very personal information and situations. Linda Lowen wrote an edgy piece for NOW, the publication for the Hobart Festival of Women Writers, using a playful form — a vacation rental listing — to show how cruel conditions were in the Japanese internment/impris-onment camps in the United States during World War II. Here is an example from her essay:

unfairbnb

Solitude, isolation & sweeping mountain views at 'Apple Orchard'
★ 5.0 Superhost Manzanar, California, United States
Check availability
Family-style camp hosted by the Owens Valley Reception Center
10,000 guests • Shared studios • Shared beds • Shared bath

CHECK-IN	CHECK OUT:
March 21, 1942	November 21, 1945

Wake up to mountain landscapes and desert beauty in our vast 5,500 acre retreat center which takes its name from the Spanish word for "apple orchard."

The space

Enjoy family-style living in our 500-acre housing section offering ample accommodations across 504 barracks. No worries about getting lost: the residential area is conveniently organized into 36 blocks of 14 barracks. Each tarpaper structure thoughtfully divided into four rooms measuring 20 × 25. Rather than solid walls, cloth partitions between rooms add to the spacious feeling, with each room designed in an open-concept style.

My former student Emily Brisse wrote a hermit crab essay using the container of the five major dance positions in ballet, through which she examines the position dance has played in her life.

She starts with her life as a child:

First position: Your feet behind your mother's waist, dangling. Music is playing. Your body rests in her arms, your head on her shoulder, your eyes closed. You sway and spin, breathing in and out of gentle pirouettes, dreaming toward the eventual dip into deeper sleep, *adagio, adagio*, where you remain elevated, where your ankles have wings.

And she goes through all the positions, and ages in her life, until she reaches the present day.

Fifth position: One foot, bare and cool, flat against the bathroom tile, the other extending six inches behind it, pointed. You are washing your face. *You always do that*, your husband says from the bed, observing you, *that little foot move*. You hadn't noticed. Had you? A moment later, water still rushing from the faucet, you tip your chest and raise your leg behind your torso, your arms and hands and fingers reaching skyward in two perfect curves. *Arabesque*, you say to the mirror. And for a moment it is all again in front of you: chassé and stage and circle and grace. But it is late. So you lower your arms, place both feet on the floor. Turn off the water, the light — the image receding in the mirror like a dream.

Braided Essays

Braided essays contain multiple interwoven threads or through lines of material, each on a different subject, each recurring several times. The story lines can also cover different time frames. The essays employ imagery and poetic tools like metaphor to evoke an emotional response in the reader. The main story line might be narrative, but the alternative story lines don't need to be. A braided essay can be written in the first person (the writer's voice), but additional information can be provided by an external (or outside) voice. Often the different threads are separated by white space or numbering. For example, Jo Ann Beard's "The Fourth State of Matter," mentioned in *Tell It Slant*, is a story about her dying collie entwined with other threads about her recent divorce, squirrels in the attic, and a shooting at the university where she works. As the authors write in the book, "All these stories weave and intersect; while we might not understand how they've all connected at first, the essay uses strong scenes, imagery, and metaphor to bring them all together in the end. It becomes a heartbreaking piece about loss of all kinds, something that would have been more difficult to do if she had focused solely on the unfolding tragedy."

Estelle's Edge: While consumer publications don't charge fees to writers for submitting work, literary ones often do. But most of them suspend these reading fees at least once a year, so if you are interested in submitting, just check on when those times are. This information is often available from the Association of Writers & Writing Programs (AWP) or sites such as Duotrope or New Pages, or a publication like *Poets & Writers*.

EXERCISE: A FLEXIBLE WRITING PRACTICE

Quickly write down a story about something that happened to you. Now try to write the same story in different formats. The first could be a narrative essay, where you are writing scenes as if from a movie. The second could be a micro memoir. The third could be a reported piece framed around your experience but with research or statistics added. With practice, you will get more versatile in writing in different formats.

CHECKLIST FOR CHOOSING A FORMAT

❏ Does your topic lend itself to lots of questions? If so, you can make it a longform essay.

❏ Does your essay fit into a single paragraph? Was it adapted from a tweet or social media post? If so, it might work as a micro memoir.

❏ Can you incorporate multiple types of information (such as scientific, medical, and philosophical) into your story along with the running narrative? If so, it might work as a braided essay.

❏ Does your story have a strong emotion running through it? You might incorporate different structures to form a hermit crab essay.

❏ Does the essay have lots of scenes you can refer to, and reflection and insight at the end? It can be a personal essay or a longform essay.

❏ Are there new research studies, TED talks, memes, or YouTube videos that complement the information in your piece? It could be a hybrid essay with reported elements.

CHAPTER SIX

The Art (and Arc) of Writing a Personal Essay

I almost always urge people to write in the first person....
Writing is an act of ego, and you might as well admit it.

— WILLIAM ZINSSER

Unusual experiences can end up as great fodder for stories.
I used to work in publicity for the PBS children's television show *Shining Time Station*, which was created to introduce *Thomas & Friends* to an American audience. The exploits of Thomas the Tank Engine and his friends first appeared in the Railway Series books by Wilbert Awdry.

I joined the company that produced the show after the role of Mr. Conductor passed from Ringo Starr (who had also narrated the British program) to George Carlin (who ties with Ernie Anastos for being one of the nicest, least ego-driven celebrities I've met). One day I was tasked with brushing George's ponytail before an appearance, and I relished the task.

One of my least favorite aspects of the job was handling the logistics of occasionally bringing a life-size Thomas the Tank Engine replica to events from the company that licensed it out. Usually staff were around to take it to and fro. But one time they weren't. I described the experience in the *New York Times*:

It was a balmy summer Friday evening in 1992. The crowd resembled a horde of marching ants as they scurried about, focused on leaving the city. I was not one of them. I had a mission.

It was to baby-sit the bright blue full-size replica of an animated train — insured for $100,000 — based on Thomas the Tank Engine, as featured on a popular British children's television series. I was a young promotions director for the show's American counterpart, which was a PBS television show called Shining Time Station. My job was to hand the train over to a security team, who would drive it into the Midtown hotel hosting the annual licensing show. The rental company that had dropped it off would pick it up afterward.

There was one problem.

"According to our insurance, I can't roll the train inside with gasoline in it," a guard informed me. "The hall closes at 9 p.m. You have till then to empty it."

I ran to the corner pay phone (before cellphones). The rental company owners and my company's top brass were nowhere to be found.

People noticed I was distraught.

One man suggested I call a gas station, so I did. They refused to come. I faced the thought that I might have to sleep in the train overnight.

As I sobbed hysterically, convinced I'd lose my job, a lanky, long-haired guy wearing ripped jeans and a stained T-shirt made me an offer: "Give me 25 bucks and I'll suck out the gas."

"Done."

As I watched, he put his mouth on the valve, sucked hard, and spit the gasoline out onto the steamy pavement. Twice.

"All gone," he said.

"Here's your money," I said.

He went on his way, as did the train to the licensing show, with minutes to spare.

So, you see, an upsetting incident early in my career later gave me a great clip.

Coming Up with a Topic, Opening, and Title That Resonate

When writing a personal essay there are certain rules that are helpful to follow.

Make It Fresh

People write about popular topics over and over, such as dating, love, death, illness, grief, and social media. So why would an editor be interested in your story? The same reason a reader would: because it's fresh and feels new either in its approach, the experience it describes, or the way it is written.

A personal essay will resonate most with the reader (and editor) when you write about a topic that you are passionate (or obsessed) about and have personal experience with. You can write about the love of your life who ditched you to become a missionary, a dream to become a vet that imploded when you developed an allergy to animals, or a mistake you made that cost you something big and important.

I wrote a piece that won a BlogHer Voice of the Year Award, "Giving Up the Ghost Baby," for Purple Clover after undergoing a devastating ectopic miscarriage. Another piece, for *Marie Claire*, was about a creepy roommate from years ago who had never left my mind because her behavior was so bizarre. For the *Washington Post* I wrote about how people constantly wanted to touch my pregnant belly.

How can you anchor your essay while elevating your personal narrative so it stands out? By starting with a strong opening, building in a narrative arc (remember, that means a beginning, middle, and end), and ending with a transformation, all the while infusing your piece with a deeper meaning.

Great first-person pieces command your attention, make you want to read on, and often pose a question that needs to be answered. Your opening scene should be one of the most exciting moments in the story.

I start by evaluating the first five sentences of an essay. Does it get you right into the action, through provocative dialogue, a timely connection to an event or holiday, a newsworthy item, setting the scene, or a controversial statement?

A powerful opening brings your reader right into the action, rather than including background information in a conversational style, also known as throat-clearing. Many of us have probably written in this style in a diary, "I woke up this morning, had coffee (black), drove to the supermarket, looked up and down the aisles searching for the perfect avocado, and then, can you believe it, a crazy man started screaming at me." A personal essay must have a carefully crafted opening. It would likely start right in the middle of the action, with perhaps a brief preface. "Standing in the supermarket, picking over the summer-fattened avocados, I heard a staccato of background noise. To my horror, the sound was housed in the body of a small, wizened man, and he was screaming at me."

Opening Sentences Should Captivate or Coax

Great opening sentences of essays can also raise questions or tensions. Here are some examples of intriguing openings from my students.

My NYU student Jenn McKee wrote a pitch about period positivity in class and sold it to *Good Housekeeping*. She began her piece with this compelling opening:

> Earlier this year, just days shy of my daughter's 12th birthday, I was changing her bed's sheets when she said, in an offhand but discreet way, "Just so you know, I started my period. But it's fine. I'm taking care of it. I'm just letting you know, because you asked me to tell you."
>
> Putting on my best poker face, I offered a quick hug and kiss and told her to let me know if she had any questions or needed anything — but I secretly marveled at how she'd seemingly taken this transition in stride, when my own first period experience, in the 1980s, had been shrouded in fear, confusion and shame. (You know. The kind that makes a frantic fifth grader wad up half a dozen tissues into her underpants.)

From a story by Angela Lundberg that I edited for Narratively:

> "I hope my dog fucking bites you on your way out!"
>
> The suburban housewife I've just served with a court summons yells that to my back as I hurry down the steps of her house.

The provocative opening makes the reader want to know more.

From a story that Susan M. Sparks wrote in my *Writer's Digest* class called "I Fell for a Catfish Who Scammed Me out of Thousands of Dollars. Here's How It Happened":

"Patrick" popped up as a match, and I clicked thumbs up.

His profile had only two grainy pictures, but he appeared to be handsome — smiling right through to me while sitting on a motorcycle — and in another close-up he was squinting slightly in the sun.

He was eager to communicate right away, which was different from the other matches I'd made on this dating site. I cringed a little at his grammatical errors in those first few messages, but they didn't really matter because soon we were talking on the phone.

His raspy voice didn't seem to match his suave appearance in photos, but it was magnetic all the same. He asked a lot of questions about me, which I found flattering. I told him I was recently divorced with two kids. I had a cool little red convertible that I liked to drive along the lake. I was a freelance writer with a lot of projects happening.

I might have been just a little cocky.

She pitched this story to *HuffPost Personal*, and they snapped it up. Not only does the title grab you for this essay, but the writer starts in the moment when "Patrick" the con artist first makes contact, hooking the reader as well as the writer.

Another example comes from a story my student Suzie Glassman wrote for AARP's *The Girlfriend*:

In the silence that came after the family and friends left, and the funeral was over, I felt a sudden sting to my heart like a jab from one of the angry yellowjackets that invade our backyard every summer. It hit me that I no longer had a best friend, and I felt like an orphan adrift at sea. By middle age, it seems everyone has their "someone," and she was mine.

The author starts this essay right in the middle of her loss, after the funeral of her best friend. The simile of the stinging yellowjacket is a vivid one. The reader connects with her pain and loss in midlife and wants to know more.

From Ivy Eisenberg's essay for Narratively:

It's 2003 and I am stuck in the bowels of Verizon's IT department, in a g-d-awful boring job. I've been working for various IT departments in Corporate America for 20 years and writing jokes for imaginary stage performances on the side. With a house, a husband, and two millennial children who need to be fed a constant diet of pizza, smoothies, and games for their Xboxes, Game Boys and PlayStations, I am resigned to staying put. October marks my 47th birthday. I only have 20 more years of this corporate drudgery, I reason. I am coming down the home stretch.

One morning, I come up with a phenomenal business idea, which will propel me out of Verizon and make me rich and famous: I'm going to start my own line of custom corporate fortune cookies. I will write up work-appropriate fortunes and stuff them into homemade fortune cookies, to be handed out as party favors. But, here's my brilliant spin: On the back, instead of "Speak Chinese" it will say "Speak Yiddish." I call my new enterprise "Work Favors the Fortune-ate."

The first paragraph shows the writer stuck in her dismal job without a discernible way out. The second paragraph propels the essay into surreal territory, because she is so certain that her new business concept is brilliant — but it clearly has flaws. The reader wants to find out what happens to Ivy's new enterprise and go on this journey with her.

From a story by Tess Clarkson for the *Independent*:

Standing in a Missouri funeral parlor, feet from my 89-year-old father's casket, the strident voice of my older sister battered my ears: My other siblings were spread around the room, including one newly contacted brother: a complete stranger to me. My eyes locked for a moment with another brother, sitting in a chair. He was the only full sibling with whom I still communicated and had been at my side at the hospital when my father died.

The narrator's annoyance with her siblings comes through in the first sentence. You know there is going to be drama, and you are eager to learn more.

From Salina Jivani's essay for *HuffPost Personal*:

As a child, my first brush with a ghost wasn't Casper or some other spook from a children's book. I encountered the real deal in the house we rented in Pennsylvania after my family emigrated from Kuwait. It was over a century old, essentially the size and strength of a wet shoebox, and was shadowed by an ominous oak tree in a rundown neighborhood.

From the moment in class when Salina first mentioned growing up in a haunted house, I knew this story would be fascinating. In the first sentence she makes it clear that this encounter wasn't with a friendly ghost from a child's storybook. That sets the scene for the rest of the piece. The reader wants to know what kind of ghost it was and what it did to the family.

Get to the Inciting Incident

So you've started your first-person piece in a provocative or compelling way that uses dialogue, scene setting, or action to get the reader into the story. What next? Cut out the backstory and get to the inciting incident — the point where something happens. For example, if you are writing about first love, start with an inciting incident that happened to you. Throughout the essay, share what you learned.

Jennie Burke's piece "The First Christmas without Him: Finding Joy in 2020 after the Loss of My Brother" appeared in the *Independent*:

I ask my family if we can put white lights on the tree this year. I will call it my Peace Tree. Something different.

"We always have colored lights!" the teens protest. "Please don't do it, Mom! We like it tacky!" My husband is against the idea too. Without an ally, I decide I'll simply add more lights to the tree, in an attempt to brighten my outlook. Besides the pandemic, besides the election, my brother died this year, of an accidental drug overdose. He was 43 years old.

Jennie first wrote this heartwarming story as a Facebook post. It was so powerful and so many people were responding that I messaged her telling her to take it off the page, write it up, and send it to the editor.

In a piece for the *Washington Post*, Tess Clarkson wrote:

I grabbed my phone and checked my Tinder profile. As a single 39-year-old lawyer, I'd scheduled a date, two days before Christmas, instead of traveling from my Manhattan apartment to Missouri to see family. There was just too much familial tension after my mother's death as we all navigated our grief.

Tapping on the app, there was a message confirming my date. I checked my emails, and found a request from Audrey, my hospice volunteer manager. On Sundays for a year, I'd been visiting patients with a life expectancy of less than six months. Sometimes, I read to them. Often, we simply chatted. Recently, I'd trained to be a vigil volunteer, learning how to serve patients expected to die within 48 hours.

Audrey said a patient near my apartment was "imminently dying." He was 91.

"Alone and dying at Christmastime," I whispered. I couldn't help but think of myself.

Two years earlier, as our family unwrapped presents, I held Mom's hand, her hair clumps under her cap, her body swollen from cancer. My father, sisters, brothers, in-laws, nieces, and nephews had gathered, spending extra time with Mom, who died weeks later. Her hospice team had provided needed support.

In my essay about people touching my pregnant belly for the *Washington Post*, I wrote:

I "popped" six months into my pregnancy, and I was thrilled to finally see my burgeoning belly jutting out under my bountiful breasts. After struggling with infertility for several years, I was ecstatic to be expecting.

Being radiant with child, however, came with unexpected side effects: I was made fair game for inappropriate comments, unwanted advice and marauding palms.

"You're carrying so well; must be a girl," my normally reserved co-worker, a father of five, said as his hand reached out and patted my bump.

"Um, thanks. Yes, I am," I hesitantly responded, unsure of how to handle this delicate situation.

A few days later the palm of my hard-driving boss snaked toward me, as she declared she was going to touch my "belly baby" and make a wish.

"Maybe now I'll meet a great guy, settle down and have a baby, too," she half-whispered, as if I were some kind of life-size lucky charm.

Title Talk

Write the title of your piece to ground the story and help you to focus it.

There are many options for writing titles, and with all my years of experience writing cover lines and headlines for glossy magazines, I love helping my students craft theirs. For starters, it's always helpful to view the titles of the publication you are interested in publishing in. Some pubs have very long titles, others are shorter. There really isn't a right or wrong, just as long as your title is compelling. It can be helpful to write up a short sentence about your essay's meaning or purpose, and then make it even shorter and punchier for the title.

Another option is to write the first part of the title as the situation or problem and then write "and that's why I realized or found X." For example, "I Lost My Sister to a Cult but Found Love with Its Leader." Or, for a story I edited for Narratively about an inappropriate talent scout, "I Survived My Own R. Kelly Story," or my essay for Scary Mommy "Mom Life Hacks to Cut through People's Crap."

Here are some more tips for crafting tantalizing titles.

Evoke Emotion

Make the reader feel something. Use active verbs such as *churned*, *sauntered*, *splintered*, *spiraled*, *peppered*, and *waltzed* to paint a picture for the reader. My essay for the *New York Times* about connecting with my dad, who has Alzheimer's, was titled "Singing My Dad Back to Me." Rochelle Newman-Carrasco's hybrid reported essay for *Next Avenue*, titled "Unmuting a Brother-Sister Relationship One Chord at a Time," played off the theme of starting guitar lessons at age sixty with her older brother as her teacher — a brother she had barely spoken to for years. A piece I wrote for Vox was called "I Had a Baby in My 40s. Part of My Job Is Preparing My Daughter for Life without Me."

Make It Specific

The title "My Husband Doesn't Post about Me on Facebook (and It Makes Me Sad)" (from a story on Your Tango) is more effective than "My Husband Isn't on Social Media Anymore."

Answer a Burning Question

One essay I wrote was titled "Love Laboratory: What I Learned from a Totally Not-My-Type Guy." I wrote a piece titled "Marry the Man, Not His Religion. Trust Me" that ran on Your Tango. The pandemic Passover piece I wrote for the *Independent* is called "Elijah the Prophet Will Toast You on Zoom: Ways to Get through a Socially Distanced Passover."

Include an Important Moment from the Essay

A piece by Suzie Glassman for Parents.com is titled "My 9-Year-Old's Unexpected Seizure Taught Me the Power of Letting Go." An essay by Tess Clarkson for *Insider* (which often uses longer titles) is called "The Man I Was Dating Publicly Shamed My Sex Preferences after We Broke Up. I Learned to Stand Up for What I Want." And an essay I wrote for Yahoo was called "The Benefits of Meeting My Mother-in-Law at My Lowest Point."

Use Numbers

Numbers in headlines promise specific information and insights. I wrote an essay for *Brain, Child* titled "15 Kinds of Kisses for my 5-Year-Old" and one for the *Washington Post* headed "6 Reasons We Don't Let

Our Daughter Sleep in Our Bed." I wrote "8 Ways to Defend Yourself from Writing Coaching Scams" for *Writer's Digest*.

Make a Statement of Fact

I wrote a five-minute memoir for *Writer's Digest* titled "I Had My Daughter in Midlife and She Became My Writing Muse" and a piece for Parenting.com called "Becoming a Mom Has Totally Transformed Me. And That's OK." Emily Brisse wrote a piece for Parents.com titled "How Paying for Daycare Helps You, Your Kids, and the Economy," and Suzie Glassman wrote a piece for *Wired* called "The Exercise Games That Can Actually Get You off the Couch."

Share Your Challenges

I wrote "What to Do When Your Tween Is Trash-Talking You," for the *New York Times*. A piece I wrote for *Salon* was titled "I Was Determined to Be a Great Mother and a Loving Daughter: This Was Easier Said Than Done." An essay I wrote for Ravishly was titled "I Was Determined to Breastfeed, but Nothing Went As Planned." A piece I wrote for Scary Mommy was called "Having a Child in Midlife Cured Me of My Klutziness" (which is so true that it really is scary).

Make a Provocative Statement

An essay I wrote for Your Tango was titled "Being Hypnotized into a Past Life as a Man Brought Me True Love." For *HuffPost Personal*, I wrote "My Blind Date Took Me to a Sex Club. Here's What Happened." My former student Juli Fraga wrote a piece for *Vice* titled "How John Mayer Helped Me Become a Better Therapist."

Estelle's Edge: If you are still struggling to define your headline, take key words out of your essay and look them up in a thesaurus to find synonyms that might work in your title. Play around till you find interesting combinations.

Title Advice from Editors

- Always include a title when you send your piece to an editor. Think of it as your thesis statement, showing us where you see the article going.
- It can be helpful if titles contain keywords that will show up in online searches.
- Create a title that is personal, emotional, surprising, relatable, or a strong statement.
- Don't be vague in the subject line.
- Don't be funny in the subject line if it isn't a humor piece.
- Send a title that matches the style of the the publication's website. If we can't figure out the title, it will be hard to assess the story.
- Submit multiple titles to choose from.

Telling the Story

Putting your essay together takes more than just a good opening and a compelling title. Once you have chosen your topic, you need to craft a strong essay that will resonate for the editor and the reader. You do that by writing evocative scenes that supply sensory details and vivid description to paint a picture.

Supply Sensory Details

Research shows that readers' brains are stimulated by reading sensory language, particularly metaphors evoking texture. Don't say the singer had a nice voice. Say she had a velvet voice.

Be specific. Don't say you had lunch: say you had a slice of veggie pizza with mushrooms (your favorite topping) and a sprinkle of Parmesan. Don't say you were angry: say you were fuming because your friend always ignores you when someone she thinks is more important enters the room. If you ate a piece of pie, describe the pie — was it apple or lemon? What did it taste or smell like, and what memories or feelings did it evoke? Here's an example:

> As I ate the slice of apple pie, with its crumbly texture, each tangy bite brought back unwilling memories of the last time I ate apple pie, visiting my dying friend in the hospital. We shared a slice each using a neon yellow fork supplied by the nurse on duty.

Examples of sights, sounds, texture, or taste (and their effect on you) invite the reader to experience the events. Instead of writing, "I went in the car with her," you might write, "I slipped into the low-to-the-ground leather seats in her white Porsche." See how much more of a story you can tell when you add the details?

> *Estelle's Edge*: Pretend you are telling your story to a friend. If after every sentence you wonder what something smelled like or looked like, add more detail and description.

To evoke the sensations of playing badminton in the backyard as a child, you might write:

> Come summer, the net would be strung out across our backyard, shadowed by the tall poplar trees that reached 80 feet up into the sky (until my dad had them cut down right before a storm). We'd barbecue hot dogs and hamburgers, have lemonade and Fresca and Mallomars, and then play a rollicking game of badminton until it was bedtime. This was precious family time.

See how the details make the story come alive?

EXERCISE: I REMEMBER CHILDHOOD

Do this exercise, inspired by Joe Brainard's memoir *I Remember*, when you are trying to evoke memories of childhood in a personal essay.

Write at the top of the page, "I remember." Then list as many memories of childhood as you can. Try to use sensory language to describe those long-gone moments. What did you smell, see, taste, hear, or feel?

Be as descriptive as possible in each sentence and try to use metaphors, similes, and analogy. Then see if you can weave the sentences together to construct an essay.

Minimize the Minutiae

Sensory details are evocative; logistical details can make a story drag. You don't need to tell the reader, "I called my mother and asked for the information for the doctor. Next, I contacted the doctor and made an appointment over the phone. I filled out the form and answered the medical questions. My appointment was set for 10:45 a.m. the next day, but I was planning to be there at 10:30 a.m." Every doctor's visit requires an appointment time and forms, so you aren't telling readers anything they don't already know. Pare it down: "I called the doctor — recommended by my mother — and made an appointment for the next day."

Picking a Personal Point of View (POV) and Adding Dimension

Displaying your voice in an essay is an important way to connect with the reader. Here's how to get out of your own way when telling your story.

Put the "I" into a Personal Essay

Some of my students try to create distance in a personal essay by using the pronoun *we* or *they*. In a personal essay, that doesn't serve the reader or the writer. You need to keep yourself visible. Use *I*. You're sharing your point of view and the way you think, so you don't ever need to use the anonymous third-person voice.

Don't Break the Fourth Wall

In theater and television, the term *fourth wall* refers to the invisible barrier between actors and audience, keeping the onstage world intact. When actors directly address the audience, it's known as breaking the fourth wall. It's a tactic that can be useful to break tension — but that is exactly what you don't want when writing a personal essay. It's okay to use an impersonal voice to give the reader information: "Claire was her best friend. She was quick to anger (her red hair gave her permission, she said)." What doesn't work is addressing the reader directly: "Dear reader, do you think I was joking?" Or "Why do you think I made that choice?"

A lot of beginner writers employ these devices hoping they will sound witty. The problem with this sort of aside is, first, that it stops the story from flowing. Second, addressing the reader makes them a character in your essay, when they should instead be an invisible (and appreciative) audience.

The same applies to rhetorical questions in a piece that interrupt the narrative, like "You don't think that made me feel crazy? It did." I would be a billionaire if I had a penny for every time I told my students just let the story unfold.

Forget about Foreshadowing

Letting the reader know what is going to happen is a surefire way to lose their interest. So leave out those sentences like "Little did he know it would be the worst day of his life," or "She saw the dark clouds, and soon her life would turn even darker." Revelations like "I'm so glad I met my husband out of this experience" are best left until the end, otherwise they interrupt the flow of the piece and give your ending away.

Just let the story unfold (yes, I said it again); tell the story in a compelling way, and the reader will follow you to the end.

Consider Chronology

While writing your essay, think about the timing of your story and scenes. Making the right choices can help move your story forward and keep the reader engaged.

You don't need to start right at the beginning: you can start in the middle (a narrative technique called in medias res, which translates as "in the middle of the thing"). Drop the reader into the action with the inciting incident or a moving piece of dialogue that also moves the story forward. Or start at a point during the action or confusion — for example, after a miscommunication or a dramatic event. That will hook your reader's attention. After that, every sentence of the story should keep moving the story or narrative along. Save the backstory for later in the piece.

Also, try to avoid a simple chronological flow and a flat recital of events: "This happened, and that happened, and that happened." Nobody wants to read a diary entry. They want to read about personal experience that becomes universal. You achieve this by showing what happened and then providing insight into it and describing your feelings about it.

For more of a narrative arc, try to create a through line, such as aging and reaching a milestone, or a fear of childbirth that you touch on throughout the essay. You could also share the emotional implications of the progression using dramatic scenes and dialogue.

Make a Scene

Each scene of your essay is a story in itself: it can depict action, narrate an incident from the past, or share a reflection. Imagine you're writing a movie scene. When the camera rolls, what does it focus on first? Write that down. What are the emotions? Emotions can't be directly described in a movie scene: you need to convey them through the setting and dialogue.

One student working on a memoir wrote about learning that his daughter had gotten a tattoo. Rather than start the scene with her telling him about the tattoo, I suggested that he note the details he saw on her body and start it that way. Judy Nelson reached out to me for help on an essay about how after losing her only child, Jason, decades earlier in a motorcycle accident, she was shocked when his college friend, Matt, contacted her out of the blue and invited her to join him at a Grateful Dead spinoff group concert. Hearing the songs Jason loved brought back her fading memories of her son. At first she started with the backstory, but then she whittled the essay down and opened with the inciting incident — the email from Matt to Judy.

I froze when I saw the subject line "Jason." I quickly opened the email and found the following message:

> Hi, Mrs. Nelson,
> I never met you, but I was friends with Jason in college and we used to hang out a lot, especially the year he died.
> We were going to be roommates senior year...
> I hope you are doing well after all these years...
> And I hope my note doesn't bring back unnecessary pain.
> I just wanted you to know that he is not forgotten.
> All the best, Matt

I wanted to hit the "delete" button — the email brought me back in time to the voicemail Jason's dad left me at midnight 29 years ago.

It was the day after Christmas and my husband Jim and I had come home late from a party. I saw the light blinking on the answering machine and pushed play.

After opening with the email and the shock it caused, she was able to add the backstory in the next paragraph. In a movie, the camera would pan down the email and then cut to Judy and her reaction. Reading the email along with Judy is more powerful than her simply telling the reader that her son died.

Lauren Stevens contacted me about a braided essay that she wanted to polish, about growing up as a military brat. Her opening needed enlivening to draw the reader into the story. She wanted to use flashbacks, and I suggested using the powerful story of how her mom was traumatized right after her birth, when a gunman came into the hospital.

Here is the original slow start, which set the scene but didn't get to the inciting incident that ignites the story:

Roughly two hours south of Atlanta, beyond the jam-packed highways and sprawling suburbs, lies an old boomtown, deep in the heart of Georgia. Dodging cars on the highway, the road opens up about an hour or so south, with views of vast fields and wild country, before we begin seeing signs of life outside of Macon. If I wasn't on a mission,

I'd wonder what the hell I was doing, driving deep into the heart of nowhere. Another half hour, we happen upon our destination: Warner Robins.

She revised her opening to recount the inciting incident and bring in the military connection, answering the question, Why should the reader care?

"Take her and hide!" Having plucked me from my warm bassinet in the nursery, the nurse rushed into my mother's room at the military hospital, panic evident in her face. She thrust me — black fuzzy hair, chubby fists, legs and all — into my mother's arms for safekeeping. Understanding the urgency and gravity of the nurse's request, my mother immediately launched into protective mode, shuffling, with her back hunched over me cradled in her arms, mustering all of her strength and channeling it to her recovering abdomen. Shocked, reacting through instinct, my mother locked herself into a bathroom stall, willing me not to utter a peep, lest we be discovered. After what seemed like hours, my mother emerged from the bathroom and was debriefed; a G.I. had entered the clinic with a gun, demanding his records and threatening all within earshot.

EXERCISE: DESCRIBE A HOT SPOT

Select a place you like to spend time in — a favorite room in your home, a vacation spot, a park, or a backyard. Then see how many ways you can describe that spot without repeating yourself. Use as much detail as you can. Pick a different spot every day and do the same exercise. It will make a big difference in the detail you use in your writing.

EXERCISE: SO WHAT?

Write one sentence that describes a person, place, relationship, or event you are interested in. After you write it, then add the words *so what*? Why should anyone reading your story care? You are a stranger to the reader, but you need to make your emotional life resonate for them.

Ask yourself what makes your story so important or interesting or different that the editor will want to share it with their readers. Write that down.

Then ask yourself what personal transformation the story describes that readers will care about. As Vivian Gornick puts it, what is the situation, and what is the underlying emotional implication? The *so what*? in your essay can illuminate a universal situation or condition, build empathy, or express an important insight.

Go Micro, Not Macro

Don't go big and broad. Home in on one person, relationship, toy, act, friend, or object of beauty. Describe smaller moments — the day your son found a shell on the beach that reminded you of the time you decided on that same beach to get over your fear of motherhood, or the day you realized the damage you were doing by repeating your mom's lament, "I'm raising an enemy in my own home," to your daughter. You can slow down the action or focus on one particular event, memory, moment, or object to show the reader its meaning.

Keep the Details Flowing and the Dramatic Tension Rising

An essay is like a shark: it must keep moving forward, or it dies. Imagine you are telling a story to people around a campfire, or at a cocktail party. How would you keep them on the edge of their seats? You would use description and details to paint a picture of escalating tension. If a sentence doesn't propel the essay forward, it needs to be scrapped, shortened, or moved somewhere else. That includes dialogue.

Dialogue Dilemmas

Dialogue should reveal details about the characters and their relationships as well as the issue at hand. It needs to provide momentum and contribute to the narrative arc. Their conversation shouldn't just transmit information, as in "Here is your phone." "Okay, thank you." I can't tell you how many times I've used my red pen to scratch out "Hi. How are you?" from sentences in my students' essays. As for the issue, it can be an external conflict — feeling scared about asking for a raise, breaking up with someone you love — or an internal conflict — wanting praise from a stoic parent, or wishing someone who treats you as invisible would finally see and appreciate you.

> *Estelle's Edge*: In a dialogue between only two people, there is no need to keep adding speech tags like "he said" or "she said." The reader can remember who is who in the conversation.

EXERCISE: DIALOGUE THIS

Write a 250-word scene using dialogue between two people you know well. Start with an inciting incident and try to show conflict. Let the dialogue show who the people are through their word choice and speech patterns and the details they reveal about their lives. Here are some options to choose from:

- A person asks for help with something, their romantic partner denies the request.
- A grandmother tries to convince her daughter to spend the holidays with her instead of the children's other grandparents.
- Someone negotiates a raise with their boss.
- Your best friend tells you she just got her dream job — at your company.
- A couple can't decide which partner they will remain friends with when their best friends get divorced.

Cancel the Cursing

Curse words can get the readers' attention, but use them sparingly — maybe only in dialogue. Overusing any word weakens its effect. In my story about an inappropriate therapist I had when I was a girl, I used the word *fuck* as the story escalated, mostly in the dialogue, to show the depravity of the therapist.

Wrapping It Up

You've written your piece, but feel the ending feels flat or hasn't emerged out of your torrent of words. A story needs some sort of insight or transformation to take place at the end. The writer is in a different place at the close of the story than they are at the beginning. If you are stymied by this part of the writing process, here are some strategies and examples of how to finish an essay with flair.

Circling Back

Circling back to something mentioned at the beginning of the article or essay provides a feeling of closure, delivers insight, and shows what the writer learned from the experience. In an essay for Parents.com, "Postpartum Rage: One Mom's Uncontrollable Anger After Giving Birth," I closed with this:

> The morning I woke up from a night-terror-free sleep, glanced over at my sweet baby sleeping soundly in her crib, and heard my husband tapping on his computer without feeling like I wanted to chuck him and it out of the window, I finally knew I'd be all right. And I was.

> *Estelle's Edge*: It helps if you write past what you think the ending of the story is. Think beyond the constraints of the story. How has the behavior or situation changed, and how will it continue to change?

My student Allison Kenien wrote an essay for *Insider* about how she felt time was flying as she watched her kids grow up in front of her (her daughter was already seven years old) and how she made an effort to slow it down, so she could enjoy them more. She realized that she was repeating the same activities, especially being in the house together since the start of the pandemic, and that her brain was on autopilot, and so she began researching time. As she writes in her piece:

I discovered that our brains perceive time moving quickly or slowly based on factors such as routine, complacency, multitasking, technology, and emotion. Routine makes time move quickly, whereas new experiences slow it down.

So she started focusing on fresh activities (creating a scooter racetrack in the basement, building a snow castle in their driveway, taking a drive to find hidden waterfalls or quiet beaches), and trying mindfulness exercises with her kids (singing feel-good songs and playing sensory games to find a sight, sound, or feeling for each letter of the alphabet) to create new memories in her brain.

Her original ending was:

Overall, I feel more in control of the ticking clock, and I'm getting more quality time with my kids. We snuggle more. We laugh more. We talk more. We're creating more special memories that will stick with us long after the moment has passed.

That was a fine but unexciting ending. Adding this line at the end took the piece full circle and brought it up a notch craftwise, because it referenced the idea of thinking beyond the essay, and even the moment, with a pithy ending sentence that brings the focus back to the writer (remember, keep the "I" in personal essays):

I haven't stopped the clock, but now when it comes to my kids, time is on my side.

Tess Clarkson wrote a piece for Scary Mommy about being a stepparent, titled "The Time I Met My Husband's Ex at Their Kid's Football Game." This was her original ending:

It's been nearly ten months since that football game, and my youngest stepson is now officially an adult like the other two. But parenting doesn't stop at a certain age, and parenting isn't severed by divorce. Since I'm planning on a till-death-do-us-part union with my husband, I'll always be the trio's stepmom.

She revised the ending by adding two sentences that take the essay full circle, incorporating a sports metaphor:

Even if I can't magically create a bond with their mom or understand football, I'm still going to show up in their lives. That's a goal I can grasp.

In Judy Nelson's essay about her son, she mentions Jason's favorite word, *awesome*:

We all chant "Hey now!" at the right moments. Jason would have loved this!
    "Awesome!" he would have said in every other sentence.

At the end of her essay, she writes:

Matt slips his arm through mine and we sway with the crowd. Each note connects me more to Jason and it offers me a sense of peace. When I hear the final words, "If I knew the way, I would take you home…" I realize Matt's gift has finally allowed me to take Jason home — if only in my heart. And I hear a voice in the breeze softly whisper, I love you, Mom. I told you you'd love the music. Isn't it awesome?

This was Lauren Stevens's first ending, where she wrote about driving away after an emotionally laden visit to her dad's old military base, leaving behind the familiar flight line that her dad, a former air traffic controller, managed from the control tower.

As we drive away from the flight line, I stop the car by the line of pines serving as a natural barrier to the world outside of the base's chain-link fences. When my father shoots me a quizzical look, I sheepishly tell him that I want to grab one of the oversized pinecones that litter the ground beneath the trees. Larger than my hand and stouter than most pinecones I see up north, I snatch two perfect specimens. The end of each of the bud scales is tipped with a thorn-like protrusion. I handle them carefully and hurry back over to the car. Hopping in and putting the car into drive, I have a sense of fulfillment, knowing that I have something tangible from inside the base gates, from the very soil of my place of birth.
    As we head back to the hotel, my eyes flit between the rearview mirror and the road as we pass through the gates, the entrance getting smaller in the distance. I've seen all that I can see here.

Travel writer Pico Iyer gave a wonderful TED talk in 2013 entitled "Where is Home?" In his talk, Iyer discusses his own mobile childhood and wrestling with both cultural and national identity, but he eloquently summarizes the plight of our increasingly mobile society, and more specifically those with mobile childhoods. Iyer says, "Their whole life will be spent taking pieces of many different places and putting them together into a stained-glass whole. Home for them is really a work in progress."

My Georgia piece of glass is now soldered and secured within lead cames [the material that holds the separate pieces of glass together].

When she revised the story, she developed the through line of pinecones more fully:

As we head back to the hotel, my eyes flit between the rearview mirror and the road as we pass through the gates, the entrance getting smaller in the distance. I've seen all that I can see here.

Travel writer Pico Iyer gave a wonderful TED talk in 2013 entitled "Where is Home?" In his talk, Iyer discusses his own mobile childhood and wrestling with both cultural and national identity, but he eloquently summarizes the plight of our increasingly mobile society, and more specifically those with mobile childhoods. Iyer says, "Their whole life will be spent taking pieces of many different places and putting them together into a stained-glass whole. Home for them is really a work in progress."

Turning the pinecone in my hand, I get lost in the seemingly endless swirls of woody bud scales fanning out from its central axis. Nothing is arbitrary in a pinecone's design. One of the many examples of the Golden Ratio in nature, my pinecone illustrates the Fibonacci sequence, with each number the sum of the two coming before it. My birthplace doesn't define me; I am the sum of the many places I have lived.

Lauren's longform piece, "Georgia on My Mind," won the Missouri Humanities Council's Proud to Be Military-Service essay competition and was printed in the seventh edition of *Proud to Be: Writing by American Warriors*.

A piece I wrote about my tween for Romper described how sheltering in place during Covid moved all my worries about her friendships offstage. In the body of the essay, I wrote:

Instead there is an invisible, silent enemy beyond the walls of our home, and the hardships are about the absence of those relationships, a coming adolescence put on pause.

I circled back with this:

Like all parents, I can't control what is happening around me and I'm struggling to adjust. I know that we will be going back and it is unrealistic to think that I can surround my daughter with a force field of love that will permanently keep her safe. I will let go once again when I need to return her to the world. I think I understand better than before what is truly worth worrying about and what isn't all that important. But just for now, before life reforms into the next new normal, I've found a safe place at home surrounded by my family, where despite being mom 24/7 I can relax.

While the world pays rapt attention to its breathing, I will exhale.

Even if it's just at home and just for the moment.

Another example of a theme running through a piece is "My Father's Fanatical Feud with the Bullies Next Door," by Mary Widdicks. I edited this piece for Narratively. The piece begins when the writer's dad starts sleeping on the sofa with a rifle. He also puts up Christmas bells in the orchard. The theme of bells runs throughout the piece, encapsulating the writer's conviction that she will never feel completely safe after her traumatic childhood.

The bells come in at the beginning of the story. Mary writes:

Lined up in neat rows along our backyard was a young orchard: spindly trees still too weak to bear fruit, propped up by wooden stakes and thick twine. Looping through the branches and woven between the trees was a series of tripwires adorned with silver Christmas bells. My father told me he put them up to keep the deer from eating our apples. That also explained the rifle, I thought. My dad wanted to protect us.

Although seven-year-old Mary thinks her dad is trying to keep the deer away, the bells are really there because the neighbor boys have been harassing Mary and her mother. The abuse had escalated from twisting Mary's arm to wrestling her dog, urinating in front of her mother, and calling her a bitch.

After Mary's mother tells the boys never to come over again, and also speaks to their mother, the bells come in again.

"I've taken care of it." My mom spoke slowly and deliberately. "They're forbidden to come to our house. I spoke to the mother, and she claims we're making things up."

"She's as crazy as they are."

"Let's just make peace and move on."

His voice boomed down the hallway toward my bedroom. "That kid needs to know what will happen if he tries putting a hand on my daughter again."

I grabbed my pillow and moved it to the foot of the bed. That was the first night I heard the bells in the yard outside my window.

Then the harassment takes a darker turn, with the neighbors anonymously making accusations to the school that Mary's father was molesting her, death threats, and a thwarted kidnapping attempt, after which the bells make another appearance.

"Mom? Why would someone want to hurt me?"

"I don't know." She clenched the steering wheel so hard her knuckles blanched. "Some things will never make sense."

"Is it because Dad tried to hurt the deer?"

She released the wheel and turned toward me. "What deer?"

"The ones in the orchard. That's why Dad has the bells and the gun, right?"

She sighed. "No, it wasn't about the deer."

"Then why did the police believe a lie?"

"They didn't. They believed you." She leaned forward and turned up the radio. It was the last time we ever spoke about the neighbors until the real estate sign appeared in their yard a few weeks later.

After the neighbors move away and the harassment stops, Mary still sees the bells as a talisman of sorts, although they're really a symbol of her dad's increasing mental illness.

It was still dark when I padded down the hallway, through the kitchen, on my way to the living room. The porch lights were on and I could see dew sparkling along the twine tied between the trees and gathering on the little metal bells. No deer. *I guess it was working.*

Everything had been quiet for weeks.

But I hadn't forgotten, and neither had my father.

I could hear him snoring before I rounded the corner. I coughed to see if he'd stir, but he didn't move.

Candy wrappers littered the coffee table and the floor beside the sofa. He'd been up late again, waiting for something to jangle the bells.

I tiptoed into the living room and eased myself onto the carpet under the coffee table. It was cold but I didn't shiver. I curled my legs into my chest, just like I had when the police had talked to me in the principal's office. Only this time I wasn't scared.

Some parents hug their kids, laugh with them, tell them they love them. My dad waited up at night for the monsters, with a rifle tucked under his arm. That was the moment that safety became elusive, and something I'd spend the rest of my life chasing like those invisible deer in the orchard.

I closed my eyes and listened for the bells until I fell asleep.

Leave the Reader with a Gift

The reader should get a takeaway message from your essay. This means that the essay offers some transformation, learning, revelation, or understanding that the reader can share. A satisfying ending ties all the threads together. The writer of the essay has grown or changed in some way, often through grasping a truth or insight that escaped them before. That insight or "aha" moment needs to be conveyed in those last sentences. Avoid summarizing what has happened or ending in a saccharine, sentimental, kumbaya kind of way. Being happy and in love is great fodder for holiday cards, but it doesn't make a story that resonates for the reader. Many writers make the mistake of trying to sum up their love for their family or children, and these attempts often come across as trite.

If the story has sad or traumatic elements, you need to offer an ending that prevents the reader from going away simply depressed.

Here's the ending of my piece "Singing My Dad Back to Me," from the *New York Times*:

> So, as I face the finality of losing my dad, I will hold on to him as long as I can, with music as our guiding force and new language. Song will let us linger in his past, until the wave of Alzheimer's overtakes us both.

Here's the closing of my essay "The Doula Who Saved My Life" for the *Washington Post*:

> My doula came back for a final visit after I went home from the hospital. She brought gifts: a rattle, poems about motherhood and a plastic container full of home-cooked quinoa.
>
> Though the leftovers lasted for days, the lessons I learned from her about self-care have lasted well beyond our contract. Would I hire her again? In a baby's heartbeat.

From "Connecting My Children to Their Heritage in Mandarin," by Connie Chang for the *New York Times*:

> Joy and wonder alighted on my father's face as he listened to the familiar verses tumble out of his grandson — verses that had been spoken by my father as a little boy in Taiwan, by my grandparents when they were students in China, and by countless boys and girls before that.

The last line in this piece conveys a sense of timelessness and history as well as pride in the author's heritage.

My former student Nicolette (Nikki) Branch writes about her one childhood encounter with her great-grandmother in her essay "Remembering Georgia" in the anthology *I'm Speaking Now*. This essay was born in one of my writing classes when I asked my students to write about a pivotal moment in their lives. Nikki asked if it was okay to share something from her childhood that she had a vivid memory of. For her it was like a movie she'd seen over and over.

> Georgia was part goddess, part saint. Her heroics run through my blood. They are the inner voices that whisper wisdom and breathe superpowers into my quest to conquer everyday mountains.
> She brought thousands of babies into this world and never lost a mother, never lost a child.
> I will always remember to draw strength from this side hustle epiphany.
> And never forget tracing the half-marble in her left wrist.
> Her sacrifice lives on.

Nikki's great-grandmother, who picked cotton, also had a side gig as a midwife. An injury sustained while delivering a baby left her with a half-marble-shaped deformity in her left wrist. This ending details the legacy Nikki has inherited from her: the power of knowing what her great-grandmother did for so many women, and the feeling that Nikki herself can conquer any obstacle.

Reviewing and Polishing Your Prose

You've written your essay and feel you have gotten your story down, but it's not quite right. Here are some steps you can take to hone your writing so it's ready to submit.

Clarity Is Key

Is your writing easy to understand? If you aren't being clear, then the reader won't want to come along on the journey with you. Clarity is more important than flowery language, or using big, impressive words. Language is a tool to move the story forward. If you are using fancy language (as some beginner writers do) but nothing is happening, it's not a story. The language must be clear, grammatically correct, and in service to the story. If you aren't conveying your message or theme through sentences that follow each other in a way that the reader can follow, you will lose them. You also need to make sure there is a logical flow to your piece and that the reader can figure out what is happening through the detail and description you offer.

Cut to the Chase

Cutting the length of a piece is an effective way to get to the meat of the story. If you are having trouble with a twelve- to fifteen-hundred-word essay, try paring it down to eight hundred or six hundred words. It helps you see what's important. It's true that you have to kill your darlings. Sometimes my favorite lines need to be sacrificed to make the piece better.

Give It a Rest

If time allows, give your essays a chance to breathe, especially if they are about heavy topics. I knew it would take a while before I felt comfortable writing about my aging parents moving into an independent living facility five hours away from me, but eventually I wrote a piece for *Salon* about the strain of navigating their needs as well as those of my child, then a toddler. Sometimes a week or two is enough; other times you may need six months or more to process all the emotions relating to a piece. And that's okay.

Once you have given your essay a few days or longer to rest, look at it again with fresh eyes. I use this next exercise to get rid of repetition in essays and to tighten writing.

Repetition Smepetition

Step 1: Go through your essays and identify the most often repeated ideas, words, phrases, or pronouns. Often writers fall in love with a phrase and then repeat it several times, each time tweaking the wording slightly. But repetition doesn't strengthen a piece; it weakens it. Here is a hypothetical example: "I left with my dad to forge a new life together in America, sadly leaving Mom behind.... I said a sad good-bye to Mom when I left for America with my dad." Both sentences say the same thing, and the first one is stronger.

In some cases, repetition can be an effective literary device to emphasize a point or a theme, but only if it's carefully used. For example, I used the words "I will" to emphasize the strong steps I would take to tame my angry self in front of my daughter.

> So, I will not yell at the cable company in front of her when they screw up the signal to our televisions for the umpteenth time. And I will not indulge in road rage (at least not in front of her) when yet another harried suburban mom cuts me off in my lane while driving my daughter to school.

That repetition lets the emotion show, but I wouldn't use it over and over again because that would dilute its power.

Step 2: Go to a site like Thesaurus.com and find words or phrases you can adopt to reduce repetition in your work. Keep them by your computer. For example, I wrote an essay for *Salon* in which the words *my daughter* appeared over and over again. To cut down the repetition, I made a list of alternatives, including C (her first initial) as well as *my child*, *little one*, and even *Princess*. In an article for the *New York Times*, "What to Do When Your Tween Is Trash-Talking You," I wanted to find a word to express how my daughter enthusiastically kisses my cheeks, with a more descriptive phrase than the word *enthusiastically*. So I wrote:

> This is the same kid who often asks me for snuggle time and kisses me on the cheeks like an out-of-control woodpecker while wildly professing how much she loves me.

Also, make sure to study the connotation and usage of any new words you are using, and run your writing through a grammar checker to make sure you are using these words correctly in your sentences and scenes.

Use Words That Work

We've all seen the words *amazing* and *incredible* a thousand times. While they may work in a quick, casual post, in an essay you need every word to work for you. The more common the word, the more readers will overlook it — and your writing. If you want to write the word *happy*, try substituting a different word, such as *elated* or *delighted*. When writing a personal essay, I write a first draft and then go through the essay, substituting more interesting or unusual words. For example, in my essay "Giving Up the Ghost Baby," I was looking for a word with medieval connotations. I ended up using a sentence with the word *portcullis* to show how my husband shut down his emotions, locked in his metaphysical castle that I couldn't get entrance to, because he was so sad.

> I couldn't tell my husband what was happening. He had already lowered the portcullis surrounding the moat containing his feelings and obvious sadness.

I tell my students to go through their drafts and replace dull verbs and nouns with more specific, active, or evocative ones.

EXERCISE: BANK YOUR WORDS

Start a word bank and make deposits in it every week, or every day if possible. Whenever I see an interesting or unusual word, I check out the definition and add it to the word bank I keep on my computer. Soon you will be rich in words that can enliven your essays and articles.

Read Your Piece Out Loud

I've said it before: words are like music. Before you send your piece out into the world, read about editing your work in chapter 17. Also, read it out loud. Record it and listen to it. Ask yourself if each sentence moves the piece forward.

Are you hearing clunky turns of phrase, misused words, clichés, convoluted sentence structures, repetition, or places where you don't sound like yourself? If so, fix them. You might also try varying the rhythm and pace of your writing and listening to it again.

Be merciless. Nothing should stay that doesn't add to the value of your piece.

Estelle's Edge: Since my motto is "Nothing is ever wasted," I usually take those "darlings" I killed, stick them in a separate file, and save them for another essay or article.

When Writing Your Truth Impacts Your Personal Life

Writing about sensitive topics can affect your personal relationships. That's why it's important to be in touch with the reason you are writing the piece in the first place — and your own emotions about it. Realize that not everyone will laud your bravery at putting your story out there, and might feel angry or respond negatively to a piece. Here is some advice I offer my students for writing about delicate issues.

Save the Venting for Your Therapist

Nobody wants to read rage on the page that has no purpose beyond trashing someone else. Your voice doesn't need to be likable, but it needs to be relatable, and that happens when the reader feels empathy for what you are going through and how you are handling it. Plus, if you are hammering on all the failings of your ex-husband, sister, mother, or former boss, your readers won't have any space to make up their own minds. So let the reader know the facts of the situation and the emotion you are feeling that moves the story forward, but don't barrage them with judgments, as if you were trying to win them over to your side. A personal essay is not a court case. Respect the reader and their critical thinking ability.

If you're writing about a personal ordeal, I also recommend not sharing every single detail unless it provides greater depth, a look at your emotional state, or further insight into your mindset.

Don't Blow Up Your Life for a Byline

We all want great bylines, but you should never blow up your life because you are desperate for one. As a writing teacher, I never encourage students to exploit their pain or put their livelihood at risk for the sake of a clip.

I've known writers who spilled the beans about embarrassing (but unseen) physical deformities, affairs with married partners, a secret life as a dominatrix, traumatic divorces, mental illness, and cheating spouses. Sometimes these revelations have serious consequences: "I wrote about cheating on my husband, and now the neighbors shun me and it's being used against me in a child custody case." "I wrote about skipping paying our taxes for years, and now people won't do business with us." "I shared about my daughter cutting herself, and now she won't talk to me."

Part of the reason this happens is that clickbait stories — even those written well — often share damning details of something that happened to the writer but offer no insight into the events. In this day of letting everything hang out, writers and storytellers need to craft a strong story that offers some sort of redemption or transformation and isn't just fodder for a reader's voyeurism. The story requires a narrative arc that helps the reader understand the emotional underpinnings of the writer's actions, and then shows some transformation or learning resulting from the experience. Writing this way requires deep emotional courage.

We tell our kids that once a post or a picture is up on social media, it's out there forever. That is just as true for your stories. If you broke the law, faced down a cop, stole money, betrayed your marital vows, or played a prank on someone that ended with tragedy, why would you want to advertise that? It can't benefit you or your family. People will get mad and may want revenge. Whether they send your essay to the cop you proudly thwarted, testify against you in a child support hearing, or take action to have you pay back what you took, writing about your own wrongdoing may come back to bite you.

If you've done something that shouldn't be publicized and you are compelled to share it with the world, write it into a novel instead.

If you write about other people in your essay, consider consulting them before putting your true feelings about them out into the world. It's true that the writer Anne Lamott says, "You own everything that happened to you. Tell your stories. If people wanted you to write warmly about them, they should have behaved better." I agree with that in principle, but some people can be very contentious and make your life miserable, so at least be prepared and gird yourself for a potential negative reaction. Also, writing about sensitive topics (such as divorce, sexual assault, fraught relationships, money issues) makes it essential for you to invest in self-care. You can cope with the emotional impact of your essay by doing what makes you happy — whether that's going for a jog, filling in an adult coloring book, painting, singing, meditating, or enjoying the beauty of nature. Make good decisions and keep writing your stories.

Please remember, it's never smart to sacrifice your integrity, sanity, health, or relationships to get that byline. You may get attention — but not for your work. Just for being a jerk.

Literary Devices to Use (but Not Abuse)

Metaphor

A metaphor is a figure of speech that directly compares two ideas or objects to suggest a similarity without using "like" or "as." This device — making the subject the object — should be used sparingly, otherwise it can seem forced and performative. Here is an effective example:

> John is a well-informed lawyer, yet his racism is a vine, weaving its way around his heart, impossible to destroy.

Using metaphor paints a picture for the reader. It can also add vividness and poetry to a piece. For example, instead of simply saying a character was angry, or describing how she acted, you might compare her to a hornet, always buzzing and ready to strike.

EXERCISE: METAPHOR MAGIC

To enliven your prose, try your hand at writing a metaphor. Take your writing and circle any boring sentences or places where you feel a visual image would help. Think of an image that would convey the same meaning, and write that down next to the sentence you are working with. Try not to make it too obvious.

If you're trying to describe rain, you might start with "It's raining cats and dogs." Yes, it is a metaphor, but it is also a cliché, so commonly used that it won't create a vivid image in the reader's mind.

Second try: "Each raindrop is a tiny sword against her skin." Can't you imagine the woman bombarded with the violence of the storm from this metaphor?

Simile

If you say explicitly how one thing is like another, you are using a simile. Similes use *like* and *as* to show comparison, and they can add color and texture to an essay.

Here are a few examples:

The ancient mansion looked as gloomy as a mausoleum.
Wagging her tail like a propeller on a helicopter.
Your hatred is as obvious as the spikes on a cactus.

Here are slightly longer examples from pieces I've written:

My hand shot up like a Bravo Housewife who had just had water thrown on her freshly-styled hair.

With a bill of good health from my doctor, I was supposed to bask in nine months of bliss, while devouring bonbons and spreading bonhomie, much like the pregnant midlife celebrities we see smiling on the covers of magazines.

Like a Midwest-born, prairie-skirt wearing Mary Poppins, sans umbrella, the doula appeared at my door, with a huge satchel filled with patchouli-scented pillows, pregnancy-approved essential oils, and home-cooked quinoa.

The difference between a simile and a metaphor is the direct comparison. A metaphor will say "she *is* a rock star" instead of saying "she plays to the crowd *like* a rock star." Similes use the words *like* and *as*, and the reader needs to interpret the statement, which isn't a literal comparison.

Analogy

An analogy is a comparison of two otherwise dissimilar things based on their resemblance in a particular respect.

"Her ideas sprouted as quickly as seedlings" is a simile suggesting that the ideas came fast and in great quantity. An analogy would say, "Ideas are like seedlings — you need to nourish them so they can flourish," which roots the comparison in the common needs of the two concepts.

Objective Correlatives (aka Necessary Objects)

Anchoring your essay with an object, like a piece of furniture, a song, or a phrase, can help tell the emotional story through the participants' evolving connection to the object. The dictionary defines *objective correlative* as "something (such as a situation or chain of events) that symbolizes or objectifies a particular emotion and that may be used in creative writing to evoke a desired emotional response in the reader." In William Dameron's *New York Times* essay, "After 264 Haircuts, a Marriage Ends" (analyzed in more detail in chapter 7), the haircut is an objective correlative for the writer's relationship. The stories of Ann Hood often start out with an ordinary object (a scarf, a recipe) that is connected to an insight about grief, loss, or love.

The idea is to turn an object or chain of events into a symbol that evokes questions and meanings not stated on the page and acts as a bridge to a larger understanding.

Alliteration

I personally love alliteration — the repetition of the same letter or sound at the beginning of multiple words in a sentence. It's much more fun to write, "I continued consuming the carrots," than "I continued eating the carrots." Or you could take it even further and write, "I continued consuming the consommé." Alliteration is a great way to imbue a piece with some personality and voice. But, as with makeup, less is more.

It can be deeply fulfilling to write an essay that shares your innermost thoughts, most difficult challenges, and powerful personal insights with the world. It also takes bravery to be your honest, most authentic self on the page.

Savannah Guthrie had this to say at a commencement speech at George Washington University, and I think it applies to writers most of all.

> And what you will find is — your obstacles, your broken places, the spots where you've healed, the things you've overcome — this is the source of your strength, and it also is the source of your beauty.

Essay Advice from Editors

- The easiest way to break into professional writing is by writing a personal essay. That's how I publish new writers. You are telling a story nobody else can tell.
- If your essay refers to other people, have you consulted them about it before putting it out into the world? Are you prepared for their potentially negative reaction?
- Tell us if you have accompanying photos or videos that you own the rights to.
- Present your story in a way that allows everyone to see their own story in your piece.
- Tell a story with an arc of insight. Not just "This sad or traumatic thing happened [such as my mother has Alzheimer's], and this is how we are dealing with it." We can't take every sad story. We also can't take every happy story about how much you love your husband or your kids or your friends. That's a testimonial, not an essay.

ESSAY CHECKLIST

- ❏ Do you have a compelling headline that evokes emotion?
- ❏ Do you have a strong opening?
- ❏ Do you have a narrative arc?
- ❏ Are you creating scenes in your writing (like movie scenes)?
- ❏ Are you using sensory language (what you hear, touch, taste, smell, and see) to paint a picture for the reader?
- ❏ Does your dialogue help portray your characters and move the story forward?
- ❏ Are you present in your essay? It is called a personal essay for a reason.
- ❏ Are you answering a reader's question of "So what"?
- ❏ Are you circling back in some way at the closing?
- ❏ Do you have a transformative ending that offers reflection, wisdom, or insight?
- ❏ Does your ending go beyond the time frame of your essay and make the reader think about how its insights will shape you (and them) in the future?

CHAPTER SEVEN

Analyzing Essays

*The first sentence can't be written
until the final sentence is written.*

— Joyce Carol Oates

I've always enjoyed analyzing processes to see how they work. I married a systems person, I've been going to a therapist for years to unravel my emotional life, and I take the same approach with my students' essays and pitches.

In this chapter, with the permission of the authors, I share three essays in full and analyze them to look at what works and why. The first, by Vishavjit Singh, appeared in *Salon*; the second, by my former star student Juli Fraga, appeared in CityLab/Bloomberg; and the third essay, by William Dameron, was published in the *Modern Love* column of the *New York Times*. The three essays approach the ideas of identity, marriage, and love in surprising ways.

The essays also follow the basic tenets for essay writing detailed in the previous chapter.

"Captain America in a Turban"

"Captain America in a Turban" is a provocative piece by Vishavjit Singh that appeared in *Salon*. It begins:

> I settled on a rock in Central Park, the New York skyline behind me.
> A glassy new skyscraper neared completion in its stretch toward the
> skies. I was striking a few poses in my superhero costume when a
> young boy perched higher on a rock chimed in.

The opening lines get you right into the action (i.e., the inciting incident) and create a sense of place. The description of the action — striking a few poses in his superhero costume — immediately makes the reader want to know more. The scenery and verbs evoke the feeling of flight, and the reader wants to know what kind of creature this is. And then he engages with the young boy (whose position on the rock creates a sense that the child is looking down, perhaps metaphorically as well as literally, on the narrator).

> "Captain America does not have a turban and beard," he said. He had
> a child's curious tone. No malevolence.

It's a great statement that shows both the innocence of the child and the "foreignness" of Vishavjit, who is Sikh. Because of the child's observation, we want to know more about the writer who is posing as Captain America. It is also important to Vishavjit that the reader doesn't feel punitive toward the child for his words.

> "Why not?" I asked him. "I was born here. We could have a new Cap-
> tain America who is Sikh or black or Hispanic."

This brief dialogue moves the story along by telling us something about Vishavjit's identity and his feelings about superheroes. It also shows that he is open to exploring these topics with the child.

> He thought about this. Finally, he conceded that yes, maybe a black
> or Hispanic Captain America would be OK. But his brain couldn't
> make sense of it: Captain America in a turban? Captain America in a
> beard? He'd never conceived of such a thing before.

This passage builds on the relationship of the writer and the child. It shows a little about how the child thinks and how he was probably raised. It is just enough. Getting further into the child's thoughts would not move the story forward. We must get back to the writer.

> That's exactly what brought me to this park on a beautiful summer day. To make fresh neural connections in our collective consciousness. To leave a new image on the hard drive of that boy's mind.

Now we are back to the writer and his motivation. That's where we should be at this juncture in the essay.

> The idea originated with Fiona Aboud, a photographer based in New York City. For seven years she has traveled the country capturing stills for her "Sikhs: An American Portrait" project. I'm an editorial cartoonist who has been documenting the thrills and travails of real-life Sikhs in the aftermath of 9/11 through illustrations made on my computer touch pad. One of those cartoons, created for my first trip to Comic-Con, featured a turbaned and bearded Captain America. It made a three-dimensional spark in Fiona's imagination.
>
> I was going to be Captain America for a day on the streets of the Big Apple.
>
> Thanks to inclement weather, we ended up shooting on Puerto Rican Day. It was bright and sunny as we stepped out of Fiona's house. I was acutely aware of my tight costume. I caught the stares of passersby in the corners of my eye. There were a few gentle smiles.

Here Vishavjit explains how this visual experiment originated, giving needed context to the essay. He also offers a setting for this piece — the streets of Manhattan on Puerto Rican Day.

> I have been skinny all my life, and I felt a stirring of anxiety to be so exposed. Family and friends have pointed out my thinness for years, and the self-consciousness has sunk deep into my psyche. Before I could even confront the political statement of my costume, I had to confront my own inhibitions and body image. But I took a deep breath, and kept walking.

As Vishavjit admits his insecurities about being thin, the personal becomes universal, enabling the reader to relate to him. Who among us doesn't feel insecure and anxious sometimes? Here he is more worried about his skinny body than about the political statement his costume makes.

> The next challenge was the reaction of my fellow Americans. I've grown accustomed to a Pavlovian response to my presence. Stares. Verbal assaults. So far, that's as far as it's gone, though for some turbaned and bearded Americans, a fearful reaction has had tragic physical consequences. So the outcome of this experiment was unknown, which felt both exhilarating and mildly terrifying.

He is taking the reader along with him on his journey and sharing how he has been bullied because of his identity. He also acknowledges that for many who look like him (bearded, turbaned), bullying has escalated to outright violence, without describing specific incidents, which would divert the reader's attention.

> We took a cab to Fifth Avenue, near Central Park, and stepped out of the safety of the car to find people coming from all directions. My breath caught in my throat, wondering what they would think of me. But I reminded myself to not focus on that. To stay in the moment. Take it all in.

Vishavjit continues to move the story forward with the arrival in Central Park. The reminder of his vulnerability keeps us engaged and rooting for him.

> As I walked down the street, it was like dominoes. People slowed down to get my attention. Fans clustered around me. Parents edged their children next to me for a shot. I urged the kids to strike a superhero pose. In front of the Metropolitan Museum, four well-built African American men surrounded me with big smiles, hands stretched out, fingers twirled with attitude and me sandwiched between them, striking a pose with my shield and a fist.

The detailed, vivid, metaphorical language paints a picture for the reader, bringing to life the mundane action of people posing for photos using active, evocative verbs like *clustered*, *twirled*, and *sandwiched*.

> The Puerto Rican Day parade was going on, and we stepped into a thicket of revelers. People did double takes like a slow-motion movie. "Hey! Check out Captain America!" people yelled from the railings. Strangers hustled over each other to snap a picture and pose. Young and old of all hues, from all walks of life. I had to be repeatedly reminded to keep moving and not hold up pedestrian traffic.
>
> People shook my hands, and a few literally congratulated me. The celebrity-of-the-moment experience was a little overwhelming. But I was jarred out of that trance by a few negative outliers. One man tried to grab my turban. Another yelled, "Captain Arab." And yet another: "Terrorista!"
>
> As we posed for a picture with one kid, he stuck his middle finger right in my face.
>
> "So you are flipping off Captain America?" I admonished him.
>
> He got red-faced, apologized, and struck a smile instead. We carried on undeterred, and the overall crowd reaction was positive and friendly.

Vishavjit offers a visual, vivid metaphor showing the depth and breadth of the crowd. He uses dialogue sparingly, to show his effect on others, and their effect on him. The kid who gives him the finger makes a dramatic conclusion to the scene.

> An NYPD officer tracked me down to take a shot together on his smartphone. He said it would be his claim to fame.
>
> As we veered off the parade route, Fiona came up with the idea to approach the FDNY staff and ask if we could enter their truck for some shots. These real-life superheroes were gracious enough to grant her wish, and the kid inside me was ecstatic. I sat on the driver's seat sticking my head out in joy.

Describing the New York firefighters as real-life superheroes elevates the story, making it a vehicle for showing others' courage.

We entered Central Park, and I found a shaded spot under a tree. In a lotus posture I meditated on the wonderful day unfolding before our eyes. Families strolling by, some lying in the shade, others baking in the sun for a tan. "This is really cool," said a young woman walking by. A baby strolling in the grass came up right next to me, intently focused on the colorful scene. A little dog barely a foot off the ground sniffed up close and barked a few words in its language. This, I thought, is the coolest urban jungle in the world.

It was the unlikeliest of days for me. Hundreds of strangers came up to me. And we were able to lay to rest any anxieties or inhibitions in those moments — about other people, about the unknown, about ourselves, about violating other people's personal spaces or not understanding their beliefs. We could simply meet. Say hi. Snap a memory of that moment. And I could leave brand-new images on the hard drive of their mind — as well as their hand-held devices, Apple clouds, virtual worlds.

Vishavjit expresses his belief in the underlying goodness of people. He also describes how he was able to lay down his inhibitions and anxieties. He circles back to the start of his essay with his invocation of the metaphor of recording new images on a hard drive.

For me, I had gigabytes of new memories tucked into the crevices of my gray matter. Enough memory snapshots to take me on repeat journeys for a lifetime.

"It takes a lot of courage to do this," a few people said during the day. I have never seen myself as courageous. But circumstances in life create moments where courage finds its way to us.

The gift he leaves the reader with is the realization that when he dressed as a superhero, he found the courage he lacked.

"Seoul Searching in San Francisco"

Juli Fraga is a San Francisco–based psychologist. She wrote a piece for CityLab/Bloomberg called "Seoul Searching in San Francisco."

> Like many Midwesterners, I was raised on casseroles created from the recipes on the back of Campbell Soup labels. My mother made comfort food like taco pie, tuna and noodles, and chicken, broccoli, and rice casserole. Our more formal dinners consisted of baked potatoes, Omaha Steaks, and corn on the cob.

I am a sucker for a good alliterative title. This title is good not just because it sounds like a song, but because it embodies the essence of the essay. It also plays on the words *soul* and *Seoul*, evoking a journey and a quest. Juli jumps right into the story, packing details into the first sentence that make you want to know more. Campbell Soup immediately evokes thoughts of Middle America. By using that term, Juli employs what I like to call a "tell," indicating where she is going in the story. In the hands of a less skilled writer, this detail might have been left out, and the sentence would have read, "Like many Midwesterners, I was raised on casseroles." Boring. Next she shares a list of other comfort foods that evoke Middle America. Notice how short she keeps the sentences, so they don't weigh down the piece.

> I never felt like I truly belonged in Omaha. I was born in Seoul, South Korea, but at three months of age, I left my home for the heartland, where I was adopted and raised by white parents.

These two clear, concise sentences convey emotion and movement. Juli shows her vulnerability with "I never felt like I truly belonged in Omaha." Then she explains how she was adopted and raised by white parents. The sparse writing suggests the emptiness she must have felt. We feel for her, so we want to go with her on her journey.

> It was difficult to find Korea in the flat lands of Nebraska. Because of this, my parents tried to expose me to Asian culture by taking me to Chu's Chop Suey House, the most popular Chinese restaurant in town.

This is a short essay, so Juli needs to get the story moving. She does that by including carefully chosen details about what passed for Asian culture in her town. Novice writers often don't offer specifics. They will say something like, "We had fun, ate food, played music, and enjoyed each other's company." It's so much better to say something like "We savored the steaks fresh off the grill as we chilled to the cool sounds of Aretha Franklin." Doesn't that say the same thing, but in a much more interesting way?

Entering Chu's felt like walking into a palace: the dark oak doors were etched with an ornate floral pattern and red lanterns with gold writing hung overhead. The waitress always spoke to me in Mandarin, because she assumed that I was Chinese, too.

I was both elated and confused by her greeting, so I remained silent. I felt validated that she acknowledged that I was not white, but I didn't know how to tell her that I wasn't Chinese. When our almond chicken, chow mein, and egg rolls arrived, she gave my mother a fork while she handed me a set of chopsticks.

Juli's description of the restaurant packs in details that let us almost see the kitsch in the decor. Next, she evokes empathy in the reader by describing her double alienation: she doesn't fit in, either with white people or with the Chinese restaurant staff. The next sentence compounds her confusion and the reader's indignation at the false assumptions made about her identity. Why should the waitress expect her to use chopsticks?

Over a decade ago, at age 29, I moved from the Midwest to San Francisco, closer to the country of my birth. In Nebraska, I felt as if my Korean identity stood at a standstill. But the Bay Area was a different story.

"I'm taking you back to your roots," my co-worker told me my first year in San Francisco. A Bay Area native, she knew about all of San Francisco's hidden culinary corners. At her urging, I tried Korean BBQ at Brother's BBQ in the Richmond district — the first time I'd tried any of the foods from my birth country.

Now that Juli has set up her background and portrayed her childhood self as a fish out of water, she turns to the discovery of her heritage.

Walking along Geary Boulevard, I was amazed by the neighborhood's diversity. People of Asian and Indian descent breezed by me on the sidewalk. In the streets of Nebraska, I had stood out as the only minority. But now, for the first time in my life, I felt at ease, because I blended in with those around me.

Inside Brother's BBQ, a grill sat in the middle of a long, wooden table. The server brought over a square silver cart holding strips of bulgogi (sirloin) and kalbi (short ribs), as well as little white dishes filled with strands of relish that resembled sea life. These dishes sat beside other petite bowls filled with cabbage covered in a bright orange sauce (kimchi) and purple pieces of eggplant (gaji-namul) covered in soy sauce. Once the meat hit the grill, a haze of smoke curled into the air. As I placed the first sizzling piece of kalbi on my tongue, it tasted as strange to me as I imagined broccoli casserole might taste to my San Francisco friend. My mouth felt like it was on fire as I tried the kalbi mixed with bright red chili sauce.

Juli shows how she finally feels like she fits in, after a lifetime of being "other." I always say that G-d is in the details. Well, look how many details she adds setting up the food scene at Brother's BBQ. Her description of the food is so vibrant that we viscerally feel her excitement at tasting all these new flavors.

When we left the restaurant that day, the waiter turned to us and said "Gomabseubnida" — "thank you" in Korean.

Those words offered me more than a polite salutation. The phrase connected me to a language I had lost when I came to America.

During that year, I visited many of San Francisco's historical sites, including curvy Lombard Street, the hippie Haight-Ashbury, and the Italian district, known as North Beach. But it wasn't until I set foot inside of the landmark Castro Theater that I felt a tug of recognition, because I finally saw other Korean adoptees wrestling with the same questions that I had struggled with throughout my life.

Being addressed in her native language is a turning point in how Juli feels about her heritage. Giving the specific words is important. Another writer might have just said, "The waiter used a Korean phrase to say goodbye." See how much more powerful it is to use the exact language?

The Castro Theater sits in the Castro district of the city, where rainbow colored stripes in hues of red, blue, yellow and green line the streets. The theater hosts several national and international film festivals each year, including the Asian American Film Festival.

I attended the festival, where Deann Borshay Liem, a Korean adoptee filmmaker, showed her documentary, *First Person Plural*. In it, she chronicles how she tried to reconcile her identity as an adopted daughter of white parents with her unknown history in Korea.

In the darkness of the theater, I saw another adoptee's story projected onto the wide screen — one that echoed my own and reflected a familiar part of my narrative back to me. After I watched the movie, I also connected with the Korean adoptee community in San Francisco, where I met two of my closest friends.

The film festival represents the essay's crescendo, culminating in Juli's discovery of a community where she finally feels she belongs. What I like about the craft here is that Juli uses specific details to describe the theater and its role in the Asian community. Then she aligns the Korean filmmaker's search for identity with her own. After taking steps to find like-minded people, she has come full circle in exploring and embracing her heritage and seeing others embracing theirs.

Two years later, I became a mother surrounded by the support of these women. We continue to talk about the unique dynamics that parenthood brings, especially when your child is your first known biological relative and the rest of your lineage is unknown.

Juli's discovery of her Korean identity enables her to share it with her daughter. The words "first known biological relative" powerfully evoke the rootlessness of an adopted child.

Now, over a decade later, I often stroll along Crissy Field with my daughter. As we look out at the water, I'm reminded of the ocean that separates me from my birth country. But despite the distance, Korea doesn't feel so far away. I've settled into a city that finally feels like home.

The gift of this essay is finding one's true home: for Juli and her daughter, it's in the Korean American community in San Francisco.

"After 264 Haircuts, a Marriage Ends"

William Dameron's 2019 debut memoir is titled *The Lie: A Memoir of Two Marriages, Catfishing and Coming Out*. He wrote this essay, "After 264 Haircuts, a Marriage Ends," for the *Modern Love* column of the *New York Times*.

> Elizabeth lofted the black cape as I watched it billow in front of me like a sheet blossoming on a clothesline. She fastened the buttons around my neck, placed her hands on either side of my head and whispered, "I can't do this anymore."

This is a powerful opening using interesting active verbs (*loft, billow*), and description (the movement of the black cape). Instead of starting with backstory ("I met my wife when…"), which won't grab the reader's attention, it starts right in the action. We don't know exactly what Elizabeth is preparing to do, although the title reveals that it is a haircut. The words "I can't do this anymore" introduce the dramatic tension.

> "Do what?" I asked.
> "This," she said, gesturing around us. "I have to let you go."
> Still, she reached into a black case and pulled out scissors and a comb. The scent of freshly cut grass drifted through an open kitchen window along with the squeals of neighborhood children.
> "Who will cut your hair?" she asked.
> I shrugged my shoulders.

Bill Dameron responds to her words of despair by questioning them: "Do what?" Elizabeth's response, "I have to let you go," adds to the tension. Then the break in the dialogue, switching to a description of the suburban scene, creates suspense. Elizabeth's question, "Who will cut your hair?," sustains the tension. Bill's noncommittal response shows us, early in the story, that Elizabeth wants more from him than he can give. We don't know why, but he is about to tell us.

> For more than 22 years, roughly 264 haircuts, we had shared this ritual. She would run her hands through my hair, nudging my head

forward and sideways, her fingers mere inches away from the secret thoughts and desires swirling inside of my skull.

Wow! The writer doesn't simply tell us, "We've been together for twenty-two years." Instead he measures the duration of the time by numbers and shared rituals (twenty-two years, 264 haircuts). Then, he uses sensual language to convey the couple's intimacy — these are not just good friends. The last few words of this paragraph tell us that in spite of this intimacy, the writer is keeping a secret from Elizabeth, and we want to know more.

She pulled up a swath of hair with a comb and began to snip.

When we first met, in the 1980s, I wore my hair parted on the side, a preppy conservative look. On our second date, she swept back my bangs with her fingertips and offered to cut my hair for the first time. Over the years, clumps of my dark hair have slid down the cape and pooled on the kitchen floor. Eventually, the side part vanished and flecks of gray started to mingle with the black. Now, the hair that fell was mostly gray, peppered with black strands.

Here the action begins: the haircut, which is the objective correlative that carries the weight of all the emotion and secrets. The haircut also represents letting go and saying goodbye. Bill shares the backstory of their relationship, but he deftly ties this to the haircut ritual, using the description of his changing hairstyles and the graying of his hair to show the passing of time. We know this relationship has been serious and consistent, and we know it is ending, though we still don't know why.

"Do you have the clippers?" I asked.

She reached into the case and pulled out the heavy Wahls. When she turned them on, they emitted a low electronic buzz.

"Cut it all off," I said.

"What?"

"I want you to buzz it all off."

If I didn't have any hair, it wouldn't matter that I no longer had her to cut it.

"Go on," I said. "Do it."

I watched the hair tumble onto the cape. Her breasts pressed against my shoulder as her hand brushed the hair from my head. And then I felt something wet fall on my cheek. I heard a sound, like a hiccup, and then I heard it again, but it was more like a sucking noise, like someone trying to catch a breath. Her tears began to fall.

"Shh, it's O.K.," I said.

She stood back, her face red and blotchy. "It's just that you look so different now."

This passage shows Bill Dameron's brilliance as a writer. He uses dialogue to move the story forward with every sentence and draws in the reader while still connecting to the main theme of the haircuts. In asking Elizabeth to cut off all his hair, he is letting go of his former look. At the same time, she is letting go of him and having the harder time. He wants the comfort of the familiar, but he also wants to be free.

She held up a mirror, and I winced. "Oh man," I said. There was something honest and bold about the look. "Shave off the rest."

"But you'll look like a cancer patient."

"It's just hair."

She finished. As if my thoughts had been laid bare, too, she said: "You know I'm stronger now. I can make it on my own."

"I know that," I said.

This paragraph offers drama through dialogue. Shaving off the hair, exposing Bill's scalp, also exposes thoughts and feelings of sadness. We know this scene is about loss, but we don't know what Elizabeth means when she says she is stronger now than before. We want to read on to find out.

For two months, ever since I moved out, we had been engaged in a weekend dance of me visiting to keep contact with our girls, staying in our home in Virginia as if nothing had changed. But everything had changed.

Now we learn that the two have separated.

She rubbed lotion on my neck and pulled out the straight razor. I felt the cool metal on my skin as she nudged my head forward and down with her fingertips.

I closed my eyes. I could hear our 14-year-old daughter chattering on the telephone and laughter coming from the TV. Our dog's claws clicked across the floor.

"I didn't cheat on you," I said, keeping my head down and my eyes closed.

The blade stood still for a moment, then skimmed down the back of my neck.

"I had to get that H.I.V. test," she said, "because you were acting so out of character."

I was offended when she had first told me this. How many times had we made love? Was it greater or fewer than the number of haircuts? Of course, the test was negative. I could count on one hand the number of people I had been intimate with before her.

This passage returns to the action, and the mention of the straight razor creates additional tension. If Elizabeth was angry and didn't love him, she could do a lot of damage. But we know that he trusts her and has children with her, including the daughter in the other room. Something happened to this former couple that is devastating, but also freeing for him. The haircut is where all the emotion is laden. The cutting of the hair represents the severing of the relationship.

At this point the reader might suspect infidelity, but Bill says he didn't cheat. Mentioning the HIV test gives a hint of the conflict's roots.

The first was my childhood neighbor in Greensboro, N.C. He and I were too young to understand our dark fumbling during sleepovers. In college, I lost my virginity to Sally, a red-haired flute player, in a rite of passage that I simply wanted to get over.

When I was 20 and in Colorado for the summer with my aunt Sheila and her psychic girlfriend, I stumbled out of a bar on the edge of town walking arm in arm with Don, my aunt's handsome young friend. Under the shadow of Pikes Peak, he and I kissed. I heard Sheila's voice in the distance calling out, "He's not sure if he's gay yet, Don!"

But I knew.

When I first started seeing Elizabeth, at 21, I told her about Sally but not Don. That part of my life was supposed to have been erased by conversion therapy, which involved me praying with my mother at the dining room table every day not to be the way I was.

Here is the reason they are splitting: he is gay. In less skilled hands, the piece might have opened with that revelation, letting the essay fill in the backstory. In Bill Dameron's hands, by using the haircut as the object, the action of the story can continue while he fills in the backstory.

The first time Elizabeth and I had sex was on a sofa in my brother's off-campus apartment in Raleigh, N.C. Neither of us was a virgin, so there was no awkward fumbling, just as there was no passionate taboo. I recognized it for what it was; this was as good as it could get.

Bill reveals here that there wasn't much passion between him and Elizabeth. That helps the reader understand why he has moved on.

For more than 22 years, after our daughters were born and as my hair became grayer and Elizabeth's body became softer, I kept my secret locked away. Then, on a Wednesday night 10 years ago in a Walmart parking lot, Elizabeth saved me. "Are you gay?" she asked.

"I don't want to be," I said.

Shortly after, our marriage ended, but while I was still making my weekend visits, there was Ray. On our second date, I ripped the clothing off his body. Afterward, he held up his pants and examined the broken zipper and popped button.

"Those were my favorite pants," he said. I laughed. He did not.

Elizabeth brushed the hair from my shoulders and removed the cape. I stood up, put on my shirt, and pulled the broom from the kitchen closet to sweep up.

Bill explains how his wife exposed his secret and how he later found passion with a man (an almost overwhelming discovery for him). This passage also shows his innocence and yearning, and his effort to suppress his forbidden desires.

When the girls went to bed, I wandered the house taking stock of things that were no longer mine. There on the dining room table was the blue metal pitcher we found in an antique shop in New Hampshire.

This painting, above the brick mantel, was my 20th wedding anniversary gift to her. Here was the sofa where Elizabeth and I once lay side by side with a sleeping dog at our feet. The wooden floors creaked as I passed.

When I reached the top of the stairs, Elizabeth stood motionless in the dark hall.

"Can I sleep with you, just sleep, this one last night?" I asked.

"Don't wake me in the morning," she said.

She removed her nightgown. I took off my shirt.

That was her side of the bed, and this used to be mine. Here was the blue comforter where we cradled our newborn girls. These were the pillows flattened with use.

Bill's wandering the house and taking stock of objects "no longer his" is a metaphor for the end of the relationship. He shows their connection and some reluctance to let her go by asking to sleep with her one last time. The blue comforter on the bed is a sign of the shared history between the two of them. The image of "the pillows flattened with use" evokes the sense of a relationship that was not exciting, but a source of comfort and familiarity.

I lay awake on my back. She rested her hand on my neck. I turned to my right side, and she to her left as we twisted in our bittersweet ballet of goodbye.

In the grainy morning light, I closed the bedroom door and tiptoed to my daughters' rooms. This was Sophie's. Those were the boxes filled with her dolls. I tucked her dark hair behind her ear and kissed her warm cheek.

Here was Marisa's. These were her glasses. I picked them up and cleaned them with the tail of my shirt.

"I'm just going to work now," I muttered, a half-truth in the half-light.

This, behind me, was the house full of secrets, and here before me was the path that lay ahead. This is what I left: an empty chair at the table, the scent of my skin on the sheets, an old painting, a sleeping dog, a blue pitcher, my lingering shadow on the front steps before I let go.

Listing these familiar objects at the end of the piece, along with the fleeting traces of his presence, is a literary device that works, because they represent the ritual and familiarity Bill is leaving behind to start his new life as a single gay man.

CHECKLIST FOR ASSESSING YOUR ESSAY

❏ Have I given the reader enough detail and insights to make the essay resonate for them?

❏ Are the scenes, descriptions, and dialogue detailed and specific?

❏ Do the detail and description move the story forward?

❏ Does every sentence of the story move it along?

❏ Can a given sentence be made even clearer?

❏ Is the narrative arc defined?

❏ Is there a clear insight that the reader can connect with?

CHAPTER EIGHT

Writing Op-Eds and Timely Cultural Pieces

You are not entitled to your opinion. You are entitled to your informed opinion. No one is entitled to be ignorant.

— HARLAN ELLISON

Writing an opinion piece (or op-ed) about a topic in the news or in the zeitgeist is one way to get the attention of editors, even if you are not an experienced writer. Almost all news outlets have op-ed sections, where writers not affiliated with the publication's editorial board can contribute. Many online publications feature op-eds as well. Most people aren't aware that the word *op-ed* is short for "opposite the editorial page," and not "opinion," as such pieces are commonly referred to today.

It always helps if you can tie your personal experience to the topic you want to write about. When Charlize Theron was in the news because someone called the police on her while she was disciplining her small child, it enraged me, and I published an opinion piece in a parenting publication about what my reaction would be should someone do that to me. I wrote about why my husband does the laundry, and should, for the *Washington Post* because research showed that fathers who participated in housework — like my husband — had a positive impact on their daughters' health, happiness, and future success. And I wrote for Romper about how sheltering in place during the pandemic removed all the usual worries about parenting.

Op-eds aim to persuade the reader to accept the writer's point of view or recommendations. The best op-eds are provocative or counterintuitive: they may be controversial, go against the conventional thinking on a subject, or add a new perspective to news stories.

When Holly Baxter from the *Independent* contributed to my *All About the Pitch* column, she told me her publication banned the word *must* from op-ed headlines. She recommends crafting a pitch that a reasonable person can disagree with, one that can start a conversation or a debate. For example, "We must do more for starving children" is not a winning op-ed idea because no reasonable person would argue against it.

With an op-ed it's always good to take an unusual or opposing viewpoint or go against the grain. If everyone agrees, then what would be the point of writing about the topic?

When it comes to arguing for an idea on the page, passion is good; ranting is not. If you are going on and on and making the piece only about you, without making it relatable or providing any new insight or information, then you risk losing your audience. A better bet is to explore the issue while sharing your personal feeling and how it is connected to the problem or solution that others are facing or dealing with, too. It's a delicate balance.

Give the Facts

Op-eds are not long diatribes or soliloquies. They start with an opinion, maybe about something that annoys you, but that opinion needs to be supported by facts. Lay out why your opinion makes sense and support it with data (such as studies, statistics, and poll results). Just make sure you cite primary sources — the original publications or websites that presented the findings, not other publications that mention or quote them.

Have a Nose for News

To find inspiration for op-eds, check out the daily news on television, online, or in the papers. Figure out whether you have something to add to the national conversation or an important point of view and use that as the basis for the piece. If you can propose solutions to the problem, even better, as I did when I wrote about my distress that Dressbarn was shutting down its brick-and-mortar stores. I wrote "Dressbarn was the perfect outlet to focus on the midlife market — and the buying power of women in their 40s and 50s — that the chain never really took seriously or tried to explore." Then I shared how important Dressbarn had been in my life — I wore a Dressbarn dress for my engagement party and another for my bridal shower — and suggested that Dressbarn ignored and didn't create partnerships with online retailers such as Amazon and QVC or on social media, they didn't have good mobile technology, and their DB dollars and loyalty codes were too complicated and confusing. This piece was published in AARP's *The Girlfriend*. The editor told me she had gotten a lot of comments about the situation, and my op-ed landed in her lap at the perfect time.

Estelle's Edge: Every day, fill out your mapping template (described in chapter 1) to keep current on news and trends.

Adapt to the Format

You might have written up something as an essay, but if you are new to publishing, it might be easier for you to get it published as an op-ed. For example, I wrote my *New York Times* piece "Singing My Dad Back to Me" as an essay, but it could have also been an op-ed, using research to support my premise that music helps Alzheimer's patients, like my dad, stay connected to what's around them. My student Jennie Burke wrote her *New York Times* piece "Defying the Family Cycle of Addiction" as an essay, with reported elements about her family's history of opioid addiction and her concern about her daughter being prescribed opioids after surgery, but it could have easily been an op-ed on how to protect teens from addiction.

Estelle's Edge: If you have a longform essay that might work as an op-ed, try to shorten it to six or seven hundred words. Tightening your writing will allow you to highlight your point of view, and writing the piece as an op-ed will increase your chances of getting it published.

Consider a Call to Action

After you have laid out your opinion and supported it with facts and information, you need to conclude. A good way to do it is to circle back to something you said in the intro of your piece and add one new insight or thought. The most persuasive op-eds often end with a call to action: a rallying cry, a way for readers to join the cause or at least think about it.

For example, in an op-ed I wrote for the *Independent* about the army of lawyers, researchers, data experts, and other professionals (called the Britney Army) supporting Britney Spears in her fight against the conservatorship she was under for thirteen years, I ended my piece with a quote from someone involved in the movement calling for the government to fund home aides who leave at night, as an alternative to providing grants to states that make it easy for unscrupulous people to get involved in corrupt conservatorships and commit conservatorship abuse.

Get Paid

Most publications pay for op-eds. Traditionally five hundred to eight hundred words in length, they now tend toward the higher end of the word count. The fee varies, but you will get paid. For information on op-ed fees, check out the site Who Pays Writers? For a list of US newspapers that publish op-eds, check out the Op-Ed Project.

Seize the Moment

Although writers can pitch and submit an op-ed whenever they have an opinion on a situation or issue, it's important to know that editors frequently send out calls for pitches for op-eds and other short pieces on social media or to writers they have worked with, pegged to new TV shows, movies, or books. Often these "rapid-response" editors commission pieces only a day or so before they run. The key to getting noticed is to get in first. The news cycle moves very fast, so when you find a topic you want to write about, act quickly.

Many of these editors also take pieces connected to major holidays and pegged to certain awareness months, because these also tend to be popular when posted on social media.

OP-ED CHECKLIST

- ❑ Is your piece connected to current events, a national holiday, or an awareness month?
- ❑ Is it provocative?
- ❑ Is it a piece that only you can write?
- ❑ Is the information you are sharing helpful to others?
- ❑ Have you read the publication you are pitching so you know what the editor wants?
- ❑ Did you pitch the piece to the right editor?
- ❑ Is it short (between 500 and 800 words)?
- ❑ Is there a dramatic arc to your piece?
- ❑ Are you telling a story and not just venting?
- ❑ Does your piece end with some sort of resolution, catharsis, transformation, or call to action (even if it's subtle)?

PART THREE

Pitch Clinic

CHAPTER NINE

How to Pitch to Publications So You Don't Get Ghosted

Most of the important things in the world have been accomplished by people who have kept on trying when there seemed to be no hope at all.
— DALE CARNEGIE

Nobody wants to get ghosted, by an editor or anyone else. I should know. I was ghosted by my peers in middle school.

I was called a nerd. I used to traverse the school halls with my nose in a book, wearing some version of my favorite pink polyester pantsuit, dodging insults, but mostly invisible. At lunchtime, I'd escape to the library, where I would pick up Nancy Drew books, fantasy stories, biographies, and the *Iliad*, and scarf down my sandwich in a corner.

One day I found a book called something like *The Art of Being Popular*. Convinced this book would be my ticket to the charmed circle of the in-crowd in my school, I pored over its text like I was studying the Talmud. I dutifully followed all the requirements (brush your hair one hundred times a day, make small talk with classmates), but it didn't help. Still, I found camaraderie in chorus and friendship with a group of older, cooler kids by the time I got to high school.

I believe my grade school experience made me a more compassionate person, a better friend — and someone determined never to be ignored. And I don't want it to happen to you either.

Editors receive hundreds of pitches a day. You need to persuade them that they want yours.

Writing a good pitch letter means thinking like an editor. So ask yourself: Why this? Why now? Why me? And convey your answers in your pitch.

Guide Yourself

Select a publication you are interested in pitching your story to, one that is a fit for your topic. Do your due diligence. Search the publication's website for a pitching guide or editorial calendar. Sometimes editors won't send you this information until they start working with you, but it never hurts to check. Also, search the site to see if your topic has already been covered and in what way. And make sure you understand who's reading this publication. Write for the audience you are pitching to. If you are pitching a teen magazine or *Rolling Stone*, you'll use different language than you would for *AARP* or *Vogue*.

My pitch to *AARP: The Magazine* focused on a foster parent over the age of fifty who was taking on a teen so that the child wouldn't have to go to a group home. I pitched the article specifically to appeal to AARP's audience of readers aged fifty and older, and it was accepted. If you forget about the reader, it doesn't matter how good your pitch is.

Acknowledgment Counts

Do your research. Editors like to know that you read their publications (you do, don't you?). So mention an article you've read. "I loved your recent article 'When the Child Becomes the Parent.' I'd like to write an 800-word parenting article called ..."

It's even better if you can reference an article or essay the editor wrote. Most editors are writers, too. Use that information to your benefit when you pitch them.

Tantalize with a Title

We know a good title is vital. It's even better if the title evokes emotion or even anger. Often an editor will assign on the basis of a compelling headline, even if the pitch isn't fully fleshed out. Try using an online phrase thesaurus, with keywords related to your topic, to get title ideas percolating. And if you want to see your byline in a particular publication, model the titles the publication uses.

Estelle's Edge: Include a pithy title in the subject line of your email submission.

Start with a Story

Pitch a story, not a topic. Instead of writing "I'd like to write about families trying to resolve conflict in the Middle East," say, "I'd like to write about the astonishing relationship between an Israeli family and an Arab family and how they managed to unite their fragmented neighborhood through their share-a-ride service through the toughest parts of town. I have access to both sides, plus commentary from the local rabbi and emir who were against it at first but have now banded together to support this peacemaking endeavor." The first example is vague and leaves the editor with pressing questions, but the second one shows that you have a clear idea of what the story is about.

Write the opening sentence of your pitch as if it were the first paragraph of the article. I often use the first paragraph of the pitch in my completed piece. You can also engage the editor with a compelling question, a dramatic anecdote, surprising (or scary) statistics, an intriguing quote from an expert you preinterviewed, or a vivid, action-packed description. Don't be afraid to be provocative. If you are pitching a reported story, list the experts you plan to quote and the research and statistics that will provide your story with credibility.

Back in the day, pitches for magazine articles were several pages long. But nobody has the time to read that much these days. Keep your pitch short, but include the information the editor will need to feel confidence in you and give you the assignment.

Estelle's Edge: While most editors prefer you to submit a complete essay or op-ed, they do not want you to submit a complete article. That's because they like to have input into the focus and scope of the article.

Pitching a Hit

There are two types of pitches. Pop-culture pitches are usually short, sweet, and very personal. They are typically pegged to a new book, movie, TV show, or public conversation or debate, and they offer commentary or analysis.

Pitches covering topics in health, science, or education are more complex. They usually cite research, experts, and statistics or polls. The process for both kinds of pitches is the same.

For pop-culture pitches, a good rule of thumb is to keep your pitch short — two to three paragraphs long, making sure that it covers the five Ws of journalism: who, what, where, when, and why.

If you are pitching a health or science topic, mention recent studies to show there is solid research behind the idea. If you have a lot of information to convey, use bullet points.

Photo Session

Good visuals can enhance your story. Let the editor know if you can supply high-resolution photos or any other media. It's important to specify that you have the rights to these works, meaning you took the photos or videos yourself, the photographer or videographer has granted you the rights, or you have a written agreement allowing you to use the images in a commercial publication. Most editors will also check that you have the rights to whatever visuals you are sharing.

Don't assume you can just pluck images from the internet and reuse them without permission. You leave yourself liable to lawsuits and big bills. Even if a friend of yours has been doing it without getting caught, don't do it. You will get caught.

What Successful Pitches Achieve

A strong pitch gives the concept of your story, details how you will approach and research the story, and explains why it's an important story to cover. If research is needed, it lists your sources. Keep in mind that editors are often not the only ones weighing in on the decision to publish. Often an editor needs to make a case for pitches to colleagues and managers at weekly or monthly pitch meetings. Of course, if you make it easy for them to sell your pitch to the team, that is a great first step toward building a solid relationship with your editor and getting assignments.

Your pitch can also convince an editor that you're right for the assignment. When I worked on a magazine for survivors and women at high risk of breast cancer, I parlayed that experience, showing I had access to experts and new solutions, into a story on breast cancer prevention to *Biography*. My interest in men's grooming and my background as a beauty editor and beauty book coauthor convinced an editor to assign me a story about men's grooming rituals for *Flair* magazine. If you have experience with a topic you are pitching, whether it is cancer, alcoholism, or adoption, that can work in your favor to convince the editor that you can bring something extra to the story.

Estelle's Edge: Always show the editor if you have a particular expertise related to what you are pitching, including lived experience — particularly if your knowledge surpasses that of the editor's.

Getting Expert Advice

For reported articles, finding experts is essential to creating a credible, newsworthy story. Look for book authors, people cited in the media, professionals who hold high positions in their industry, professors at major universities, and researchers who have published articles in peer-reviewed journals. (See chapters 13 and 14 for advice on finding and interviewing experts.)

Estelle's Edge: Editors today are very focused on diversity, so take that into account when you are selecting people to speak to.

Include statistics and the latest research — material that makes your pitch stand out as timely, compelling, and credible. If it's about your struggle with substance abuse, look for recent research cited by the National Institute for Drug Abuse. Look for online fact sheets or reports (check the public relations part of the site) that give you the background you need.

Savvy Sleuthing

Make sure you can support any claims you make and that there is a real story there, not just one you wish were there. If you are pitching a reported story, research the topic beforehand. If you are pitching a celebrity or author interview or profile, you need to assure the editor that you can get access through the person's publicist.

Estelle's Edge: Give the editor proof that you can deliver what you're promising. For a pitch on how teens can save money, provide new tips, maybe suggest a new app, or get quotes from an author of a related book. If you plan to offer fifteen tips in the piece, provide at least four or five solid tips to the editor in your pitch.

Outline It

Some editors might be intrigued with your pitch and ask for a detailed outline. The best way to create one is to write down your opening and your main points, and then delineate how you will support each point.

The outline below demonstrates that the article will be informative, narrative in focus, and provocative (drawing on groundbreaking research), and it will have a greater application or demonstrate a continuing and positive trend.

Sample Outline: Mindful Eating Class

1. Scenario of a mindful eating class at Waddell Academy, with the teacher leading the class through a mindfulness exercise
2. Applying the latest psychological research about how mindful eating prevents eating disorders
   a. Eating disorders background
   b. Rates of eating disorders in the United States
   c. Mortality rates
   d. Barriers to treatment
   e. Quotes from prominent eating-disorders psychologists about the effectiveness of school-based prevention programs and how mindful eating education improves students' body image
   f. Mindful eating and better body awareness
   g. Developing intuitive eating skills so students make healthier food choices
   h. Costs of the curriculum and different ways mindful eating classes can be introduced
3. Examples and narratives of students who have benefited from school-based mindful eating programs
4. Testimonials from teachers who have taught these programs
5. Ideas about how educational systems can implement these programs and how they will help children and teens

> *Estelle's Edge*: An outline can be very dry, so if you submit one, reassure the editor that you can write the article in a style similar to the publication's.

It doesn't matter what outline style you use, as long as you specify exactly what you plan to include in the article. Below is an example of an outline using a less rigid format.

Sample Outline: Kid Fears: Helping Children and
Adolescents Cope with Worries

- Worrying is a normal part of childhood and adolescence. Preparing and teaching kids how to face their fears can prevent concerns from spiraling out of control.
- The Worry: Here I'll list possible worries that kids and adolescents face at each stage of development.
  - ○ Infants and toddlers (ages 1–4)
    Possible worries: first day with a new childcare provider, nightmares, loud noises, going to the doctor, first shots.
  - ○ Big kids (ages 5–10)
    Possible worries: first day of school, the death of a pet, natural disasters, school shootings, making friends.
  - ○ Tweens and teens
    Possible worries: First breakup, fitting in with peers, being included on social media, applying to college.
- Helping your child prepare: Worries may be inevitable, but we can make them less scary by helping our kids prepare for them in advance.
  - ○ In this section I'll share how parents can prepare kids to face challenges. I'll interview child and adolescent experts, like psychologists, pediatricians, and educators.
  - ○ For example, even though separation anxiety is inevitable, research shows that introducing an infant to friends, family members, and babysitters can show them that other people love and care about them, which can help them adjust to new care providers.
- How to cope when the worry appears
  - ○ Here I'll share tips and tricks from child and adolescent experts on how parents can help kids cope when worries arise.
  - ○ For example, once separation anxiety appears, parents can say things like, "Mommy always comes back," and "I know it's upsetting when Mommy leaves." Parents can also read their kids age-appropriate books about saying goodbye. Imaginative play can also help kids cope with stress.

- Sidebar 1: How parents' worries and anxiety can affect kids
  - A few tips and tricks for parents, teaching them how to cope with their worries before talking about them with their kids. I'll interview an expert.
- Sidebar 2: How to tell if your kids' worries are something more serious (I'll interview an expert).
  - List of signs that worries could be something more serious, like chronic anxiety.
  - How parents should intervene if they're concerned (e.g., talk to a school counselor, make an appointment with a mental health provider, find a support group).

Estelle's Edge: If you find that a similar story to the one you're pitching ran in the past few years, be prepared to address any questions the editor might have about how your story would be different from the previous story.

Shine with SEO

Search engine optimization (SEO) is important to editors, because if your articles don't show up in online searches on the topic, people won't find them and read them. Identify relevant keywords and incorporate them into your piece.

Several of my students have gotten assignments on pitches after showing the editors that the topic they want to cover is a popular one in searches.

To see what search terms are the best matches for your topic, go to Google Trends, which analyzes the popularity of Google search terms using real-time data. When you enter your search terms, you will find out how many times the terms come up in different geographic locations. You can also compare terms to see which are more popular. Other online SEO-checking sites include fee-based ones, such as Keywords Everywhere and Ubersuggest. When you pitch the editor, list relevant keywords and include data to show that searches for these keywords are up.

End Eloquently

At the end of your pitch, include a brief bio (two to three sentences), along with your bylines (if you have any), any other important credentials, and up to three clips related to your pitch. I don't advise including a link to your website or portfolio unless you are also providing pertinent clips, because most editors don't have time to browse through your website to find samples.

If you have a beat, mention it so the editor will keep you top of mind when they want a writer covering your area. I used to say I cover the three Ps — parenting, publishing, and psychology — plus health, beauty, and aging. That makes it easy for editors to think of me for future assignments, if they are looking for a writer with my expertise.

Always end your pitch with the sentence "Thanks for your consideration" and not "I look forward to hearing from you." One reads as polite, the other as pushy.

> *Estelle's Edge*: Email your pitch to yourself before you send it to the editor. This way you can review it and make any corrections, so it's pitch perfect once it lands in your editor's inbox.

About Timing

Most people send their pitches for magazines and online publications first thing in the morning, Tuesday through Thursday. This avoids the risk of your pitch getting buried among emails that pile up over the weekend. Still, you never know when an editor may be working. I received an acceptance for my first piece in the *New York Times* on July 4, and my first piece for the *Washington Post* was accepted the day after Christmas.

Making Holidays Work for You,
Even If You're Taking Time Off

Most publications feature personal essays focused on national holidays such as Chanukah, Christmas, Diwali, Kwanzaa, Mother's Day, and

Father's Day. One way to get a byline is to think ahead about national holidays and gear your essays and articles toward them with a newsy peg. I did a story for *Insider* titled "I Never Let My Daughter Sit on Santa's Lap. Now She's Old Enough to Tell Me I Made the Right Choice" and another, titled "How We Celebrate Both Hanukkah and Christmas," for Kveller. Editors may also appreciate seeing how your pitch is linked to awareness months, like Breast Cancer Awareness Month, Mental Health Awareness Month, or National Safety Month, to mention a few.

If you're pitching an article or essay linked to a specific holiday, remember the mantra for print publications: "Think Christmas in July." That's how far out they usually plan.

Stories on stress and other mental health topics are perennials, with publications covering and repackaging many stories on related issues throughout the year. Why shouldn't that next assignment go to you?

The Compunction for Celebrity Conjunction

I'm not trying to be macabre, but there is a market for essays with connections to recently deceased celebrities. I wrote about the death of Carrie Fisher and Debbie Reynolds and their effect on me for Quartz. When the actor Penny Marshall died, I wrote a piece about her influence on my life (as Laverne on the sitcom *Laverne & Shirley*), but by the time I finished writing the essay, it was too late to sell it. I held on to the piece for a few years (because nothing is ever wasted when you're a writer) and eventually tweaked the lede, pegging it to the reboot of her movie *A League of Their Own* as a series on Amazon Prime. I titled it "How Penny Marshall's 'Laverne' Was the Role Model That Saved Me." Using the new series as a way to make the story timely, I sold that essay to AARP's *The Ethel* digital publication.

This was my lede:

Director Penny Marshall's 30-year-old female baseball movie *A League of Their Own* is finding a new fan base in its latest incarnation on Amazon Prime as a video series, shining a light on multiple story lines the movie left out. With that hit film coupled with *Big*, Marshall was the first woman in history to break the $100 million mark at the box office.

When Abbi Jacobson, star and series cocreator of *Broad City*, spoke with Marshall in 2018, the director — who died in December 2018 — supported the then-controversial idea of focusing on the private lives of athletes who were LGBTQ+ and persons of color during World War II.

Given her notorious chutzpah — on- and off-screen — it isn't surprising that Marshall was not afraid to tell someone to take a creative risk. It only makes me value her more.

The television show *Happy Days*, which ran on Tuesday nights in the '70s, was part of the soundtrack of my life growing up. Since that show mainly focused on the dating life of boys, I was thrilled when the 1976 spinoff *Laverne & Shirley* aired starring female characters, Penny Marshall as Laverne DeFazio and Cindy Williams as Shirley Feeney.

Their blue-collar lifestyle as friends and roommates working as bottle cappers at Shotz Brewery in the late 1950s in Milwaukee was a far cry from my childhood in Long Island growing up the daughter of a white-collar executive in strip-mall suburbia. But the character of Laverne captivated me.

Editors are always looking for stories connected to new television series, movies, controversial or popular books, and celebrities, so give yourself a leg up by preparing.

Estelle's Edge: Peruse PubMed and Google Scholar by inputting keywords for topics you are interested in writing about, and look at alerts from your mapping template to see if there is something new that you can spin into a story. Once you become known to public relations companies, they may add you to their mailing list for press releases. You can sometimes find story ideas through those, too.

No Clips, No Problem

Clips are simply examples of your published writing that you share in a pitch to show the editor that you have been published before. For your first pitch to a specific editor, it's helpful to include clips of published pieces that are close in topic to the piece you're pitching.

"But, Estelle, what if I don't have clips?" is a question I hear a lot, especially from academics, ghostwriters, and people who write in some capacity for their jobs but aren't published freelance writers. Others have clips that are very dated.

If you lack good (or any) clips, build on other experience and information that makes a case for you as a writer. For example, you can say, "I've contributed to academic publications or books," "I've been a ghostwriter," or "I specialize in advertising copy." Given the importance of search engines today, experience working in advertising or some other business writing arena that has you working with keywords can be a selling point for an editor.

Never identify yourself as a new writer. While most editors want to present different, emerging voices, few want to risk assigning an article to someone who is unproven. It's best to simply say you are a freelance writer and showcase your writing with the first paragraph of your pitch, written as if it were the opening paragraph of your article or essay.

Estelle's Edge: If you have never been published before, don't worry. All you need to show is how your personal experience gives you insight into your topic. Frame your value to the editor in terms of the special perspective you can offer. For example, if you are pitching a story about the perils of freezing eggs for IVF, it helps if you have gone through that experience. If you are proposing an article on running, you can say "I have been a marathon runner for a decade." Make your pitch answer the question, Why you?

Make Bylines Your Business

You can get published without prior experience (most often with an essay or op-ed), but there's no denying that clips help writers land new assignments. If you have no published articles, work on getting bylines like it's your job. Try your local paper, local magazines, regional publications, and neighborhood rags. Also, go to a newsstand or local bookstore and check out the niche magazines.

If you haven't been published before, essays and op-eds are the best formats to pick, since the quality of your writing is what counts most there.

Estelle's Edge: Get into a big print pub by pitching a smaller feature for the front-of-book section (FOB).

Changing Your Niche

If up till now you've been focused on one kind of writing, you can take steps to pivot into a different area. For example, if you write about fashion but want to move into travel writing, you can start building a new niche for yourself.

Start by pitching stories that span both areas: a story on the best clothing for travel, environmentally friendly fashion for traveling, or how to pick the hotels with the most fashionable guests. So start incorporating the elements of the topic you want to write about into your pitches and work.

Getting Paid

Usually an editor will tell you what they pay, and you can often also find that information in the publication's writer's guidelines or through asking other writers. You can also check the site Who Pays Writers? While there might be set rates, the pay you are offered by the editor will depend on your experience, knowledge of the subject, and status in the industry.

Sometimes an editor will ask what you charge. That's when you need to check with writer friends who have written for that publication, or ask what the rate is. When I started out freelancing, an editor for a digital publication asked me my rate. I quoted them a standard rate for print articles — a dollar a word — and the editor told me that was way over their budget, leaving me no room to negotiate. If I'd checked with colleagues or done some research beforehand, I would have known not to quote so high.

> *Estelle's Edge*: When an editor quotes me a rate, I often ask, "Do you have any wiggle room on the fee?" I've had my pay increased by hundreds of dollars and my students have doubled their payment by asking that one question. But if you are a newbie, don't expect to be paid the same as a pro who has worked with the publication before and knows their process and style. You may turn out to be the best writer the editor has ever worked with, but at this moment you are a question mark.

Writers often ask me if they should ever work for free. I believe that you should be paid for your work. I also believe that working for free devalues the hard work and craft of writers everywhere. I have to admit I've done it, but today I won't write for free unless it's really a big gain for a small amount of writing (like *Tiny Love Stories* in the *New York Times*). There is a simple rule of thumb: if you need to be paid, send your work only to places that pay.

Find Pitching Help

Whatever your subject, there is a publication for it. Many editors call for pitches on social media. You can also sign up for pitching newsletters like Freedom with Writing, the Open Notebook (which focuses on pitching science stories), or, for a fee, Sonia Weiser's newsletter. When publications like the *New York Times* tweet about their newest editors, see if they're a match for your interests.

> *Estelle's Edge*: If you are interested in getting a regular column in a publication, start by writing individual pieces for the

publication (and make sure they love your work) before pitching your idea to the editor. Otherwise, it's similar to going on a first date and asking the person if they'd like to marry you.

Editors' Best Advice for Writers

- Include new, diverse readers by giving voice to their experiences in religion, age, culture, economics, and race.
- The best pieces come from writers who are visionary and observe something everybody else missed.
- Since we are a print magazine and it is there till you recycle, every word is really important.
- Take a course on how to interpret medical studies.
- Make sure you can support your premise (e.g., "print magazines are dying") with research and credible sources.
- Don't tell me, "As so-and-so wrote in *Psychology Today*." Talk to the psychologist yourself and get fresh quotes for the story.

CHAPTER TEN

Best Practices for Pitching

*It is good to obey all the rules when you're young,
so you'll have the strength to break them when you're old.*

— MARK TWAIN

Someone years ago told me that you should think about pitches as if you were an alien coming down from outer space and looking at humanity with fresh eyes. What would you want to say? What question would you start with? Here's what I've learned over the years.

Recipe for a Powerful Pitch

The Preparation Phase

1. Mine your life for ideas. (See chapter 2.)
2. Find an idea that is newsworthy, timely, provocative, culturally significant, trending, or based on new research and information. (See chapters 2 and 11.)
3. Search the website of the publication you are most interested in pitching to see if your idea has already been covered. Search the internet for terms related to your idea. (See chapter 9.)

4. If you plan to cite expert sources, see if you can do a preinterview or get information about them online, such as descriptions of projects they are working on, to use in the pitch. (See chapters 13 and 14.)

The Active Writing Phase

1. In the opening of your pitch, mention something you've read in the publication to show the editor you've been paying attention to it. (See chapter 9.)
2. Include a clear and compelling title, using devices like alliteration, active verbs, and interesting words. Boldface the title so that it stands out. (See chapter 6.)
3. Include a peg or hook to show that the story is timely, provocative, personal, trending, cultural, or connected to an awareness month or major national holiday. (See chapters 2, 9, and 11.)
4. Write the opening or lede as if you are already writing the article. Include a dramatic anecdote, compelling statistics, and vivid description. (See chapters 3, 4, and 11.)
5. Make sure you are covering the important points, including the 5 Ws, and can boil down your pitch into a one- or two-sentence explanation. The editor shouldn't have any big, pressing questions after reading your pitch. (See chapter 9.)
6. Include pertinent new research or studies, statistics, and information to demonstrate that you have a plan for researching and writing the story. Show that your story will be one many people relate to and has the potential to move the conversation on the topic forward. Include hyperlinks for any statistics or studies mentioned in the pitch. Make sure your topic isn't too obscure for the publication's readers (that's where online searches and SEO help — see chapter 9).
7. Buzzy words that are new to the editor and related to the topic are always good to include and build a pitch around. Students of mine have used the terms *emotional cushioning*, *revenge shopping*, and *mommy mentoring programs*. (See chapter 11.)

8. Let the editor know if you have relevant visuals you own the rights to. (See chapter 9.)
9. Show your credentials and what makes you the perfect writer for this piece. (See chapter 9.)
10. Include your short bio and pertinent clips, if any. If you don't have clips, find a way to relate your experience to the subject matter. (See chapter 9.)
11. At the end of your pitch, thank the editor for their consideration. Don't say, "I look forward to hearing from you." (See chapter 9.)
12. Email your pitch to yourself, check it for spelling and grammar, and then read it over to make sure it is clear, concise, information-packed, and current. You are working on building trust with an editor, and especially if they haven't worked with you before, the pitch needs to show that you are professional and organized. It's all about gaining their confidence, and you are in it to win it. (See chapter 9.)
13. Email the pitch to the editor. If you don't have a personal email address for the editor, you may have to send your pitch to the publication's pitch box or to an online submission system like Submittable. (See chapter 16.)

> *Estelle's Edge*: Write "Freelance Pitch" in the subject line of your email, so the editor knows the pitch is not coming from a publicist. Then include your pithy title.

The Follow-Up Phase

1. Review the advice about editor etiquette and how to follow up after pitching the editor in chapter 16, and if your pitch is rejected, think about whether you can refine your pitch.
2. If your pitch is accepted, congratulations! (Head to chapter 12.)
3. If it's rejected, better luck next time. Tweak your pitch for another publication. Keep looking for those timely bits of news and great anecdotes and tips and begin again. (See chapter 19.)

Estelle's Edge: When you put together a pitch, keep a file of all the material you collected. It gives you fodder for pitching pieces on the same topic, with different angles and approaches. You'll have key information on experts and studies at your fingertips.

To keep track of the pitches you've sent out, create a running list of your pitches, with the name of the publication, the editor, whether it was accepted, the fee, any expenses, and the date you sent in your invoice. You can use a spreadsheet, a Word document (like I do), or project management software, like Trello.

You can also keep a separate document where you note editors and publications that you plan to send your pitch to if it isn't accepted by your first choice. That way, even if your pitch gets rejected, you already know where you are sending it next.

Advice from Editors on Pitching

- Pitch stories about something unusual or interesting. We love stories that put a human face and voice to a news story or trending topic, or break a big issue down into a personal story.
- Successful pitches aren't about topics (e.g., parenting during a pandemic). Instead, they explain the concept, how you plan to research it, your sources, key points you'll cover, and why it's important.
- Any new twist will help sell an editor on a story. If you are writing about families, showcase the modern family: for example, include blended families, nonbinary parents and children, raising children who are transgender, or a grandparent raising a child.
- News organizations want stories to have a news hook, and they will say no to pieces they feel they have seen before.
- The writing is so important. Try to wow the editor with the first paragraph of your pitch.

CHAPTER ELEVEN

Analyzing Pitches

The desire to reach the stars is ambitious.
The desire to reach hearts is wise and most possible.
— Maya Angelou

Among the many regular columns I've written for magazines was the *All About the Pitch* column for *Writer's Digest* where I interviewed editors and analyzed pitches to see what works and why. Here are some takeaways from this column, plus additional pitches from me and my students. We'll look at what works in a pitch and what doesn't. The examples cover a wide range of publications, topics, and genres.

A Pitch Works…

When Quotes Make the Pitch

Some pitches, like the one below, which was sent to *Good Housekeeping*, arrive fully formed, which helps the editor envision the finished piece. The quote from the nurse helps make the story personal and relatable, and it helped the editor, Marisa LaScala, make a case for the story during the magazine's pitch meeting.

Estelle's Edge: When you are interviewing sources, be alert for brief, powerful quotes.

Where Have All the School Nurses Gone?

I would like to pitch a reported piece exploring the school nurse shortage, why it's happening, and how it puts kids at risk. As a mom of two daughters, I believe this is an often-overlooked health issue that deserves more awareness.

I met my children's school nurse for the first time earlier this year, when our district invited parents to preview the puberty video our fourth- and fifth-graders would soon be watching. After the video, we listened to a presentation by the district nurse. Her closing remarks made my jaw drop: "Please email me if your student is going through something major. I have 3,800 kids at six schools, so it's hard to keep track sometimes."

Like many parents, I was surprised and concerned when I realized my children's school does not have a full-time nurse — and I wanted to learn more. According to the National Association of School Nurses (NASN), only about 40 percent of all schools across the United States have a full-time nurse, 35 percent have a part-time nurse, and 25 percent have no nurse at all. While the projected overall U.S. nurse shortage has received a lot of media attention, there are deeper reasons why schools are struggling.

This piece would discuss:

- The factors that make it especially difficult to recruit and retain school nurses: limited funding, dangerously high and complex caseloads, and not enough opportunities for advancement.
- How the school nurse shortage puts kids at risk, particularly those of lower socioeconomic status and those with chronic health conditions. Stephanie Prince Alexander, a mom in Denver, spent months trying unsuccessfully to secure a spot at a school with a full-time nurse for her 4.5-year-old daughter, who has type 1 diabetes and needs continuous monitoring. "My child could have a seizure, slip into a coma, or even die from mismanagement of her disease," she said.

- How schools without full-time nurses are coping (often by sharing a part-time nurse or assigning other staff to cover medical tasks), and why this is "asking for trouble," according to Nina Fekaris, immediate past president of NASN.
- How school nurses make a positive difference for students — not only by identifying critical health issues, but also by teaching kids about self-care and healthy lifestyles.

The writer also shared other sources and her website.

When You Bring Up a Trending Topic and Cultural Conversation Starter

The editor said she liked the pitch below, also to *Good Housekeeping*, because she knew it would attract a lot of comments, both from readers proud to stick with the traditional names for grandparents and those wanting to tell the story of their unique name. By referencing a previously published piece that also talked about names, the pitch showed that the writer had been reading the publication. It also showed that she would be happy to add in an engaging element to the pitch, such as her intent to cover "wilder names."

A pitch can cover a question or situation that is already part of the conversation in the group it's targeted toward.

> *Estelle's Edge*: Your mapping template can help you find cultural trends you can peg to.

Why Doesn't Anyone Want to be Called Grandma (or Grandpa) Anymore?

I see this along the lines of the "I'm not crazy about my grandkids' names" piece. I want to write a humorous look at a phenomenon I've noticed among my baby boomer cohort: Everyone in my expanded circle seems to be either requesting or being assigned weird names other than Grandma or Nona, like Mi Mi or Pup Pup. My theory is they want to appear young and hip and not stodgy. I'd interview a psychologist for their take on this trend and grandparents as well, including some of the wilder names out there.

When You Show the Editor
a Deep Understanding of the Topic

The pitch below might not mean much to you if you aren't an online gamer, but it told Alan Henry, an editor at *Wired*, that the writer knew what he was talking about. It used language specific to gaming and the Twitch platform and mentioned his career as an ESL teacher to demonstrate his knowledge about both gaming and language acquisition.

The writer also suggested alternative ways of focusing the topic, which can be helpful to an editor who isn't as well versed in it.

I've been watching a lot of Twitch lately. I see we both use the C920 for live-streaming purposes (I'm an online ESL teacher). One thing that has always struck me is how pervasive the emotes were in the chat and how quickly and easily I learned them all...even if I couldn't always remember if it was KKona or Kkona each time. It told me something deep about humans and language in such a surreal place.

How Twitch Chat Convinced Me I Could Learn Mandarin Chinese

This article would explore:

- A (brief) History of Twitch Emotes/BTTV/FFZ, etc.
- The "Grammar" of emotes (Why is PepeLaugh camel case and Pepepains not?)
- The link between pictures/sounds (I know 我 is wo3...but how? What does the brain do to make me say this? Why do I know that the lovable gray face with no space is "Kappa"?)
- Engaged, fun, repetition drives language creativity and learning.
- If you know Twitch-speak, you can learn any language. (Language learning processes)

The article will make the average reader feel smarter and more capable without having to lift a finger. "I don't remember any French/ Spanish from high school, and that's not my fault." This should go well as an upbeat counterpart to [a recent *Wired* piece, to which the writer included a link]. An alternative and less personal title could be "Mandarin Chinese and Twitch Chat, Not So Different." If this doesn't interest you, I could also write about the many ESL personalities of Twitch, including their usage of Twitch-speak.

When You Include a Clear Community Tie-In

This writer did something clever in pitching to *Wired* by showing through one of their writing samples that they are queer. Because the story was about queer appeal, the clip showed Alan that the writer was writing their lived experience without them having to say it explicitly.

If you are writing about a diverse community, it's good to show your connection to it in your pitch. And of course a great, pithy title always helps, too.

I am a gamer and a freelance writer from Kansas. Saw your post about *WIRED* Games and wanted to reach out with a pitch!

Headline: The Queer Appeal of "Dead by Daylight"

Subhead: Is the LGBTQ+ community a driving force behind the popularity of this asymmetrical multiplayer horror game?

In June, the development team behind "Dead by Daylight" acknowledged a lack of diversity in the game's lore. "We set our characters' preferences in the past, notably in heterosexual relationships." In a recent Nielsen study, 10 percent of gamers self-identified as LGBTQ+. In addition, the study found that LGBTQ+ gamers spent 8 percent more per month [than the general population of gamers].

For *WIRED* Games, I would love to chat with a few queer Twitch streamers who play "Dead by Daylight" to get their perspective on this horror game and its current cultural significance. In addition, I could reach out to the development team at "Dead by Daylight" to see if they have any concrete plans for queer representation in upcoming game lore. [The writer included three writing samples.]

When You Approach Sex or Other Sensitive Subjects in an Honest Way

HuffPost Personal editor Noah Michelson liked this piece because the author approached it in a no-fuss way. Her essay wasn't salacious, just open, honest, and practical.

You can formulate a pitch that covers a topic that people are dealing with but not talking about. As long as you are candid with your story, you can use it to continue or start an important conversation.

> I never imagined I'd be telling my two children exactly when and where I was having sex with their father, but just like this pandemic has changed school, work, dating, parenting, and even grocery shopping, COVID-19 has changed my sex life, too. While I didn't feel like I had much choice — given that we've basically been living on top of each other in our small townhouse for the last eight months — it's been amazing how much more enjoyable having sex with my husband is now that we're being transparent about it.

When You Peg It to a Movie, Book, or Cultural Phenomenon

Although this pitch to *HuffPost Personal* is framed around the movie *Promising Young Woman*, Noah thought it was more about how the writer continues to take revenge on her rapist, in a way the reader doesn't expect.

If you have a personal situation connected to something in the cultural zeitgeist, try using it as the basis for a pitch. In addition to referencing films and books, you can source topics being discussed in social media, such as Instagram, Reddit, and TikTok.

> The topic of my piece is the film *Promising Young Woman* and how it affected me as a rape survivor. "Trigger warning!" my sister announced, when she called me a week ago. "That new film, *Promising Young Woman*...the guy is Declan. You probably shouldn't watch it. But you should. I don't know." Declan (not his real name) is the man who raped me 14 years ago in college. After a few days of thought, I sat down to watch the film.
>
> Trigger warning, indeed. Many aspects of the story rang true to memories which once sent me into full-blown panic. And yet there was one fatal flaw to my empathic journey down PTSD lane: Cassie's revenge story was *so* not my revenge story. Among the details: I spoke to Declan, years after the assault. I forgave him. Yet I still

take my revenge every week in my volunteer role as a sexual assault advocate, a job I've been doing in three cities for over 10 years. I still take my revenge as a mother of two sons, who I will raise to honor and respect every single living thing on this earth and cherish their and others' sovereignty of self.

When You Tailor the Pitch to the Publication's Style

Sierra magazine has a literary bent to it, so the writer used phrases like "nature's soothing fractals" to show her skill with words. The editor, Katie O'Reilly, knew this thoughtful take on a low-impact activity would inspire the reader.

If you know a publication has a literary style, try incorporating more figurative devices, like metaphors and similes, and rich syntax and language, into your pitch.

Study articles in publications you want to be published in to become familiar with the way they use language to engage the reader.

In the first year of Covid-19, I learned to fish. It's a small thing, in the scope of all that's happened. But miles off the shore of remote Alaska, I hauled a halibut up from the floor of the North Pacific, shoulders burning with the effort, and it was the first time in months that I didn't feel utterly, overwhelmingly helpless.

In a Tennessee mountain stream, I learned — by trial and a lot of error — to fly fish, and earned an afternoon-long respite from the constant risk-assessment of pandemic living. Fly fishing is a personal festival of renewal. A reverent observance of the earth going on: Years pass, bad things happen, rivers run, and the fish come back.

And on the last sunny summer day, I stood on a breezy New Jersey jetty with my fisherman friend Rodney — each of us on our own rock — and dropped a crab-baited jig over and over for tautog. We talked about big things, the slow march of his dad's cancer, how losses pile up, and the nature of grief. But we talked like you do while you fish; long pauses and eyes on the rod tip, the conversation running somehow deeper with fewer words than it ever does away from the water.

And while my time on the water was spent mostly, blessedly, away from other people, I'm certainly not alone in my new hobby. After years of free-falling numbers, Fish and Game departments across the country are reporting unprecedented spikes in fishing license purchases. While most industries struggled, this one thrived: in many places, sales of boats, bait, and tackle reached all-time highs in 2020, and I was among the huge number of Americans who got a new rod and reel this past Christmas.

Millions of people have discovered the balm that is fishing. Credit the calming, repetitive nature of the cast. Or the psychological benefits of being well away from other people, out in a wild place with nature's soothing fractals as a backdrop. Or the surety that comes with ability — while I'm no master angler, I can put good food on my table in a pinch. But really, I think it's just this: while I'm fishing, I feel safe in the world again.

It's a pursuit that doesn't take much — a body of water, a pole and some line — but it requires things of you. Focus and mindfulness, a quiet composure and confidence. And a willingness to cast, and cast again, and again, and again. It's deep and very simple, the thing I learned in the first year of the pandemic and am carrying with me into the next: fishing requires you to hope.

I'd love to expand this one into a reported essay, and I've got great photos to go with it.

When You Pick a Topic or Setting That Hasn't Been Widely Covered

Although Katie gets a ton of pitches about hiking stories, she hadn't heard of the Great Plains Trail and had seen little reporting on the Great Plains states. She also liked the idea because the writer showed the personality of her subject in the pitch.

You can pick a setting that is not much written about and use vivid anecdotes and interesting quotes to insert yourself and other characters into the story.

Estelle's Edge: Research the setting you want to feature. You may find some great descriptive content you can add to your pitches. And, not to sound like a broken record, but you should also set up online alerts for that setting.

Luke "Strider" Jordan, the only person to have thru-hiked the 2,200-mile Great Plains Trail, pulls out one particular photo when someone asks about his trek. In it, he's standing in Nebraska's Oglala National Grassland, on a hilly sea of gold at sunset. "No one's ever seen anything like it," he tells me. "It's stunning. But if you say, 'Hey, go to Nebraska!' to anyone, they're just gonna walk away from you."

That's what Steve Myers, the man behind the GPT, is up against — getting hikers to believe that the "Great Plains" *is* that first word but *not* the second. The trail is his proof: It crosses six national parks and monuments, ten national forests and grasslands — statistics that would make the Appalachian Trail blush — five state high points, and fifteen state parks. It is not a poor substitute for the wild: with permits issued for the PCT tripling in the last eight years, with AT thru hikers more than doubling in that same timeframe, perhaps it's one of the wilder places left.

"We don't have a huge following," Myers admits. "We need users. We're trying to get people to go out there and experience it however they can. Foot, bike, 15 seconds, 15 miles — it doesn't matter." But Myers knows full well that the GPT doesn't just need hikers — it needs visionaries, those willing to buck the trend. "You're gonna have to take the sharp end of the rope," he says. "You'll need that pioneer spirit, same as 200 years ago."

He may not know it, but all this makes him the bearer of good news: In 2021, there is still a frontier to explore — should we decide it's worth exploring…

I plan on hiking a portion of the GPT this spring.

When You Tie In to a Celebrity Moment

Editor Holly Baxter, of the *Independent*, liked the honesty in this pitch. She'd seen a lot of pitches saying that older motherhood is fantastic. But people want to read a nuanced piece and see their experience reflected.

If you want to write about a novel or challenging personal experience, consider linking your story to a celebrity who is going through something similar. Include juicy scenes in your pitch.

> *Estelle's Edge*: When you mine a celebrity's story to tie in with your own, do a deep dive to find out what else you might have in common that you could include in your story.

I would like to pitch something on the pros and cons of older motherhood, pegged to Naomi Campbell's announcement [of her pregnancy at age 50]. I had my first and only child at age 43. He's now 13, and I'm now 56, almost 57. There were definitely ups and downs in the early years, including being called Grandma by someone in Starbucks; dealing with post-partum depression in the first six weeks (which was attributed to a variety of factors); and now getting teased for having wrinkles by my newly minted teen. It was much harder to bond with the younger moms in the new parent groups.

I did a piece a long time ago called "Don't Call Me Grandma" for Kveller, a Jewish parenting site, and also wrote other essays about this in the early years. I'd be happy to write a 650-word op-ed on this for you — on the challenges and joys of becoming a mother so late in life.

When the Tone Matches the Pitch

Hattie Fletcher, the former editor of *Creative Nonfiction*, liked this pitch because it's engaging and a little funny. You get a sense of the writer's personality and voice. She sets up the situation and then matches the tone to it.

If you're writing on an academic subject, try spicing it up by using your voice in the pitch.

Estelle's Edge: When pitching to a publication you aren't familiar with, read several issues to see the style and tone, because it will give you a glimpse into the editor's tastes. (Yes, editors are people, too, with their own attitudes and preferences. Why not work with that?)

An Argument for Humor in the Addiction Memoir

Addiction memoirs continue to be published at astonishing rates, and as the opioid epidemic gains more visibility and victims, there's no sign of the trend slowing down....Too often, readers are exposed to the nightmare scenarios of rock-bottom, leaving the impression that there was never an alluring or just plain fun reason that people start drinking and using drugs in the first place. It can also reduce people's experiences to sad-sack statistics rather than fully complex human beings who experience the full range of human emotion. The role of the writer, and of creative nonfiction, is not limited to the functions of acknowledging pain and sorrow, and the addiction memoir can be a surprising and ripe opportunity for reminding people of the absurdity and humor in even the bleakest situations. As my drunk grandmother liked to say after her third gin gimlet, "You catch more flies with honey, my dear." Cliché? Yes, but she was drunk, and it's true: readers respond more positively to a little light than an endless tunnel of darkness. I know there was a recent call for "intoxication" stories for the magazine, and I thought this would be timely. I will give a concise overview of the addiction memoir and establish that the genre includes some of our most celebrated and notorious writers (Mary Karr vs. James Frey). I'll then argue that the genre is unbalanced in terms of tone, with many memoirs focusing almost exclusively on desperation and damage. I'll argue that this reflects our societal discomfort with allowing addicts and alcoholics any room for joy or humor once they've gone public, admitting their problems.

Ultimately, I'll argue, all the doom and gloom doesn't just damage the perception of addicts, but it's poor writing, because it doesn't attempt to illuminate the whole truth of a story. Humor allows the memoirist to avoid the clichés of addiction, a topic replete with cli-chés because so much of the experience itself is about repetition.

I co-founded and teach in the Words Without Walls program, which brings creative writing classes to jails, prisons, and rehab centers in Pittsburgh. Through that work, I read a lot of writing about addiction. And because of it, I've sought out a lot of addiction memoirs, both as a way of understanding students and for class resource material. In addition to the study of the addiction memoir, it's always struck me that in my classes at rehab centers we do a lot of laughing, but rarely does that humor make it to the page.

When the Headline Tells the Story

The editor-at-large of the love and relationship website Your Tango, Andrea Zimmerman, kept the headline from this pitch exactly as it was, because it was so clear. By linking a home remodel to all that it churned up in the couple's marriage, the writer created a compelling story out of two common situations.

> *Estelle's Edge*: You've been keeping your mapping template up to date, right? Can you connect two situations the way this writer did? Can you play around with active verbs or nouns connected to your topic and use them in the title or the pitch? The one below uses the verbs *collapse* and *churned* and the noun *turbulence* to show the chaos in the relationship.

I Learned the Hard Way That My Marriage Was on the Edge of Collapse — Again

The article is 1,030 words and is a personal story of how my husband and I took on a house remodeling project that ultimately churned up the problems, issues, and underlying turbulence of our marriage. As the project progressed, things got worse — both with the home and our relationship. Let me know if you'd like to take a look.

When You Can Relate to Topics That People Are Thinking about but Not Talking About

Andrea was struck by this pitch because she had experienced body dysmorphia during her pregnancy and had never spoken or written about it.

What is going on in your life that you can write about clearly, perhaps even with humor, that is relatable to everyone?

Estelle's Edge: Look at your mapping template to see what is fresh and new that you have been dealing with. If you follow an editor on social media, they might reveal information about their lives, family, kids, origin, and interests that you can use in your pitches to them. Even without you mentioning their situation, the editor will make the personal connection, and it might help you get the assignment. (Make sure, though, that the information is appropriate to include. If your pitch is about divorce, you might not want to disclose that you know the editor is getting divorced.)

The Bitter Truths I Learned about My Eating Disorder — after Being Pregnant

This article is a personal story about my experience with eating disorders. I recovered from bulimia in my 20s, or so I thought. In hindsight, I must have been in quasi-recovery, because my experience during pregnancy sent me headfirst into orthorexia after my babies were born. A combination of diet culture's obsession with women regaining their pre-pregnancy weight and body, and how alluring it can be to "bounce back."

I will share the key things I learned: not only that diet culture is obsessed with women's bodies both during and after pregnancy, but also that this can be extremely damaging to body image. It's very easy to jump onto a "healthy eating plan" but there's a fine line between getting healthy and disordered eating.

When It's Framed around Pitching Prevention, Not Cure

Rather than frame this as a cautionary tale, Jennie Burke wrote a piece for the *New York Times* about the protocol she followed to ensure that her daughter didn't fall into the family cycle of addiction. As she wrote, she added reported elements, citing a prominent study and a TED talk on addiction.

Any kind of prevention story with a personal angle and supportive research could make a good basis for a pitch.

> With the help of our family, my 13-year-old daughter recovered from hernia surgery without the use of narcotics. (Although she was sent home with 44 Oxycodone [pills].) Our strategy was not New Age or Woo Woo, nor did she suffer. We simply kept her company, administered treats, listened to her fears and had fun. Before her surgery, we devised a pain protocol based on a study from the American Academy of Pediatrics and this research from journalist Johann Hari. [The writer included a link to Hari's TED talk.]
>
> I come from a long tradition of addicts, from my grandparents and in-laws to my very own brother, who died of a heroin overdose during the pandemic. He became addicted to opiates following an appendectomy.
>
> This 1,000-word piece is timely as many parents are deciding to complete elective surgeries (such as tonsillectomies and wisdom tooth removal) once postponed due to COVID-19. Narcotics are prescribed for pain following these surgeries, and parents are unaware of simple alternatives for pain mitigation. My hope is that sharing our successful experience will encourage parents to consider other avenues to ease adolescent surgical recovery.
>
> I'm vocal about our experience with my friends, and I frequently receive calls from other moms and dads asking how we went about avoiding painkillers. I'm always happy to share.

When You Start with a Provocative Question

This pitch to *Wired* was born out of an experience I had with someone who was baiting me in a Facebook group. I thought others could relate to it and got a team of experts to share their advice, framed around my story. Citing the British royal family's motto gave my story a celebrity tie-in.

Any kind of provocation or annoyance could lend itself to a pitch like this one:

Sometimes the Best Thing to Do on Social Media Is Just Shut Up ... Isn't It?

This piece will cover the power of not engaging in social media, and when you absolutely should. The royal family's motto is "never complain, never explain," which is a surprisingly empowering stance to take — if you are already in power. But not everybody is. When it comes to social media snafus, when should you give oxygen to people's fire? I'll give examples from my and others' experiences, and advice from experts on how to navigate through it. I'll get a therapist's perspective on what makes other people think they have the right to tell you that you are wrong, how not to be disempowered, and how exactly to handle these scenarios — supported by research and empirical data.

When the Writer Includes a Fresh, Buzzy Term

The editor who read this pitch to the *New York Times* from my student Emily P. G. Erickson agreed with my assessment that the term *emotional cushioning* felt fresh and new.

Do your research and uncover an accepted psychological, medical, or cultural phrase, word, or term that hasn't been explored widely and put it into a pitch. If you get press releases or online alerts, scour them to see any new terms you haven't yet heard about, and make a note to explore them further.

I loved your piece this summer "Becoming a Dad Meant Losing My Edge." This line, in particular, connected with me as a writer and a human: "I have always been led by what I felt were the most important stories to tell, those that make differences in people's lives."

I'm writing to you with one of my own ideas about what I believe is an important and difference-making story. "What to Expect

When You're Expecting the Worst" is an evidence-based service piece geared toward NYT Parenting readers who are expecting again after a loss. Every year in the United States, over one million pregnancies end in a loss, an umbrella term that includes miscarriage, ectopic pregnancy, molar pregnancy, and stillbirth. Eighty percent of people who've experienced a pregnancy loss go on to be pregnant again within five years.

The reported article, framed around my own experiences of expecting the worst during pregnancy after loss, will focus on emotional cushioning — a common but rarely-talked-about phenomenon that includes tactics like expecting the worst and delaying purchasing items for the baby. In a 2011 study published in the *Journal of Reproductive and Infant Psychology*, 59% of people pregnant after loss reported using emotional cushioning. The idea is that emotional cushioning protects pregnant people's feelings so they can do what they need to do during their stressful pregnancies — but does it work?

Emotional cushioning may be normal, but I've uncovered some related research that indicates that expecting the worst may not help anxiety or mood. However, the research also indicates that there are other things people pregnant after a loss can do to cope. In fact, a study published this May explored how a list of 10 simple strategies called the Positive Reappraisal Coping Intervention, which includes items like "learn from the experience," could be helpful to people pregnant after recurrent pregnancy loss.

When It Focuses on a Trending Health Issue

This pitch to Narratively tied in to an interesting and little-explored area of health and healing that has documented science behind it. The writer started the pitch with a powerful scene.

If you have authoritative sources and a narrative arc, a health issue like this could make a good story. Make sure to include compelling scenes highlighting sensory details, and include the science to ensure your story's credibility.

I have a pitch for Narratively: "Music Saved My Life: How Sound Healing Helped One Woman Recover From Trauma," an "as-told-to" story about the psychological benefits of sound healing, and how it helped one woman heal from trauma.

The concert arena vibrated from the sound of the bass and the heavy beat of the drums. "Suddenly everything has changed," sang Wayne Coyne, lead singer of the rock band the Flaming Lips. Fans screeched with delight as they danced along to the music.

When Jacqui McLoughlin heard these lyrics, the music moved through her body. Her chest tightened, and a tingly sensation tickled her throat, pushing painful emotions to the surface. Tears fell from her eyes, but instead of feeling sad, she felt cathartic.

"I was in a meditative state; it was the first time I'd released emotion since my friends and loved ones had died."

I'll tell the story of a trauma survivor and artist/musician Jacqui McLoughlin, and how attending the Flaming Lips concert led her to study sound healing — a type of music therapy shown to help people recover from trauma, anxiety, and depression. [Bio information.]

A Pitch Doesn't Work...

When It Can't Prove the Topic Is a Popular Trend

Though this pitch starts with a promising, visually evocative opening, it leaves the editor with too many questions.

The pitch makes it seem as if the writer is pulling this notion out of a hat. It doesn't mention any credible experts or any new research. The therapeutic benefits of expressing anger are well documented, so that part isn't new.

To fix it, the writer needs to prove this is a trend. The writer states that couples are choosing anger gyms over traditional couples therapy, but what is the evidence? The pitch needs to state how many gyms there are and where they are located, and to cite research that supports the effectiveness of the practice: for example, "In *Frontiers in Psychology*, a study showed ..." Is there a poll or other statistic demonstrating this trend? Editors are always looking for veracity and substantiation.

The Psychological Benefits of Going to an "Anger Gym"

Feeling enraged and want to give something a whack?

Try working out your emotions at an "anger gym." These smash houses feature everything you need for a cathartic rage attack, including hammers, old televisions, and mirrors.

While visiting an "anger gym" might seem entertaining, research suggests taking your aggression out on objects, instead of people can be therapeutic. In fact, letting emotions out in this way has become so popular that couples are choosing "anger gyms" over traditional couples therapy.

I'd like to write a story profiling the psychological benefits of anger gyms. I'll talk with people who've benefited from it. I'll also include research that discusses the therapeutic benefits of expressing one's anger, as well as an outside expert who can comment on these smash houses.

When a Fun Topic Just Isn't Supported by Research

An editor won't assign a story unless the trend or concept it describes has wide appeal to the readership. The writer didn't convince the editor that this solution would work.

This is an interesting premise, but I haven't seen one link to a study or piece of research that supports what the writer is saying or the need for a story. If the writer did find the research, it would be helpful to write the first paragraph as if it were the actual story, to show their voice. Also, how did this approach work for the writer? Have they continued doing this? Is anyone else doing it?

Sleeping with Stuffed Animals Is the New Ambien

As an occasional insomnia sufferer, I've spent many nights trying to coax my body into a sleepy state. Following the advice from yogis, I've tried taking deep, meditative breaths while folding my body into the downward-facing dog or child's pose. When my Zen attempt to cure my sleeplessness fails, I've taken medication. Recently, however, I discovered a remedy for my insomnia—hugging my daughter's over-sized stuffed bear.

That being said, if you're an insomniac looking for an "off-label" use for your kid's Beanie Boo (and the Pokémon size-eyes don't creep you out), consider substituting stuffies for Ambien.

I'd like to write an essay about how hugging my daughter's stuffed animal helped ease my sleeping woes. I'll also include research that backs up my personal discovery, discussing how hugging an object (even a nonhuman one) can help calm the body's nervous system, eliciting the body's relaxation response.

EXERCISE: PITCHCRAFT

Craft a pitch. Research a topic or issue you want to explore. If your family is struggling with sibling rivalry, review the latest psychology research about what it is, why it happens, and how to build a more harmonious home. Want to quit smoking, but can't seem to commit? Try acupuncture, meditation, or guided imagery, then write a pitch about what you learned.

EXERCISE: STRAIGHT FROM THE HEADLINES

Take a headline from a newspaper's lifestyle section about an interesting issue and craft a pitch around it for an article. Or try crafting a pitch from what a TV commentator says on a newsworthy topic.

Pitch Tips from Editors

- Find new ways to speak about issues that might not have been approached in the same way in older articles.
- Once in a while, pitch a humor piece. Editors often clamor for humor because their readers want to be entertained.
- Know the service aspect of your piece before pitching it. How will it help the reader?

- Pitch a story, not a topic. What would you say about it at a cocktail party? Is it compelling, fresh, interesting, and useful? Why are you the person to tell it: do you have a strong opinion or viewpoint or special expertise?
- Is your topic a widespread problem? Can you sum up your pitch in a single question the reader can ask?
- Give a tip or two in your pitch to intrigue the editor and show you know what you are doing.
- Offer acknowledgment. Mention different options and experiences for the reader and help them feel understood. Here is an example: "If possible, consider seeking out a therapist. If that seems too time consuming or financially draining, look at our roundup of digital therapy apps, or virtual support groups."
- If I tell you to pitch me again, pitch me again. I'm not doing that to be nice.

PITCH CHECKLIST

❏ Does your pitch show that you're familiar with the publication and/or the editor's preferences?

❏ Do you have a compelling title that evokes emotion and uses active verbs?

❏ Did you start with a reference to something timely, newsy, or culturally relevant?

❏ Is your pitch provocative? Does it answer a question?

❏ Do you have a lede that hooks the editor from the first paragraph? Will you surprise the editor in some way?

❏ Did you keep it short?

❏ For a complex pitch, did you include bullet points or outlines to break up the copy?

❏ Does an online keyword search demonstrate a demand for your story?

❏ Did you explain who you will interview or who your sources are? Are your sources diverse?

❑ Did you show how you will support your spin or angle by citing interviews, research, quotes, and statistics?
❑ Did you explain why you are the perfect person to write the
story?
❑ Did you include a bio (and clips if you have them)?
❑ Did you end with a thank-you that doesn't insist the editor get
back to you?

CHAPTER TWELVE

Your Pitch Landed

What Happens Now?

Raise your word, not your voice.
It is rain that grows flowers, not thunder.

— Jalāl al-Dīn Muhammad Rūmī

Congratulations! You got the assignment. I remember the joy of getting an email with my first assignment that wasn't from the magazine where I worked. It was from the now-defunct *Longevity* magazine. I wrote a short item, probably only three hundred words, for the front of the book (FOB), the pages after the masthead that are typically filled with short, newsy items, about a special weekend for couples in a hotel in San Francisco that focused on aphrodisiac foods. The magazine spelled my name wrong in the byline, but I didn't care. I was overjoyed to be in print. The next time, I made sure they got it right. And there was a next time, and a bigger assignment. But I had to start somewhere, and so do you.

Now that your pitch has landed, take a moment to give yourself some well-deserved praise, and then take these steps to success.

In the meantime, don't announce your wonderful new assignment or dream publication on social media. Not until it's published. Please, I beg you. Stories get killed; editors leave.

Before you start work on the piece, get a contract or written agreement. At the very least, get the information in writing in an email from your editor. It should specify the following:

- Word count.
- Deadline (the date the piece is due).
- How much you will be paid.
- When you will be paid. Payment within thirty days of submission is optimal. Try to avoid agreements that say you will be paid on publication, which could mean a long wait (or never getting paid if the piece is not published).
- Kill fee: what happens if the publication kills or never runs the story?
- Publication rights. Copyright can be complex to understand, but there is one main set of rights you should always try for — see below.

Negotiating an Agreement

If you aren't satisfied with the terms the editor proposes, you may be able to negotiate. Negotiating for what you want is a skill that anyone can learn.

With every negotiation, it's important to have a BATNA, short for the "best alternative to a negotiated agreement." It means going into a negotiation knowing what your bottom line is (the lowest offer you're prepared to accept) and the value of what you are negotiating. It means understanding what your alternatives are if negotiations fall through. For example, if you are asking for an extra $100 to do a freelance assignment, and the editor offers you $75, you can say, "I can do that, but can you assign me two articles, instead of one?" Or ask, "Instead of transcribing my interviews myself, can I have the company transcribe them?"

The negotiating experts Roger Fisher and William Ury outline this process to develop the best alternative to a negotiated agreement in their book *Getting to Yes*:

- List all the alternatives to the current negotiation — the things you could do if negotiations fall through.
- Evaluate how much each alternative is worth to you.
- Select the alternative that would provide the highest value to you (this is your BATNA).
- After determining your BATNA, calculate the lowest-value deal that you're willing to accept.

Being bold enough to negotiate takes practice. It takes knowing your worth. But each time you ask for what you deserve, you build confidence. Even if you don't get the result you want, you can give yourself points for asking.

If you don't get what you want the first time, don't get mad — get prepared. You will most likely get another chance to negotiate. Just have your BATNA ready.

Estelle's Edge: If you are afraid to step up to negotiate for yourself, write down why you deserve whatever you are asking for, so you don't get thrown when making your ask.

Going for Your Rights

Assuming you have negotiated payment terms, you are ready to address the complex subject of rights: the question of who has the legal right to determine future uses of your piece. This can be a tricky area to negotiate, and what follows should not be regarded as legal advice.

Your best bet is to ask the publisher to take first North American serial rights, also known as first rights. These give the publisher the right to put your work (whether it's a single piece or all future work for the publication) into a magazine or newspaper in North America. (An alternative is first world rights, which cover publication anywhere in the world.) After a specified period following publication, the rights to the material revert to you, and you can do what you want with it.

I recommend retaining movie rights, particularly if you wrote a narrative piece.

Publishers often ask for exclusive rights for a period of time (anywhere from three months to a year), and for nonexclusive rights for an additional period, meaning they still have certain rights to the material, but now so do you and anyone else you'd like to assign rights to.

Here is an example of a good contract. It doesn't just cover a specific work: it covers all work for a specific period of time (which seems to be the direction publishers are headed in). Every publisher has their own wording for contracts, differing slightly in certain parts. You can find more information on contracts through the Author's Guild, the American Society of Journalists and Authors, the National Writers Union, and other professional organizations.

To: [FREELANCE NAME]

This will confirm the agreement pursuant to which [PUBLISHER NAME] has acquired the nonexclusive rights to reproduce, upon the terms and conditions set forth below, all Articles written by you, as assigned by, and written for, [PUBLISHER NAME] in the year/s [YEAR/S].

1. You hereby grant to the Publisher the following rights with respect to all Articles covered by this contract:
    a. First world editorial rights to the Article(s);
    b. The right to use the Article(s), together with your name and pertinent biographical data, in advertising and promotion of the Article(s) and the publication (s) in which they appear;
    c. The right to publish the Article(s) on internet and digital platforms owned and operated by [PUBLISHER];
    d. The right to reprint the Article(s) in [PUBLICATION's] special interest publications (SIP).
2. You will deliver to the Publisher written materials acceptable for publication. In the event an article is determined not to be acceptable, you will be given an opportunity to revise it. If the revision is deemed not to be acceptable, the Publisher may cancel the assignment and pay you a fee equal to 40% of the original amount. The decision as to whether an article is acceptable for publication rests solely with the Publisher.

3. You shall retain all other rights to the Article(s); provided, how-
    ever, that you shall not authorize or permit the publication of
    any of the following Articles in any medium or publication until
    60 days after publication by the Publisher. The Publisher shall
    pay to you, in consideration:

    a. [PAYMENT AMOUNT] for successful delivery to the Publisher
        of a [WORD COUNT] article about [TITLE] due no later than
        [DATE] and approved in accordance with section 2 above.

    b. In the event that an article is digitally reprinted on any other
        [PUBLICATION] websites, pursuant to the provision in Sec-
        tion 1c above, you will be paid [AMOUNT] upon the publica-
        tion of such reuse.

    c. In the event that your article is reprinted in an SIP, pursuant
        to the provision in Section 1 (d) above, you will be paid 25%
        of the original fee upon the publication of such reuse.

4. You represent and warrant that:

    a. You are acting as an independent contractor and not as an
        employee or agent of the Publisher;

    b. You have the power and authority to enter into this letter
        agreement as the author and copyright owner of the Arti-
        cle(s);

    c. Each Article is original except for material in the public do-
        main;

    d. Each Article has not been previously published, in whole or
        in part;

    e. To the best of your knowledge each Article does not contain
        any defamatory material or any injurious instructions; and

    f. To the best of your knowledge each Article does not violate
        or infringe any right, including the copyright, of any person.

5. This letter agreement is the entire agreement between you and
    the Publisher and may not be altered except by written agree-
    ment of both parties. Please indicate your acceptance of this let-
    ter agreement by signing below and returning the original to us.

Please confirm that the foregoing accurately and completely
sets forth our agreement by signing and returning the enclosed copy.

Getting into the Mire with Work for Hire

Try to avoid an all-rights grab also known as a work-for-hire agreement from the publisher, which means that they own the rights to your work in perpetuity. That means they can change it at will, put someone else's byline on it, make it into a brochure, sell it overseas, place it in a book, and never have to pay you another dime.

Here is an example of language for a work-for-hire contract:

All Work shall be considered "work(s) made for hire" for [PUBLISHER] and shall belong exclusively to [PUBLISHER] and its designees. To the extent that under applicable law any such Work may not be considered a "work(s) made for hire," Writer agrees to assign and upon its creation automatically assigns exclusively to [PUBLISHER] for the full period allowable under law, all its rights, title, and interest, including all statutory and common law copyright, and any other intellectual property in such Work, without the necessity of any further considerations.

Get the picture? This publisher is effectively taking all your rights to the work.

Unfortunately, this seems to be the direction that publishers are heading in, so I would recommend that if you are writing about a personal experience, or a personal experience with a reported element, you should negotiate with the publisher so that you retain the rights to publish the piece in an anthology or a memoir. Sometimes, if you agree to share the work in a publisher's other print or online outlets or syndicates, you might get some other rights back.

You can try renegotiating a work-for-hire agreement along these lines: "You hereby grant and assign to Publisher first worldwide serial publication rights, exclusive for three [or six] months from the on-sale date of the issue in which the work appears." This means that after the specified period, you can do whatever you want with your work. The publisher may not accept the proposal, but it's worth a shot.

The Dreaded Indemnification Clause

Most contracts include an indemnification clause. This makes the writer responsible for paying the publisher for any damages arising from legal claims made against the work and puts the onus on the writer to defend themselves.

This is the language you want to avoid if at all possible:

Writer will indemnify and hold Publisher harmless against all claims settled by Publisher or reduced to judgment, including all court costs and reasonable attorney's fees and expenses, provided the basis of such claim or judgment constitutes a breach of any of the Writer's representations or warranties; and until such claim or suit has been settled or withdrawn. Publisher may withhold any sums due writer under this Agreement or otherwise.

A contract containing the following language is usually fine to sign because the phrase "to the best of the writer's knowledge" (italicized in the example below) gives the writer some protection.

Writer's Representations and Warranties

Writer warrants that with respect to Writer's contributions to the Work: Writer is the sole and original author of the Work (excepting any material identified in the Work as third party material) and has full power and authority to make the grant of rights set forth herein: Writer is not restricted by contract from entering into this Agreement or carrying out Writer's obligations hereunder; *to the best of the writer's knowledge* the Work contains no matter that is libelous, an invasion of privacy, or otherwise unlawful; the Work does not infringe upon any statutory copyright, common-in-law literary right, or proprietary right of any third party; Writer has used and will use all reasonable care in the creation, research and preparation of the Work to ensure that all facts and statements in the Work are true and correct in all material respects; and no instruction, formula, direction, recipe, prescription, or other matter contained in the Work will cause injury or damage.

Years ago it was possible to strike an indemnity clause out of the printed contract or add "to the best of my knowledge." Today, most contracts are automated through DocuSign or other services, making it impossible to change anything without trying to find out who handles legal issues at the publisher. Most writers I've spoken to don't even try to change the wording of contracts anymore.

Remember, a good contract protects both you and the publisher, but a bad one protects only the publisher, so please watch what you are signing. If possible, have a lawyer friend, or someone who deals with corporations, look over the contract to make sure you are protected.

What If You Didn't Get a Contract?

Some publications don't provide their freelance writers with a contract. In that case, you should email them an agreement letter like the one below. Examples can also be found on the websites of the writers' organizations mentioned above.

Again, please note that this is not to be construed as legal advice.

[DATE]

Dear [EDITOR]:

It was great speaking with you yesterday about an assignment for [MAGAZINE/PUBLICATION] on the hazards of headache medications and ways to mitigate their side effects.

To confirm our discussion: the 1,200-word story is due on [DATE] and will include real-life stories from four women who have had bad side effects from these medications. In addition, I will include a short, 300-word sidebar that lists advocacy organizations that patients can reach out to for help.

The fee for this assignment is [DOLLAR AMOUNT], to be paid on acceptance. You will also have first North American serial rights (FNASR) for this assignment.

If the manuscript does not satisfy the requirements stated above, you will give me the chance to revise it. If it still does not work, you will pay me a 25% kill fee of ([DOLLAR AMOUNT]).

If I don't hear from you, I will assume that these terms are agreeable. I'm looking forward to working with you.

Sincerely,

[YOUR NAME]

Keep copies of all written or email contracts, agreements, and related correspondence. Once an agreement is finalized, send a confirmation message and keep a record of that, too.

Estelle's Edge: You need to be comfortable with the pay, word count, and deadline specified in your contract or agreement. If you aren't, discuss your concerns with the editor right away.

What Can Go Wrong?

- **You get a deadline that you can't make.**

  Gentle pushback: Say "I already have commitments that week, can we move the deadline to [alternative date]?"

  Keep in mind: If the editor won't budge, you may have to walk away, unless you can meet the original deadline.

- **You aren't satisfied with the payment they are offering.**

  Gentle pushback: Remember your BATNA and say, "I was wondering if you had any room to move that fee up?"

  Keep in mind: The editor may not have much discretion over the budget.

- **The specified word count is too low for your topic or too high for the fee the editor is offering.**

  Gentle pushback: Ask for an adjusted word count to meet your needs.

  Keep in mind: The editor may have a set word count for those types of pieces, articles, or essays.

Writing and Delivery

Once you have an agreement you are happy with, it's time to write your piece.

Before you begin, make sure your vision of the piece is aligned with the editor's. Ideally, the editor has already told you the word count and fee, shared any style guidelines, deadlines, and other instructions with you, and given you specific guidance about the story (or, ideally, is happy with what you pitched and doesn't have any tweaks).

If you have any questions, problems with a source bailing, or other issues that will affect the content or delivery of the final article, contact your editor right away. Keep your emails short and to the point. Use the email address that the editor last used to contact you, and change the subject line to say "URGENT: Quick question about [ARTICLE] from [YOUR NAME]." (I know my editors are laughing now as they see this.)

This is a good tactic because at this point, any questions about your assignment affect not only you but also the editor and the reader, and it's in everyone's interest to get the issue resolved. Make your questions specific: for example, "My expert decided not to do interviews. Is it okay if I replace expert A with expert B?" Or, "My expert is going out of the country and will be back on [DATE]. Can I speak with him on [DATE] and move the deadline to the following week?"

When I was writing an article for the *Washington Post* about supportive male partners, I mentioned Sheryl Sandberg, then the chief operating officer of Facebook. Right before I submitted the piece, her husband died suddenly. I emailed my editor about it, and we added in an extra paragraph addressing the tragedy. Thanks to clear and prompt communication, we were able to handle the situation gracefully.

Now it's time to get writing. Here are the steps you should take to move forward with your assignment.

1. **Organize.** Have a place where you can sit and write; ideally at a desk or other place where you can organize your materials. The longer, more complicated, or more data-driven your piece, the more materials you will accrue. I organize my print materials in colored see-through snap folders with a label for each project. I also keep a digital file, but being able to spread out all your information on paper can be helpful in organizing your thoughts.

   If you will be interviewing experts, plan how to record your interviews and where to keep the recordings (and backups).

You can record interviews with your computer or phone. I like to use the phone app TapeACall (which has an option for transcription), in case your editor asks you to provide a transcript.

2. **Research your subject.** For the pitch you wrote, you've already done a deep dive into the subject matter, vetted your experts, chosen anecdotes to include, and selected diverse subjects and sources.

    Now it's time to flesh out your piece. If you are writing a profile or including someone prominent in your article, do a thorough internet search for your subject. If you find disturbing or incriminating information about the person or their business, alert your editor right away, so the publisher can either change the focus of the profile or prompt their legal team to review the article. It's always best to notify your editor of anything unusual you come across before you do the actual write-up.

3. **Write a headline and dek for your piece.** The dek is the text underneath an article's headline that provides additional information on the story. For example, a story I wrote for *First for Women* called "Sex in the Workplace," sharing stories of people who got caught up in their passion, had this in the dek:

    Office romances can turn lives upside down, destroy careers and tear families apart.

    Then take your original pitch and paste it at the top of your draft manuscript, along with a reminder of your word count and deadline, to help you stay on track.

4. **Ask yourself these questions**: What is the point of my story? Am I fulfilling what I promised in the pitch? Am I writing for the target audience of the publication? Why is this important? What will people learn? The story should answer the questions posed in the pitch.

5. **Set up interviews with sources.** For short, reported pieces (up to one thousand words), try for two or three interviews. Some newspapers require consulting a minimum of three experts per story.

6. **Incorporate research and statistics.** Include hyperlinks to your sources. They may not be included in the published piece, but you'll find them useful to refer to as you write, and fact checkers at the publication (if any) will appreciate them.

7. **Include tips and expert advice if the piece requires them.**

8. **Add subheads to guide the reader and structure the story (see chapter 4).**

9. **Do your own fact checking.** Check every URL, study, poll, organization, term, and name.

10. **Edit your piece.** (See chapter 17.)

11. **Print out and read over your final version.** Make sure your piece matches or is very close to the assigned word count. Before emailing it to the editor, email it to yourself for another final check.

12. **Craft or polish your bio.** Include a short author bio or write-up for the publication, following the format on the publication's author pages. Include a photo. If the photo is by a professional photographer or from another website (rather than taken by a friend or family member), make sure you own the rights. If you don't, you'll have to make a separate arrangement with the photographer. If you hired a photographer for a photo shoot, then you own the rights.

13. **Send the piece and your bio to the editor by your deadline or a little before.** In the subject line, put "Article [TITLE OF ARTICLE] delivered by [YOUR NAME]" and then copy the piece into the body of the email (in case the editor doesn't like to open attachments from external sources), and also attach it as a Word document, so that the editor can get started working on it right away. Here's an example of a cover note:

Dear [EDITOR],

Thank you for this assignment. I really enjoyed working on it. Attached, and also pasted in below, is my [WORD COUNT] piece [TITLE OF PIECE].

I look forward to hearing your thoughts.

Please confirm receipt and let me know if you have any questions. If possible, I would love to review it before it goes live [or, for print publication, ask to see the galleys].

Sincerely,

[YOUR NAME]

Deliver What You Promised

Did you make sure you delivered what you said you'd write? It means that your research is current, accurate, and on topic. That your data supports the premise of the article and is correct and up to date. That your piece focused on what you said it would in the pitch. That you edited your work, so it's clear and each sentence flows into the next. That you didn't obscure points with flowery, academic, or jargon language. That you included the sources you said you would include, or had good replacements.

What Can Go Wrong?

- **The editor tells you that the article isn't what they wanted.**
    Gentle pushback: Say, "I'm so sorry, there must have been a miscommunication. Can we speak on the phone about this?"
    Keep in mind: The editor may be annoyed and frustrated at the delay, so you may need to deal with the situation with kid gloves (no matter who might be at fault). Check to see whether you had any guidance in writing from the editor that you might have overlooked. If you didn't, it is a good reminder to always make sure you understand the nature and scope of an assignment and ask for clarification if necessary.
    Realize that revisions may take more time than you expected, without additional pay.

Reviewing Your Edited Article

Once you've submitted your piece, the editor will review it and send it when they've had a chance to attend to it — which, for shorter, less complex pieces, sometimes isn't until right before publication. If the editor gave you a target date for when the piece would run and you still haven't heard anything from them, it's always okay to send a polite email reminding them that you had the pub date in your calendar and asking if they've reviewed the piece yet.

After the editor has reviewed the piece, they will send it back to you marked up with questions and suggestions on changing words, sentences, and paragraphs. Most editors use software (usually Microsoft Word or Google Docs) that shows suggested deletions and insertions as tracked changes. Make sure that you understand and follow their instructions on working with the edited document: for example, some editors may ask you to "accept" their changes before making more revisions, while others will ask you to leave their tracked changes in the file. If you don't agree with the changes proposed, or if you can't meet the suggested deadline, contact the editor. An article may go through more than one pass of editing before it's finalized.

Bring in the Backup

Most large circulation print magazines that hire fact checkers will not pay you unless you provide the sources for the fact checker to confirm. When I wrote for *Family Circle, Glamour, AARP: The Magazine*, and other magazines, they required the following backup for fact checking.

- An annotated copy of the final manuscript (with links for any info that came from websites). *Annotated* means providing a credible source for every statistic, poll, study, or figure you cite, such as a fact sheet or a link to a primary source. If original sources for scientific research are unavailable, most magazines accept an abstract or a press release from the relevant research university or institution.
- A source list with email addresses, telephone numbers, and/or public relations contacts for each person quoted in the story.
- Transcripts, emails, and/or notes of all interviews. Some publications will also ask for recordings of your phone, Zoom, or Skype interviews.

- For stories referring to commercial products: the manufacturer's press release, a public relations contact, and/or a link to a website with those materials.

For scientific and health data, information must come from reputable websites, such as government agencies, official organizations (e.g., the American Cancer Society), universities, and research hospitals (e.g., the Mayo Clinic) and professional (ideally peer-reviewed) journals. Unacceptable sources include newspaper or magazine articles, Wikipedia, blogs, fan sites, and medical information from non-medical sources (e.g., patient support groups).

You can make a great impression on both the fact checker and your editor by providing them with a well-organized package of everything they need.

Estelle's Edge: Although your published essay may not include footnotes, using footnotes in your draft will allow you to keep complete and readily accessible documentation of your sources for facts, quotes, references, statistics, and assertions.

Final Review

Always ask if the editor will send the piece to you for proofreading before it goes live on a website or in print. You'd be surprised what errors you can catch by carefully reading your piece over in a different format.

Keep in mind that if a publication is digital, you may not have a chance to review the piece before it's live, mainly because errors are easy to correct later if necessary.

What Can Go Wrong?

- **The edited version of your piece contains errors.**
    Gentle pushback: Correct the errors using tracked changes and include a comment explaining why changes are needed.
    Keep in mind: This is part of the editing process, and gives you a chance to participate.

- **Your voice has completely been stripped out of the piece.**

  Gentle pushback: Ask politely if some of your voice or personality can be put back in, giving examples of the places where this is most important to you. Focus on having your voice come through at the beginning and end of the piece.

  Keep in mind: Sometimes publications have very specific styles and voices. In that case, you can decide whether or not you want to still keep your byline on the piece.

- **The editor asks you to make revisions that are outside the scope of your agreement** (for example, asking for an article twice as long as specified or a completely different article than you agreed to).

  Gentle pushback: Ask for a phone call to discuss. If the editor doesn't respond in a day, email them saying politely that you feel the changes requested are outside the scope of your agreement. If you are willing to make the changes, ask for additional remuneration.

  Keep in mind: The editor may say no to additional payment. If it seems like it's the editor's style to make unreasonable demands, think about whether you are willing to go on working with them. It's up to you, but I would probably decline to make the changes and ask to be paid for the work already done, which fulfilled the agreement.

Make the Choice to Invoice

Once the editor signs off on your piece, you can send in your invoice. Many companies use online invoicing systems. Check with the publication on their requirements. In general, an invoice requires your name, address, phone number, email, the title of the article, the name of the assigning editor, and the amount due. You may also need to complete a tax form. After you file, note the invoice date, and put a reminder on your calendar to follow up in thirty days (or whenever the scheduled payment terms are set for) if you haven't received payment.

Being Published

When your piece is ready for publication, you'll most likely hear from your editor telling you that the piece is up or will appear on a specified date. You may want to ask the editor to send you a PDF or a printed copy of the article. It is courteous to send the PDF to any sources you used in the story. For a piece in a print publication, you can provide the sources' addresses and ask your editor to mail them a copy of the article.

What Can Go Wrong?

- **Your published piece contains errors.**

   Gentle pushback: If there are errors, don't hesitate to point them out. I say, "The essay looks great, and I'm so happy to promote it. I noticed one misspelling in line ___." I often also highlight the error in yellow and give the correct version to make the editor's job easier. Usually they will change it right away.

   Keep in mind: Editors have a lot on their plates, from conceptual planning to correcting typos on the website. Be patient and polite.

- **Your piece came out, and it's a mess. It's lacking your voice and riddled with inaccuracies introduced by other people.**

   Gentle pushback: None. You have to take action. Your professional reputation is at stake.

   Keep in mind: With legitimate publishers this rarely happens, but if the errors are embarrassing, or someone has added weird sidebars or other information that doesn't belong in the piece, screwed up the quotes from experts, or misrepresented someone in the story, you can ask your editor to fix it via email (so you have a record). If they won't or don't make corrections, ask them to take your name off the piece. I would not work with that publisher again.

Best-Case Scenario

Your published piece looks perfect. Everyone is happy. Congratulations!

I always ask the editor to let me know when the story is up so I can promote it on my blog and my social media channels. Once you receive the link, as promised, promote your story on social media and tag your editor and the publication.

If your story is digital, immediately save a PDF copy of it. Many of my colleagues have lost their valuable online work because it was taken down without their knowing. Also, send links or PDFs to your sources and experts. Everyone will appreciate the effort.

Estelle's Edge: If you and your editor are both happy with the story, now is the time to pitch another one.

What to Do If You Don't Get Paid

If you haven't been paid within thirty days (or the publisher's stated payment period), first send a gentle nudge to your editor. Processing invoices promptly should be standard office procedure, but sometimes this important step falls through the cracks. An editor who doesn't respond to this kind of request may be changing jobs or having personal issues. Try to find out if they are still there. If not, try contacting the publisher's accounting department. If accounting doesn't respond, go to the top of the masthead — the publisher.

When dealing with recalcitrant publishers, it is a good idea to mention that you belong to writers' organizations such as the American Society of Journalists and Authors, or even Facebook groups where writers share information on publications. This can gently persuade them to be fair with you.

Be cautious about payment arrangements, especially when you are working for publications with no track record. One time a publisher who was new to publishing got so annoyed with my repeated requests for payment over a three-month period that he dropped off $300 worth of pennies at my home. It just so happened that when the "payment" arrived, I was on the phone with a colleague who was considering writing for the publication. This rude behavior was enough to make the other well-connected writer shy away, and he shared the story with other writers. Shortly after, the publisher shuttered his business.

PART FOUR

All about

the Expert

CHAPTER THIRTEEN

Finding and Vetting Sources

Live the full life of the mind, exhilarated by new ideas,
intoxicated by the romance of the unusual.

— ERNEST HEMINGWAY

My first job in magazines was as associate beauty editor for *Woman's World*, where I was trained in service journalism. In that job, besides writing my "beauty tips" column and all the beauty features, I helped prep for and direct beauty photo shoots, maintained the beauty supply closet, selected makeover candidates, and hired models.

My boss used to let me clean out the beauty closet and take products home to make room for the new ones each season. That's how, on a pauper's salary, I ended up with huge bottles of Chanel perfume and a "goody bag" I would bring out for friends visiting me in my tiny New York apartment. Everyone got to choose a gift, from fire-engine red lipsticks to new skincare creams. But the biggest perk of the job was the crash course in journalism. With seven deadlines a week, I needed a constant supply of beauty experts.

Your experts must have credibility. So how do you find them?

Go for the Authority Figure

The higher a potential expert has risen in their field, the more credible they will seem.

Start by looking in your own backyard. Perhaps someone you know wrote a book on the topic you're researching. If the book was published by a major publisher, that makes the author a credible expert. Self-published books are harder to evaluate because they are not vetted by other experts or knowledgeable editors, so some editors of national publications don't see them as proof of expertise.

Look for experts who hold high positions in their industries. Your uncle may be a terrific realtor, but your editor will probably prefer a source with more name recognition.

> *Estelle's Edge*: While many publications allow you to quote your friends or relatives as sources, as long as you reveal the connection, news organizations generally do not allow it, because it can compromise journalistic credibility.

Other great sources are professors at major universities and authors of studies published in peer-reviewed journals (whose articles are vetted by other experts in the field).

One way to find medical experts is to contact research hospitals like the Johns Hopkins Hospital or nationally renowned medical centers like the Mayo Clinic. You can also contact the authors of a study recently published in a peer-reviewed journal, such as the *New England Journal of Medicine* or *JAMA*. Search for relevant journals by name or look for studies on PubMed (PubMed.ncbi.nlm.nih.gov), a database maintained by the National Library of Medicine.

When I look for a physician to interview, I try to find someone who has already appeared on television or in a magazine or publication. People with media experience understand what is involved in being interviewed for an article and won't have false expectations, like thinking they will get to review the article beforehand, as if they were the author.

Once your first byline comes out, PR firms take notice, and you may end up getting press releases sent to your email inbox. Personally, since my days as a magazine editor, I have been inundated, but I often find useful information in the releases, such as contact information for experts I want to quote in my articles.

> *Estelle's Edge*: To make life easier for yourself (and your editor), you want to interview someone who knows how to speak in concise sound bites. People who drone on and on before getting to the point are not helpful.

Making the Contact Count

Once you identify an expert you want to interview, you need to reach out to them via their website, email, or social media. To find contact information, try checking their websites, articles, and books. Many times, I direct message experts on social media sites. Most respond.

The Power of Preinterview Preparation

If you have a story that includes interviews, line up and confirm your sources beforehand and see if you can preinterview them. It's not always possible, but being able to say you're already in contact with a source can often make a difference when you are first pitching an editor. Read more about interviewing in chapter 14.

Nailing the Interview Request

To increase your chances of getting an interview, plan your approach ahead of time. Experts with something to promote (like a book, podcast, or YouTube channel) are often accommodating and happy to be interviewed because they want the exposure. You also up your chances of getting an acceptance by doing a preinterview before pitching an article.

Here is an example of how I approach a potential source:

Dear [NAME],

Hope you are well. I am a widely published journalist writing an article about [TOPIC] for [PUBLICATION NAME IF YOU HAVE IT]. I would love to interview you for my piece. I would like to interview you by [DATE]. Please let me know your availability, as I'm on a tight deadline. [I almost always include this phrase to create a sense of urgency.] Looking forward to chatting. [I always use the word *chat*, because it sounds friendlier and less formal, and it makes sources less nervous.]

If you don't have a set assignment for the piece, or are doing a pre-interview before you pitch an editor, here is an example I suggest my students use.

Hi, I enjoyed reading an article in [PUBLICATION] that you were interviewed for. I would love to speak with you for a piece I'm pitching to one of my many outlets. I've written for [PUBLICATIONS]. Happy to include a mention of your new book and your website. I'm on a tight deadline so would appreciate hearing back ASAP, please, on what day and time works for you this week. Looking forward to chatting.

Estelle's Edge: Often I contact people via an email address on their website (rather than a contact form on the site). As with pitches, I use descriptive subject lines such as "Journalist writing a story for [OUTLET] would like to interview you."

If I don't get a response via regular channels, I try direct messaging on Twitter, LinkedIn, or another platform. Most professionals have their messaging open, in case they get a business opportunity or a new client. If they have a business, you can also try to message them on the business's website or Facebook page. For book authors, you can look for a public relations contact on the publisher's website. Never give up. If it works, do it. If it doesn't work, try something else.

If I was referred to the source by another expert or a colleague of theirs, I always mention that person's name. If I found them through an article they were quoted in, or through their publisher or agent, I mention that, too.

What If You Don't Have Bylines?

Everyone is a marketer, and everyone has something to sell. Use that as your strategy when you are making contact. Here is how I suggested one of my students who hadn't yet been published approach a source:

> Hi, I'm a freelance writer working on a story about [TOPIC]. I plan to pitch it to a variety of health publications. I am happy to share information on your [new book, website, initiative, research, YouTube channel, etc.].

Another approach is to find a connection between yourself and the person you want to interview. Perhaps you are both alumni of the same university, or you both moved to a city from another country, or you both have twins. You won't always be able to find a connection, but it's worth a shot.

Looking for Anecdotal Evidence

Often editors will ask you to include brief anecdotes of people dealing with the issue you are writing about, particularly if it's health, psychology, parenting, or money. Anecdotes are a great way to begin a piece, and a hook to make the reader want to read on.

For example, for a piece for a beauty and cosmetic surgery site, I started a story this way:

> Mary, 52, and Sophie, 27 (names changed for privacy), are a mother and daughter whose relationship is so close that they can finish each other's sentences — much like the fictional Lorelai and Rory from the *Gilmore Girls* television series. The difference — this mother-daughter duo is real.
>
> I recently spoke with them about their cosmetic surgery choices.

Here is an anecdote I wrote to start off a piece for a health magazine:

> "I feel like every day, I lose my memory more and more. It started when I couldn't find my car keys, sometimes I forget directions. My mother has Alzheimer's, so I'm concerned," says Jerry Solowitz, a 63-year-old man.

Ellen Lerner, 37, sometimes worries that she can't keep track of everything in her job as a public relations executive. "I feel like stress can get to me easily, and I worry because I forget simple things like where I put a file."

Should these people be concerned?

Anecdotes are an effective way to get the reader invested in your story from the beginning.

You can find sources for anecdotes by crowdsourcing on social media or emailing friends and other writers to ask for suggestions. I've also had luck by tweeting using the hashtag of the topic I'm writing about, and some writers swear by reaching out to people through sites like NextDoor (for local connections) and Reddit, though I haven't tried that myself — yet.

> *Estelle's Edge*: Be careful when posting requests on big sites, because if you identify yourself as a journalist, you may not be welcome in some forums. A better bet is to read through the site for potential sources and then see if you can reach out to people through email or social media.

Vetting Sources and Experts

Crowdsourcing can also be a way of locating experts, but it requires care. Often when writers post on a site that refers queries to experts, they get deluged by people trying to make a name for themselves who are answering every query and trying to make their experience fit, regardless of its relevance. In addition, they may not be who they say they are. That's how you get a veterinarian claiming to be a parenting expert. (That actually happened to me.)

To avoid being scammed, check to see if the source has been written about before, and try to verify their credentials, particularly if they were profiled for their research or something they created, launched, or invented.

Start with a Credential Check

To make sure the expert you are approaching has appropriate credentials, ask yourself these questions before making contact.

- Have they achieved national professional success or met the top criteria in their field?
- Have they published a bestselling book? Is it highly rated on sites that sell books, or by book reviewers?
- Have they received prestigious awards?
- Are they frequently quoted in the media?
- Can you locate the articles they have been quoted in?
- Do they host or cohost a highly rated podcast or TV program?
- Did another vetted expert recommend them?

Questions to Ask When Vetting a Research Scientist or Academic

- What studies have they been involved with?
- How were the studies funded?
- Have they been the lead researcher on any studies?
- Have they been published in peer-reviewed journals?
- Can you find their work on PubMed?
- Do they teach at a university? (Not all do. In that case, check the other information.)
- Do they speak at industry or professional association conferences?

Red Flags

- You can't find their work published or cited anywhere.
- They were published in an obscure journal you've never heard of.
- Their research is funded by a company, not a university.
- They are the spokesperson for a company that they are doing research for (this makes them a public relations vehicle and not an appropriate source for journalism).
- They work in one area of medicine but say they are an expert in another, without any proof.

- They have started up or invented something that you can't locate information on.

Questions to Ask When Vetting a Medical Professional

- Are they licensed and board certified in their field?
- Do they speak at conferences in their field?
- Have they published journal articles in their area of expertise?
- Are they affiliated with a major hospital?
- Do they teach at a university?

Red Flags

- They don't have a major hospital affiliation.
- They want to speak about a topic completely outside the field they are certified in. For example, a dentist is not a credible source on cosmetic procedures. Sure, they may be trained to administer Botox, but they don't have the credentials of a board-certified plastic surgeon or cosmetic dermatologist.
- They are on the board of a pharmaceutical company.
- Their research is funded by a pharmaceutical company.

The Ethics of Being an Expert (and Working with One)

While many experts will be happy to share their expertise with readers, occasionally you may find that there are strings attached or that you're being asked to spin the story in a way that makes you uncomfortable. Here are some situations to watch out for:

- Avoid conflicts of interest: for example, be cautious about interviewing a friend, relative, or business contact. Many news publications define specific conflicts of interest in their agreements and ask the writer to disclose them.
- Don't work with sources who want favors or money in exchange for information (also called "pay to play").
- Refuse gifts, money, and any other kind of deal to provide media exposure for the source.

The reader (and your editor) is relying on you for objective, accurate information. Don't let them down.

Where to Find Experts

There are many ways to locate expert sources for your articles — including searching on LinkedIn and social media — with new ones emerging every year. Here are some of the most widely used. See chapter 15 for a more extensive listing of databases.

Academia.edu: A search engine that helps you find academics and researchers. You can see their research topics and send them messages.

Amazon: Search for relevant recent books and note their authors.

The American Academy of Religion (AARWeb.org): Lists experts in religion.

Data.gov: Website providing publicly accessible data collected by the US government. Other government agencies such as the US Census Bureau (Census.gov) and the Centers for Disease Control and Prevention (CDC.gov) are also great places to locate experts.

DiverseSources (DiverseSources.org): This is a large database of experts focused on science, health, and environmental work.

Editors of Color (EditorsOfColor.com/diverse-databases/): Offers more than one hundred databases featuring talent from underrepresented groups.

Expert Click (ExpertClick.com): An online directory of expert sources with some free search functions for journalists. Part of the Yearbook of Experts directory.

Expert Engine (ExpertEngine.com): Lists experts in different fields.

ExpertiseFinder (ExpertiseFinder.com): A search engine that locates academic experts.

Experts.com: Lists experts in business, insurance, law, and media.

Google Scholar (Scholar.Google.com): This is part of the Google toolbox that allows you to access research and studies and find their authors. If you don't find a study you are looking for, try checking open-access journals.

Help a Reporter Out (Haro.com): Connects journalists with media outlets. I've used this resource a lot over the years. It works best if you frame your requests very specifically (e.g., "I'm only looking for therapists, not social workers or PR professionals"). You can make same-day urgent requests on Twitter (using #URGHARO) if you sign up in advance.

Hospitals: Research hospitals and institutes such as the Mayo Clinic and Johns Hopkins that conduct cutting-edge medical research have media sections on their websites that can help you locate experts.

Journalist's Toolbox (JournalistsToolbox.org): Offers expert sources and lots of helpful information, including where to locate diverse experts.

Local continuing education courses: These can be a good resource if you are working with a regional publication.

Newswise (Newswise.com/journalists): A database of news releases and experts in science, business, lifestyle, and medicine.

NPR Diverse Sources Database (Training.NPR.org/sources): A platform maintained by NPR that focuses on underrepresented voices.

People of Color Also Know Stuff (Sites.Google.com/view/pocexperts /home): This platform connects journalists with subject-matter experts and people of color who are available for interviews.

Profnet (Profnet.com): A database maintained by PR Newswire listing more than fourteen thousand public relations professionals and experts. The site is free for media professionals. You can submit a query stating the type of expert you are looking for, along with your deadline and contact information. Queries can be targeted by company, organization, or geographic area.

Public-relations agencies: PR agencies are often willing to put writers in contact with their clients for interviews and media coverage. Search online for names of agencies or get access to the database Cision (Cision.com). Media releases from the Public Relations Society of America (PRSA.org) can help you find out what agencies work with the type of experts you are looking for.

Publishers: Publishers welcome media interest in authors of new books. Look for their media releases online.

Qwoted (Qwoted.com): A source of both ideas and experts.

SciLine (Sciline.org): A free service for journalists and scientists offered by the American Association for the Advancement of Science (AAAS). It's ideal if you need an expert for a science article.

Sources of Color (SourcesOfColor.com): A free site for journalists offered by PRSA, the Society of Professional Journalists, and other organizations.

Speakers.com: A site that television producers often use to find talk-show guests and speakers.

University websites: Most university websites have individual pages for departments and faculty members, with contact information and descriptions of their current research. Some universities also have media outreach pages, such as the University of Southern California's Expert Service (Pressroom.USC.edu).

Vetted (JoinVetted.com): A website that matches journalists with industry sources and PR specialists. Signup required.

Women's Media Center SheSource (WomensMediaCenter.com/She Source): A list of media-experienced women experts on various topics.

Estelle's Edge: If you've interviewed people before, one great way to find other experts and sources is by going back to those people and asking them for recommendations.

The next chapter discusses how to interview a source once you've found and vetted them.

CHAPTER FOURTEEN

Interviewing Experts

Interviewing someone is very similar to preparing a character, isn't it?
You're just asking questions: "Who is this person? Why did they make
that choice? Why are they doing that?" You're being Sherlock Holmes.

— FELICITY JONES

Throughout my career, I've interviewed thousands of people from all walks of life and all areas of expertise.

When I was a magazine editor, I had the chance to interview celebrities and media stars. Some of my highlights include speaking to Christie Brinkley when she was married to Billy Joel, a grown-up Maureen McCormick (aka Marcia from *The Brady Bunch*), the Romanian gymnast and former Olympic star Nadia Comăneci, the breast cancer expert Susan Love, MD, the nutritionist and author Ann Louise Gittleman, the actress Patricia Heaton, and the former infomercial queen Susan Powter. Each time I interviewed someone, I focused on learning at least one interesting fact about them. For example, when I interviewed the financial journalist Maria Bartiromo for W.I.T. (Women in Touch), when I was the editor in chief there, she revealed to me some of the steps she takes to stay ahead of the pack on financial news.

She told me: "Each day I get to the office at about 6:30 a.m., then I go through the wires and the newspapers. When I'm through reading, I start my phone calls and search out information before it's widely distributed to the market." When I asked her about her nickname, Money Honey, she said, "I was flattered initially, but after a while it got tedious. Bottom line: You can't fool our viewers. They're looking for substance and breaking news about money — a topic which people take very seriously — and I deliver."

What I Learned from My Brief Role on *Guiding Light*

When I was senior editor at *American Woman* magazine, the PR department of the network set me up with a tiny one-day role on the long-running soap opera *Guiding Light*. I wrote about my experience in a behind-the-scenes story, describing what happened from 7 a.m., when I left my home, to 7:30 p.m., when shooting ended for the day. I loved interviewing the actors and production people on the set.

The story included these moments:

9:15 a.m.: Joe (the makeup artist) tells me some gossip. It seems that at some other soaps (not GL), the makeup people give actors a mini "lift" using tapes and thin wires to pull up the skin under the hair.

10:30 a.m.: For some of the scenes featuring babies, they use a doll for blocking (setting up where the actor will stand or walk across the stage). The doll is used because a baby actor is only allowed to work four hours a day.

11 a.m.: The costume designer tells me he buys a large percentage of the cast's clothes at Saks, Bergdorf's, Bloomingdales, Lord & Taylor, and Macy's.

5 p.m.: For many of the scenes, we go straight from block rehearsal to taping (skipping the dress rehearsal).

I end my piece with:

7:30 p.m.: As I trek back to New Jersey, I wonder if a star was born today (namely me). Will I get a call back? You'll have to stay tuned...

It just so happened that a friend of mine worked for a company that was auditing the corporation that ran the show. I shared the tape I'd made of my day, on which the head of the costume department revealed that at the end of every season, he sold the clothing that had been used on the show to cast and crew at a deep discount. My friend listened to the tape and said, "Um, Estelle, that is illegal. He is not allowed to do this." I kept the information about the sale to myself, since I was a journalist, not a spy, and the person who needed the information (my friend) already had it.

Estelle's Edge: Always assume somebody is watching and listening. Learning this has taught me to be professional in every situation — in person, in emails, and on the phone.

Phone versus Email

I prefer phone interviews over Zoom interviews, because it's hard to take notes while being on camera. Most newspapers only accept in-person or phone interviews, but some publications, especially those with a tight timeline, allow email interviews. This format allows you to narrow down your topic and think through your questions, and it also saves time because the interview doesn't require transcription. When I wrote a *Mom's Talk* column for Patch, I always started my interviews via email. As I did, you can always follow up by phone to get clarification on certain points.

One of the reasons newspapers disallow email interviews is that they may enable unethical sources to plagiarize answers from other interviews. That's why I follow up the rare email interviews I do with a brief phone call, and I also run the file through plagiarism detection software to see if material has appeared elsewhere online. One example is Turnitin, to which many educators have access. In addition, some sites, including Grammarly.com, offer free plagiarism checkers.

Some sources may insist on email communication if they've had negative experiences with the media before and felt that they were misrepresented or misquoted. In that case, you might try assuring them that you aren't interested in making them look bad, but you might also want to find a more trusting source.

Working with a Publicist

Sometimes when you request an interview with a well-known figure, you'll be intercepted by a publicist, media relations professional, or someone from the communications department, who may be employed either by the individual or by a company or publisher with which they're affiliated. The job of these professionals is to make sure their client or spokesperson is favorably represented in the media, which means deciding where and how the person appears in public, on TV and radio, in social media, and in publications. I saw this experience from the other side when I wrote my viral story for the *New York Times*. Lots of people reached out to me to be on their blogs and podcasts, but the *New York Times* connected me with the executive director of the communications department, who vetted incoming requests, asked me how I wanted to handle them, and set up interviews, including my appearance on *Good Morning America*.

A publicist may insist on being present during an interview. This has happened to me a couple of times, and I agree, but I focus on the expert and what I need for my story. The publicist will also sometimes want to see the questions beforehand, which I always agree to. Because I once worked in public relations, I understand their job and try not to get in the way. If the publicist wants a particular issue addressed, they usually ask in advance. If I can accommodate it and it works for my story, I will include it.

Planning the Interview

Once I've set up an interview, I add a reminder to my Outlook calendar. To prepare, I create a text file containing my questions. At the top of that document, I post my pitch, to help me focus the questions. When I do the interview, I have this document in front of me, with the questions in large type so they are easy for me to read.

Next I research the expert or subject I'm interviewing. I like to do a deep dive into who they are. I look at their public social media, website, and YouTube site, if any; read about any books they have written; look for media appearances like TED talks; and do a Google search on them. I also look at older interviews and articles by or about them. For scientific experts, I search online for peer-reviewed research they've contributed to. If they have recently written a book, I purchase and read it. As I research, I keep adding to my list of questions.

I let the interview subject know that I will be recording the call (I use TapeACall, which has a transcription option). Other journalists use voice recorders or the voice memo feature on their phones, or they record the interview on their computers and use a transcription service like Otter or Temi. Make sure to test your recording device or software beforehand and learn about all its features before you use it for an interview.

Letting an interviewee know you will be taping them is required by law in certain states. I always ask, and I've never had anyone say no.

Coming Up with Interview Questions

It's essential to know what you want to achieve in the interview, whether it's corroborating something you learned, getting other connections or information, or finding interesting anecdotes. Your source may have their own agenda, but you need to keep your eye on the prize.

- To get them feeling comfortable, start with easy questions about something they know about, and let them know a little bit about you. Congratulate them on some news (a new book, research study, media interview) and ask them about it. You can also warm them up with factual questions that are easy to answer: age, where they live or lived, family situation, jobs.
- Remind them why you are doing the story and what your timeline and deadline are, and tell them what is interesting to you about their background, experience, and research.
- Ask questions about their interests and passions, as they relate to your story. Use words like *how*, *what*, and *who* to elicit information.
- Don't be afraid to ask the source to fill gaps in your knowledge or explain concepts to you.
- For interviews with experts, you can get them to expand

on their work with a question like, "I'm aware of your [RE-SEARCH, STUDY, BOOK, PAPER]. Can you share any other research studies, books, or papers that make an impact on [TOPIC]?"

- For service pieces, you can also ask something like "What kinds of activities or approaches help (or don't help) with [TOPIC]?"
- Ask for examples and anecdotes to support and fill out the story.
- If the interview relates to a traumatic incident, it is best to ask the person to tell you about it in their own words.
- For any incident or situation, ask questions that establish who, what, when, where, and why.
- To draw out more details, you could ask someone about the pivotal moment of some significant discovery, accomplishment, or life change and their state of mind about it. For a story I wrote for PBS's *Next Avenue* about how a woman found purpose in a preretirement trip to Ecuador, I asked her, "Describe your career up till retirement, and its spiritual and emotional impact on you."
- Just as you do in your own writing, try to get your source to describe their interests and experiences in detailed, vivid terms. If they say an experience was great, ask them what was great about it. What specific moments can they share? What special memories do they have? Boil it down and boil it down some more to get the tasty nuggets you need for your story.
- If they are making a big move or change, ask what compelled them to make that decision.
- If they make a statement about themselves, such as "I'm not an extroverted person," or "I'm not a sporty person," dig deeper to find out why they said that.
- If I'm interviewing an expert, I always ask, "What is coming up for you in your career/research/studies? Where can people find you or your book/website/social media for more information?"

Nailing Your Interview

When the day comes for the interview, I like to start with some small talk, and then I remind them that I'm recording the call.

To get your subject to relax and reveal themselves, you need to show that you are calm yourself. Until the day we speak, I always refer to the interview as a "conversation" or "chat," which sounds less intimidating.

If you find something in your research that connects you with the subject (you went to the same university, you both wrote for the same publication), mention that to break the ice.

This should go without saying, but if you are speaking with someone who has been affected by tragedy, always show empathy and sensitivity when interviewing them. Sometimes a source will want to tell you something off the record. What that means is you can't use it for publication, even if it provides background information or important context.

Get into the Groove

Rather than go abruptly from one question the next, try for a conversational flow. If you have prepared well and know the key points you want to ask about, you won't have to stick rigidly to your script, and you can cover your topics even if the interview veers in a different direction.

Take Notes While Talking

Even if you are recording the interview, take notes on your laptop, or mobile device, or notepad. Ask the subject to spell out any unfamiliar words or terms, especially names of people, organizations, or locations that aren't easy to verify. Recording devices can fail, and transcripts are not always accurate.

I often check off or cross out questions during the interview and jot notes on the printout of my interview questions.

Grab the Good Stuff

The best interviews reveal new info, interesting details, or maybe even something provocative or controversial. Don't just read the press releases. Go deeper into what really matters to your subject.

I try to highlight great quotes as I hear them, and I sometimes even note the time, so I can find a quote easily on the recording.

Hang on to sensitive questions until you've established a good rapport.

Stay Focused

You have written out your questions in a large font and placed your pitch at the top of the sheet. You know what you need from the person you are interviewing. Many people love to talk, especially to a journalist doing a story, but they may wander off track. If they're providing material you can use for another article, then let them speak. If they are veering way off into territory you aren't interested in, say, "You are saying such good stuff, and I really appreciate it, but I would like to focus on [TOPIC]." That will politely bring them back to what you need. Continue following that process.

Estelle's Edge: It's always good to ask what someone has learned from a new or challenging experience. What would they do differently another time? And how was their thinking changed (or not changed)? Just as a story needs a narrative arc, questions need to take an interview in a specific direction.

Make It Reader Friendly

Academics, researchers, and physicians often use complex terminology when discussing their subject. You may be able to follow this, at least some of the time, but your reader may not. Ask your subject to explain their meaning in layperson's terms: "Can you tell this to me as if I weren't in your field, so I can understand and convey it to the reader, who doesn't have the benefit of your expertise and experience?"

Ask Open-Ended Questions

Try to formulate your questions in a way that invites a long, detailed answer. Closed-ended questions like "Where did you grow up?" can be answered by a single word or statement: "New Jersey." But "Where did you grow up, and what did you most enjoy about your childhood?" is an open-ended question. The person can answer, "New Jersey, and I loved going to the Jersey shore with my family during the summer. We would open the top of the car and smell the salt of the ocean in the air as we got closer to the shore." The second answer reveals far more about your subject and lends itself to a more interesting article.

The Million Dollar Question

Since I started in publishing, I have been ending my interviews with a variation of this question: "We've covered a lot, is there anything that I haven't asked you that you want to tell me?" That's often where the gold is. Through asking that question, I've learned of new studies and interesting anecdotes to add to my story, found ways to pull different threads of a story together, and come up with ideas for other articles. Wherever you are in your career, I guarantee that adding that simple question to your repertoire will reap rewards.

Another question I always ask is "Who else should I talk to about this?" It's especially helpful if I need more sources. I follow up by asking if I can use their name when I contact the person or people they suggest. When contacting the other potential sources, I say, "[NAME] highly recommended I speak with you." I've never had anyone say no. I think being recommended by a peer or a friend makes the other person feel good and provides me with added credibility.

End with a Powerful Statement

I can tell when an interview has a good ending. Usually it's a powerful quote or statement, which I highlight in my notes.

Finessing the Follow-Up

Always thank the person you interviewed for taking the time to speak with you. Ask them how they would like to be credited. If I'm writing for a digital publication, I usually offer to include a link to their website or book. Some people (or their publicists) want to make sure that the credit includes professional affiliations, though your editor has the final say on that point. Confirm that you are spelling their name correctly — don't be afraid to ask. If you need photos or documentation, mention it now, and emphasize that the person needs to own the rights to any images. Also, let them know if a fact checker from the publication will be reaching out to them.

I also ask if I can contact them again before my deadline if I have other questions or need clarification. Then I ask for their direct cell phone number or email address, especially if I originally made contact through a public relations professional or personal assistant.

I explain that when my editor receives the piece, we may need to follow up with last-minute questions or changes. This is important to communicate, to be sure that you have a way to reach them after the interview, especially if they have travel plans. It's just how life is: people get busy, and once the interview is over, it won't have the same priority for them unless you emphasize that this is just the first step. I don't want to scare you, but editors have killed stories when key sources turn out to be impossible to reach.

Most professionals are on social media, so let them know when the piece will run. When it appears, send them a link or PDF copy with another note of thanks.

How to Write Quotes

The best quotes move the story forward in some way. If your source states a tangible, verifiable fact, such as "George Washington's birthday is on February 22," it's best to paraphrase it and treat it as part of your running text, rather than as a quote. Quotes should elicit emotion or provide information in a way that adds to the story and supports the expert's credibility. Don't feel compelled to include a quote if it isn't interesting. Here is a made-up example of what a source might have said:

> The meeting between the faculty, parents, and students took place on Friday. Our kids said they were not engaged in their studies, and it was the teachers' fault.

It is fine for you to put it like this:

> The meeting between the students, parents and faculty took place last Friday. "Our kids said they were not engaged in their studies, and it was the teachers' fault," said Jeff Miller, one parent at the meeting.

The powerful part of the sentence is not the logistics, but the way the parent is blaming the teachers.

Nir Eyal, the author of *Indistractable: How to Control Your Attention and Choose Your Life* and *Hooked: How to Build Habit-Forming Products*, writes about the intersection of psychology, technology, and business. He had been trying to get published in his goal publication, the *New York Times*, for years. During a brainstorming call, he told me some of his ideas for articles.

I immediately homed in on one about homeschooling teens and tweens. This was just at the beginning of the pandemic, and schools were closing across the nation. I thought it was the perfect confluence of events and his expertise. Knowing that the *New York Times* likes to be first to publish on trending issues, I guided him through the pitch process. His pitch was accepted, and he submitted his piece three days later. (When you want to be first, you have to be fast.)

The piece includes several quotes from experts, deftly interwoven with the writer's own statements:

> No matter the child's age, educators recommend providing structure.
>   "It's important kids don't see this as an indefinite snow day," said Dr. Michael Rich, director of the Center on Media and Child Health at Harvard Medical School.
>   School-age children can learn to school themselves, as long as a caregiver has set the groundwork to help them succeed.
>   At home, there are no bells ringing to tell students when it's time

for their next class. But apportioning time and sticking to plans are valuable life skills kids can learn while school is canceled. Dr. Rich believes families can take advantage of the change in the schooling environment. "I see this as an opportunity to help kids become more self-regulated," he said.

Estelle's Edge: The best interviews reveal new information, or something compelling or controversial. Don't just mirror the press releases. Go deeper into what really matters to your subject.

Make Your Sources Look Good

In your article, you want your subject to appear in their best light. So edit wordy quotes by removing filler words (see the advice on editing in chapter 17). Don't use the sentence fragments that people use in regular speech. Get rid of the person's "uhs" and "ahs."

Listen to the recording of the interview, even if you have a transcript and took notes. Often nuances that you might have overlooked in your notes become apparent from listening to the person's voice and inflection. Also, your notes and the transcript can contain mistakes, so it's best to go directly to the primary source — your recording.

Use Attribution

Let's say you love a quote from a subject that ran in another magazine, and you want to use it in your story. For many publications, particularly newspapers, this is absolutely verboten. They want you to interview the person directly and use those fresh quotes in your piece.

If you do reuse a great quote from another source, with the approval of your publication, you must mention the other publication and (if applicable) link to the original source. For example, for an article about beauty in a publication focused on people interested in cosmetic procedures, I prefaced the quote with "As cosmetic dermatologist Dr. David Bank said in *Allure* magazine, ..."

Don't Allow Sneak Peeks

Many times, experts who are new to being interviewed ask, "Can I see the article before it's published?" There is only one answer to that question: "No, I'm sorry. That goes against the publication's policy."

The reason you don't send the whole article to a source or expert is that previewing an article can lead a source to try to influence changes in the piece or give themselves an advantage over other experts. Any changes dictated by a source change the article from journalism to a public-relations puff piece.

To mollify the experts, I tell them I will run anything past them that I'm not clear about, but they do not get to see the entire article.

If a source pushes you on this issue, you can offer to send them only the text of their quotes that you plan to use (with the rest of the article stripped out), with the proviso that you can't make any changes unless the quoted material is incorrect (meaning they can't revise their on-record quotes). Sending quotes out of context can be helpful for ensuring accuracy if you are interviewing someone who uses complex terminology, like a scientist, especially if the article will appear in a print publication that can't be quickly corrected the way an online article can. (Also, newspapers generally list corrections made to articles on their websites, which can be embarrassing.)

If You Don't Use a Source

If you don't end up quoting a source you interviewed, it's a good idea to let them know after the piece is published that during the editing process their quotes were cut for space, but you are grateful for their time and will keep them in mind for future articles.

What If a Source Turns on You?

It has never happened to me, but if a source tries to retract or alter what they said or their participation in a story, or threatens legal action, it is best to escalate that situation to your editor immediately. Publications have policies in place to address those behaviors, and your editor needs to decide how to handle it. If you report the situation promptly and without complicating it, you will retain your editor's trust, making it easier to get additional assignments.

CHECKLIST FOR ASKING THE RIGHT QUESTIONS

❑ Did you ask the key questions that you needed answered to support the premise in your pitch?

❑ Did you ask questions that will confirm that your story is relevant, trending, important, surprising, newsworthy, or culturally significant?

❑ Did you find out what people most need to know about your topic?

❑ Is your research current and credible?

❑ Did your source refer you to further research and sources?

❑ Did you find pithy quotes from your source?

❑ Do you have an easy way to go back to your expert or source if you need more quotes or information?

CHAPTER FIFTEEN

Data Rush
Resources for Your Research

Writing is its own reward.
— HENRY MILLER

When I was in high school, I worked in our local library. I didn't love the hours, but I did love being surrounded by books and magazines. As a child, I kept a running tally of the books I read and wrote short book reports for all of them without anyone asking for them. I preferred fantasy books like *A Wrinkle in Time, The Princess and the Goblin,* and Julie Andrews's book *The Last of the Really Great Whangdoodles.* So I was thrilled to snag a job handling my beloved books. Unfortunately, I was fired after a few months for reading on the job.

My experience there made me value the work of libraries and librarians and was good practice for my later work as a magazine editor, where I read on the job for hours each day, selecting and curating the content for each print issue, much of it excerpts from books. I think I read hundreds of books a month, and I was on every publisher's list to receive new releases.

After I edited the *American Breast Cancer Guide* in the early aughts,

I became editorial director for a large medical publishing company. In the short term, this career twist allowed me to pay off debt from being a perk-rich, cash-poor magazine editor, and being in a nine-to-five job gave me the time to enjoy my nascent relationship with Werner, the man who would become my husband. A year later, it allowed me to navigate the early days of marriage, and later to grapple with the drain on my body and finances from infertility treatments.

In my job, I worked directly with physicians as our company developed continuing medical education (CME) programs for physicians on new treatments like Eli Lilly's Cialis (for erectile dysfunction), Allergan's Botox for hyperhidrosis (excessive sweating), and drugs for treating acne and diabetes. Over seven years, I worked on the educational side and later on the promotional side, organizing symposiums and developing web initiatives. It was not the most creative environment, but there were some real highs. I'll never forget how the team celebrated with cupcakes when a $320,000 grant proposal we submitted to the biotechnology company Genentech got approved.

From that career pivot, I learned how to read and write abstracts and work with medical studies, and I learned good research habits that have helped me land prestigious assignments and earn the respect of editors.

Researching the Right Way

Researching a story means scouring documents, files, and other information to verify your story and bring it to life.

Being able to locate and assess studies, census information, statistical data, and archival clips can help you in every aspect of your writing. Whatever area or subject you are writing about, editors appreciate it when a writer includes studies, research, statistics, credible polls, and compelling facts to make a pitch and later an article more impactful.

When you are looking for information for a story, you might be inclined to start with a Google search, but you need to keep in mind that the internet is full of false information. Citing unreliable or biased sources will torpedo any assignment.

Say you are researching a health story and come across a website that purports to share the latest research, touting one drug in particular. What you don't know is that somewhere on this site, in very fine print, is a statement that the site is sponsored by the pharmaceutical company that makes the drug. Suppose you rely on this site and the company's own research in your story. Your editor will tell you that you screwed up. If you're lucky, they'll let you fix the story. If you're not lucky, they'll kill it, or take it in-house, and vow never to work with you again. Instead of producing a reported piece, you've created a puff piece for the pharma company, destroying your journalistic integrity.

Journalistic integrity means remaining impartial and offering data that supports the story, but not allowing any source of information, like a big pharma company, to drive the story. It also means not accepting money or favors to mention a company, product, or individual in your story. If you were a patient of a physician pushing a drug on you, and you later found out the physician was paid by the company manufacturing the drug, you would think that the physician recommended the drug only because of their financial ties to it. Well, that's how journalism works, too.

You need to be skeptical.

Before citing a website, you have to see who sponsors or owns it, because some sites take great pains to hide the fact that they are promotional tools.

So instead of painstakingly combing your Google search results for information that may or may not be true, where can you go?

The answer is to seek out credible sources for your data and market research. Here are a few examples.

Universities

Universities offer access to research, journals, data, and reference databases, including many that require paid subscriptions. If you teach at or work for a university, you should have access to its reference library resources. Alternatively, try asking a friend who does, or see if your alma mater offers library privileges to alumni.

University websites typically have pages offering information about different departments and individual faculty members. These often include links to journal articles or research and the email addresses of researchers.

Professional Associations

Some associations for writers and journalists offer valuable resources, including access to subscription-only reference databases.

Companies

Many companies and corporations provide databases of news, journal subscriptions, and other information (some proprietary) and offer access to employees and affiliates. It never hurts to ask.

Government Sites

Sites that are funded by the US government (with URLs ending in .gov) are ideal for fact-finding, statistics, and research, and are generally free.

Government health websites include PubMed and the website for the National Institutes of Health (NIH.gov). Others include the National Center for Education Statistics (NCES.ed.gov) and the CIA's World Factbook (CIA.gov/the-world-factbook). This was produced for policymakers, but everyone can access it for basic information on almost all the world's countries and territories. See chapter 13 for other useful sites.

Journals

Every academic discipline and professional field, not just medical fields, has a journal for sharing the latest research and information from people in the field.

A number of scholarly journals are open access, which means that the information is free and open to everyone.

- DOAJ (Directory of Open Access Journals, DOAJ.org) is a community-curated online directory that indexes and provides access to open-access peer-reviewed journals.

- *Sage Open* (Journals.SagePub.com/home/sgo), a peer-reviewed journal from Sage Publishing, offers original research and review articles in the full spectrum of social and behavioral sciences and humanities.

It's important to understand that not all journals are reputable and reliable. Most professional journals have a peer-review system that vets articles to ensure that the content is original and valid. They are selective in what they publish. In recent decades, other journals, known as predatory journals, have offered paths to publication that bypass peer review and often charge authors hefty fees to appear in the journal. Some of these journals falsely claim affiliations with prestigious institutions and researchers. As a result, the information they contain is of questionable accuracy and value. So how can you tell the difference between a reliable journal and a predatory one?

- *JAMA*, the *Lancet*, the *New England Journal of Medicine*, and *BMJ* (published by the British Medical Association) are the gold standard for health and medical information.
- Journals included in databases such as PubMed and Scopus (maintained by the publisher Elsevier) have been vetted by a board of reviewers.
- Beall's List (BeallsList.net), compiled by a librarian, is a list of predatory journals and publishers, with links to other helpful sites. Unfortunately, the list is infrequently updated.
- Journalytics (Cabells.com/about-journalytics), a subscription-based list of over eleven thousand academic journals curated and maintained by Cabells Scholarly Analytics, also shares reports on predatory journals.

Another way to gauge the reputability of a journal is by checking a statistic called the impact factor (often found on the home page or "About" page). This shows how often the journal is cited by other researchers in their work. And articles in reputable journals will usually cite other reputable journals, so you can assume those have been vetted, too. If you find an interesting study, you can also look at the papers it cites (which will be in the "Works Cited" or "References" section at the very end of the study or paper and sometimes hyperlinked in the paper or study itself).

Although subscriptions to specialized journals can be expensive, many offer free email newsletters highlighting recent articles. It's worth subscribing to these newsletters in your area of interest.

Sometimes significant research findings are embargoed (meaning they aren't released to media or the public until a certain date). If you keep up with the news in your areas of interest, you may be able to get leads on these breaking stories and be ready to pitch an article as soon as they're released.

Your Editor

If you're having trouble getting access to information from professional associations, you might try asking your editor if they belong or subscribe. I had connections like these when I was a glossy magazine editor, and others may, too.

Librarians Are the Heroes of Your Story

What if you can't access these important databases and journals? What if they require a fee? There is one source that will help you get access, usually within easy reach. And that is a reference librarian.

Librarians are fantastic and so helpful. To this day, if I ever need a hard-to-access document that I can't get from the university libraries I have access to, they are who I call.

Your neighborhood librarian can help you access online resources such as websites, newspapers, and journals. You can talk to your local librarian in person, by email, or via online chat. Librarians are great at accessing resources like these:

- EBSCO: Academic Search Complete — a cross-disciplinary database
- ProQuest Central: a multidisciplinary research database
- Gale Academic OneFile: a source of peer-reviewed full text scholarly content
- rare historical material

- embargoed research and studies
- databases and information on publicly traded companies (most sources are fee-based)
- obscure but important organization databases that only a librarian has access to
- databases and other online resources from other countries

Citing Research

When you are citing research or statistics in your pitch or article, it's imperative to use primary sources: the original documents produced by the research group (journal articles, statistical data, or polls), notes from your one-on-one interviews, or a press release from an author's own institution or company (not a press release from somewhere else that happens to mention them). This is important because any time information is relayed through another source — called a secondary source — there's a chance that errors could have been introduced, and data could be misreported or misinterpreted. If you read about a research study in a magazine article, it's not a primary source. Instead, go to the original source — that is, the journal, study, poll, or press release where the information was first presented.

The most recent studies are the most newsworthy. They will often link to previous studies, which may provide helpful background and other information you can use in your article. If you are looking at health or medical studies, you want to cite clinical studies done on humans, not in vitro studies (which are done in a lab), or in silico (computer modeling or simulations).

You want to cite studies published in a peer-reviewed journal, as opposed to studies funded by a pharmaceutical company or another organization with a vested interest.

The abstract, which appears at the beginning of a study, is the most important part. It summarizes the objective of the study, the methods, and the results. The discussion section, usually near the end, is helpful, too, because it elaborates on the significance of the study.

The reference section at the end lists the other articles the researchers cite in their study, often with links.

If you can't get access to the full text of the article describing the work, you can try emailing the first author listed in the paper to request a copy. If contact information for the author isn't available, look for their faculty page on the website of the university they are affiliated with. I've had great luck finding phone numbers this way.

Like professional journals, some book publishers require manuscripts to go through peer review before publication. These publishers include Wiley, Emerald Publishing, most university presses (such as MIT Press), Springer Nature, Nova Science Publishers, and Rowman & Littlefield.

> *Estelle's Edge*: Many study authors post their work on ResearchGate.net, especially older papers that aren't under copyright restrictions.

Doing Your Research: An Example

Here's a step-by-step example of rapid primary-source research: a story I wrote in a single day for Parents.com.

1. The editor sent out an email to regular contributors in the morning asking for a story they wanted to run the same day with the title "PSA: It's Totally Fine to Have Babies After 35; Science Backs It Up." The country singer Carrie Underwood had recently said that at age thirty-five, she had missed her chance at having a baby. Clearly, a lot of people didn't agree. The editor wanted a hot-take reaction story by a writer who'd had a baby after thirty-five.

2. Since I got pregnant in my forties and had written a lot about it (see chapter 19 on repurposing your work), *and* I disagreed with Underwood's statement, I had some statistics and information already, so I knew that as long as I updated my facts, figures, and statistics, I could pull off this story. I emailed the editor telling her it's okay to get pregnant after thirty-five and that I could prove it with studies and statistics. We negotiated the fee (see chapter 12), and I got the assignment at 1:18 p.m. It was due at the end of the day.

I had never worked with this editor before, although I had written for another editor at the same publication. This story seemed like a great opportunity to get the new editor to notice me and my writing. I had the information I needed, I knew how to do additional research, and I felt passionate about the subject.

3. I started with the premise that what medicine calls "advanced maternal age" doesn't mean someone can't get pregnant and give birth to a healthy baby. Adoption, which Underwood was considering, is a fine choice, but it's wrong to think it is impossible or irresponsible to conceive after thirty-five. I did, and so did many of my friends and colleagues.

4. I wrote my lede using what I already knew:

When Grammy-winning singer Carrie Underwood opens her mouth, people pay attention — and not just when she sings. What she says counts, too. Case in point: In a 2018 cover story for *Redbook* magazine, Underwood said that she believed that she and her husband Mike Fisher may have missed their "chance to have a big family" and give her son, Isaiah Michael, siblings because she was 35. She, therefore, planned to explore her options, including adoption.

Then I wrote:

There's just one problem. Many Parents.com readers believe Underwood misspoke.

The publication kept my original first paragraph but later changed the second one to this version, addressing the comments from social media:

In addition to comments of support and encouragement, many of Underwood's Twitter followers expressed their feeling that she was either misguided or not sharing all the information regarding her viewpoint.

5. I delved into the science. I found a study from my regular ScienceDaily.com email about a new Harvard School of Public

Health study, published in *JAMA*, showing that patients over thirty-five had better prenatal care and pregnancy outcomes than those slightly younger. Perfect. Since I didn't have access to the *JAMA* study yet, I cited the announcement from Harvard as a valid primary source.

6. Searching a government database (a source of reliable, peer-reviewed research), I found support for these findings in an article that appeared in the *Journal of Family and Reproductive Health*, and I included a link to that information.

7. For a piece for a different publication on the topic of age-related infertility, I had looked at the New England Centenarian Study (a study of people who live to age one hundred or older). I went back to it and found information I could use for this piece, too.

    The study found that people who gave birth after the age of 40 were four times more likely to live to 100 than those who had children younger.

8. Looking at studies related to the centenarian study, I found another relevant study and added it in:

    One study published in the *Journal of the American Geriatric Society* found that people who have birthed children can benefit from the hormones that flood the body and brain during pregnancy, which can help improve cognition including problem-solving, mental reasoning, and memory in postmenopausal stages of life.

9. With my data in hand, I needed to create some subheads. I framed them around all the studies. The editor liked the structure that subheads provided but changed most of them. For example, I wrote "Giving Birth at This Age Will Make Her Smart" (referring to Carrie Underwood), and the editor changed it to "Giving Birth After 35 Might Make You Smart," which put the focus back on the reader. I also submitted the subhead "Having a Child Later In Life Keeps You Young," and the editor changed it to "Older Parents Might Live Longer."

10. Since this piece was focused on the science and only eight hundred words in total, there wasn't a lot of room to add my own voice, but I found a way to express it:

    Many of my friends and colleagues had their first children in their late 30s and early 40s. With a little help from modern medicine, I had my own daughter in my mid-40s as well and had a healthy — if heavily-monitored — pregnancy. And I wouldn't change a thing.

11. To add quotes from an authoritative source, I made a quick call to Juli Fraga, a San Francisco–based psychologist specializing in reproductive health. She had recently written for the publication, so the editor knew who she was and her credentials.

    "It's normal to be concerned about later age pregnancy, and yet women at the age of 35 are generally healthy and can have babies," says Dr. Fraga. "Even with fertility issues, there are many ways to help families have children, through IVF, donor eggs, or surrogacy," she adds.

    Dr. Fraga believes she knows why Underwood brought out the old belief about not being fertile after the age of 35. "She is probably responding more to the cultural message that women over 35 are no longer able to bear children, which is not true. This pre-pregnancy-related anxiety about one's fertility being finished is more of a worry than a reality."

12. I submitted the story at 4:51 p.m. The editor tweaked the ending — to include the news that Underwood had just announced her pregnancy — and it ran later that day. She told me it was doing very well on the site, thanked me for the quick turnaround, and said she was looking forward to working with me again. And I'm happy to say we did.

Databases

Databases organize large quantities of information in searchable form. The following lists provide a basis for compiling your own reference list of publication databases. Unless otherwise noted, most of these databases are free. Those that are subscription based may still offer limited free features, and you can often sign up for a free trial period.

Your local librarian can give you the latest and greatest information and help with access to these and other databases. Remember, whatever you find, it's just a start. You need to go through the material and read it to make sure it fits your article's purpose.

Health Databases

Google Scholar (Scholar.Google.com): A large (though not exhaustive) source of studies on any topic. Simply type in keywords.

JSTOR (About.JSTOR.org): Database offering access to more than twelve million journal articles on a variety of topics.

National Library of Medicine (NLM.NIH.gov/bsd/journals/online .html): A database of journal citations and abstracts that are indexed in Medline.

PubMed (PubMed.ncbi.nlm.nih.gov): Also maintained by the National Library of Medicine, this is an extensive database of articles on medical research. PubMed does not do the research itself; it just provides abstracts (brief summaries) and links to the research. To access an article, you must click on a link that takes you to the journal in which the article was published.

Sage Journals (Journals.SagePub.com): A fee-based database offering access to more than one thousand journals published by Sage Publishing.

Scopus (Scopus.com): Maintained by Elsevier publishing, Scopus lists journal articles published after 1995. It is subscription based but offers limited free features.

The differences between PubMed, NLM, and Medline are often confusing to writers. PubMed is a database run by the National Center for Biotechnology Information (NCBI), a subsection of the NLM. Medline is the largest component of the database. PubMed provides free access to Medline and links to full-text articles when possible.

Databases for Academic Sources and Journalism

Academic Search Premier (Ebsco.com/products/research-databases /academic-search-premier): A fee-based database of more than 3,600 peer-reviewed publications on every subject.

African American Newspapers Archives (1827–1998) (libraries .indiana.edu/african-american-newspapers-1827-1998): A database of more than 350 newspapers from every region of the United States. Direct access is restricted to affiliates of Indiana University–Bloomington, but you can message the librarian to ask for help.

Alternative Press and Index Guide (AltPress.org): Offers articles from alternative periodicals, newspapers, and magazines.

American Periodical Series Online (1740–1940) (libraries.indiana .edu/american-periodicals-series-online): A treasure trove of digitized images of the pages of American magazines and journals published from colonial days to the dawn of the twentieth century. Another resource at Indiana University–Bloomington for which you can request assistance from the librarian.

American University Library (subjectguides.library.american.edu): A great, publicly accessible list of databases of scholarly journals.

Bartleby (Bartleby.com/quotations): A searchable collection of more than one hundred thousand quotations, including the contents of *Bartlett's Familiar Quotations.*

Encyclopedia.com: A free online resource that offers a searchable database of over two hundred individual encyclopedias and reference books.

Factiva (DowJones.com/professional/factiva): A fee-based database maintained by Dow Jones that offers news and data from over thirty thousand sources — newspapers, newswires, industry publications, websites, company reports, and more — from two hundred countries, in thirty-two languages. You don't need a subscription to search by journal title or subject.

LexisNexis (LexisNexis.com/en-us/gateway.page): This fee-based database offers business and legal articles. You can get a one-week free trial.

Statista (Statista.com): Offers statistics, insights, facts, and studies on a variety of topics. Fee-based, but access is available through many public libraries, schools, universities, and government agencies.

Databases for General News, Trends, Market Research, and Polls

Dow Jones News Retrieval (DowJones.com): This subscription-based site offers business and financial news from the *Wall Street Journal*, Dow Jones Newswires, Factiva, *Barron's*, MarketWatch, and *Financial News*.

The Harris Poll (TheHarrisPoll.com): A leading source of opinion-poll data.

Newsbank (Newsbank.com): A large archive of news articles accessible through many libraries.

Pew Research Center (PewResearch.org): A nonpartisan research organization that conducts public opinion polling, demographic research, and data-driven social science.

ProPublica (ProPublica.org): An investigative journalism website that makes data available to journalists for free.

ProQuest (ProQuest.com): Lets users search hundreds of newspapers, magazines, and broadcast reports. Access available through public libraries and universities.

Solutions Story Tracker (SolutionsJournalism.org/storytracker): A database of reported stories on social problems and issues from around the world.

Spokeo (Spokeo.com): Enables searches of data from public records, social media, and email.

The Wayback Machine (Archive.org/web/): An archive of material originally published online that may no longer be accessible on the original publication site.

PART FIVE

All about Editors

and Editing

CHAPTER SIXTEEN

Researching Publications and Editor Etiquette

Words are a lens to focus one's mind.
— AYN RAND

When I was a magazine editor, I loved being able to reach out to people I thought would enhance the magazine by covering specific topics. That's how I ended up giving the legendary divorce lawyer Raoul Felder his own legal column in *American Woman* magazine and worked with a famous body-language expert who analyzed photos of celebrities. Each time, I knew I was providing value to our readers.

In addition to carefully researching the topics you want to write about, it pays to research the places where you want to publish. One of the ways to make a positive impression on an editor — besides your pitch or essay — is to show you understand their publication and the kinds of articles the editor is looking for.

Aim for the most prestigious or well-known publications, but prepare well. After working with well-established magazines, I pivoted into creating and editing new publications when I impressed the former CEO of Hachette Filipacchi, David Pecker, with my research and analysis of his publishing empire. I saw him at a press event and was determined to meet him. At the time, I was editor in chief of a woman's magazine that had a midsize circulation. My colleagues told me, "Don't do it. Why would he be interested in talking to you?" I thought about it for a moment and decided I wouldn't allow anyone else to decide my actions. I walked up to him, introduced myself, and shared my knowledge about his publications, which then included *George* (the most famous new magazine of the 1990s), *Elle*, *Mirabella*, and *Woman's Day*.

We met for lunch at Le Bernardin. After a few more meetings, he hired me as a consultant, and later I became the editorial director of Hachette's newest magazine from the custom publishing division.

The publication, *Body by Jake* (the celebrity fitness trainer Jake Steinfeld), ended up closing a year later, but my role there positioned me to launch other publications, such as W.I.T. (Women in Touch), *The American Breast Cancer Guide* (a magazine for women with or at high risk of breast cancer), and *Esthétique* (a skincare and plastic surgery magazine).

When I was consulting at Hachette, I got to work with Frank Pellegrino Sr., the famous "Frankie No" of the restaurant Rao's and actor on *Goodfellas* and *The Sopranos*, who was also consulting for the company.

One day he invited me to dine at Rao's — where, according to the Zagat restaurant guide, it "practically takes an act of Congress" to score a table.

"Why don't you come to my restaurant, Rao's, one night as my guest?" he offered. "It's a fun joint. We eat Italian food and sing along to the jukebox till three in the morning. You have an open invitation."

Although I unfortunately never took him up on his invitation, I did parlay my experience with Frank into an essay for Ozy called "Blowing the Best Invite of My Life." I love telling people that even though I never made it to Rao's, and regret that very much, I was one of the few people that Frankie No gave a yes to.

To get a yes from editors, it helps to understand what they do. Editors have a lot on their plates. They have to come up with ideas, select content (sometimes including book excerpts), work with writers, edit articles, write headlines and cover lines, work with designers and production staff, submit invoices, troubleshoot, and more. The easier you make their job, with strong, relevant pitches and (later) articles that require minimal reworking, the more likely they are to say yes.

Read the Publication to Prepare Your Pitch

Editors are people. They like to feel you have taken the trouble to get to know their publication and interests. If you're planning to pitch to an online publication, look at what it has covered over the past six months, including regular columns. For a print publication, buy the most recent issue, read it cover to cover, and consider subscribing. If a publication you're interested in writing for has an email newsletter — and most do — sign up.

Before you pitch a story, check that it fits with the magazine's mission. When I was the editor in chief of *Woman's Own*, a magazine for single and divorced women, I wasn't happy when writers submitted pitches for stories centered on men (read the title, people). Also, check that your story hasn't been covered already.

Putting Your Best Pitch Forward

I talk to editors every week for my classes, and so I hear firsthand what they are looking for and what annoys them.

Offer Original Material

Editors want your piece to be new and original. If you try to pitch a story that you have already featured on your blog, or on Medium, don't think the editor won't find out. Most editors do a preliminary Google search to confirm that an article hasn't been published somewhere else, and that it's original, particularly the first time they work with a writer.

Estelle's Edge: If a version of the story you're pitching appears on your blog, you can probably unpublish it or make it private, as long as it hasn't already gone viral.

Keep Your Social Media Clean

Make sure your Facebook page is locked down so that only the people you have accepted as your friends can see your posts, and avoid getting into wars on social media. An editor could see this as confrontational behavior and think you may be a headache not worth betting on.

Follow Submission Guidelines

Become familiar with the voice and style of the publication you're pitching, and take the trouble to read its submission guidelines, if they're available. You can find them online or request them through the contact information on the publication's website. (Some publications send guidelines only when a writer is under contract.)

If an editor gives you specific guidelines, stick to them. If the publication wants 700 words, don't send 1,500.

> *Estelle's Edge*: Cut and paste a few of the articles or essays from your target publication into a document on your computer. Follow their word count and pacing as you write your piece.

Follow the Publication's Prose Style

Most pubs have a specific style and tone. If the style is conversational, don't make yours overly academic. Also, pay attention to style issues, such as how the magazine uses quotes and formats their pieces with subheads or sidebars.

Avoid the IT Axe

Unless editors request submissions as word processor files, it's wise to paste them into the body of your email, since many publications' IT departments block incoming attachments. Also, if your email signature line contains numerous social media and publication links, you should trim them, because they may cause your message to be blocked by spam filters. Although tracking apps showing whether the recipient has read your email are popular, a lot of IT departments block them, and if editors know their email reading habits are being tracked, they may become annoyed and avoid you.

Get the Editor's Name Right

Unless you have met the editor, were introduced by a colleague, or have seen a call for pitches or their regular posts on social media, begin your email with "Dear Full Name." The days of formally addressing editors as Mr. or Ms. (or, G-d forbid, Mrs.) are long gone. Check the spelling (again) before sending your email.

Be Ready to Hear "It's Not a Fit"

The response "It's not a fit" is editors' favorite form of rejection. It's sort of the equivalent of a breakup when the person says, "It's not you, it's me." It usually *isn't* you (though sometimes it can be). Editors can reject a piece for myriad reasons: they have a similar piece in the works; your writing style, while good, didn't fit theirs; they do those kinds of pieces in-house; they don't think the piece is timely; or they don't like the ending.

When they tell you no, don't annoy them with a ton of questions asking why. Take no for an answer. Editors hate getting into dialogues about why a piece was rejected. Also, don't ask them to help you with your writing. If they accept the piece, they will work with you to polish it. If you start acting needy before they even come to that decision, you will never get your foot in the door.

How to Piss Off an Editor — from Editors

- If I reject your piece, please don't argue with me about it. I don't have time to explain why it's not a fit and then go back and forth. I'm more likely to consider another idea than the one I've already rejected.
- When an editor passes on a pitch, it is not a good idea to send ten or fifteen new ideas right away.
- Please send your final version, not a draft that you expect to revise and resend after we accept it.

- No pestering. Responding to email can't be my full-time job.
- If I see "Hey [EDITOR NAME]" and the rest of the email is in a different font, I wonder how many people it has gone out to.
- I dislike misspellings, missing words, and sloppy work. As careful as you are when writing the piece, be careful about making sure the email is conversational. It shouldn't be stilted or overly academic.
- Try to find the right person to send your pitch to. I get pitches from staff, and from public relations people, not just freelance writers. So if you send your pitch to six people on my staff, I will end up getting the pitch in my box six times, and that is annoying.
- I can see if a writer hasn't looked at the site. All you need to do is search on the site for five minutes and see recent topics and headlines. If you send me three ideas that I just covered, that doesn't look good, because it shouldn't have been hard to find them.
- If we ask for a story of 750 words, don't submit a 2,000-word draft and say it can be cut down.
- Don't ask me who you should speak to for your piece. I'm paying for the reporting. You should know how to figure out who the experts and authors are.
- The number one way to annoy an editor is to state, "I'd love to write for you," without mentioning a specific story, article, or essay.

Find the Right Editor

It's always best to send your pitch or piece to an individual editor rather than to a general email address. Pick the editor for the section you want to publish in (e.g., beauty, health, parenting, science, technology, money). To find the right editor, check out the masthead of a publication for names and email addresses, or search its website. If you don't know who to send it to and aren't sure of the right section for your pitch, it's always a good idea to send it to the managing editor, if the publication has one. They can decide who to funnel your pitch to. If the publication doesn't have a managing editor, an associate or senior editor would be my next pick — better than the editor in chief, who doesn't have the time to review pitches from writers they don't know. If you are looking for new publications or just want to browse potential new outlets for your writing, the website Issuu (which requires a subscription fee) offers PDF versions of many magazines. You can search for titles and peruse mastheads through the site's publisher directory (Issuu .com/publishers) without subscribing. You can also find magazines through Amazon Kindle Magazines, which shows bestselling publications); Magazine Agent (Magazine-Agent.com); and Magazines.com. Or you can browse magazines and mastheads in a bookstore.

Locate editors through searches on LinkedIn, Google, and Twitter. Search for the publication's name and the word *editor*.

Although I don't recommend cold calling editors directly, an alternative tactic is to call the customer service line for the publisher and ask who the editor is for a specific section. The person responding may even give you a direct email address for the editor.

Some publications use Submittable, a cloud-based submission management system. This allows writers to submit articles but does not disclose the names or email addresses of editors. It makes the process impersonal, since the site also issues acceptances and rejections.

Don't forget your personal networks. Writers you meet through events, conferences, Facebook groups, and classes will often share the names of editors they've had recent success with.

Many editors use social media to share calls for writers and tout their own achievements. If possible, sign up to get notifications from those editors, so you see what they post the minute it happens.

If you've got the name of an editor but are struggling to find an email address (which many editors don't make public so they can avoid being swamped), you can try some sleuthing. Many corporate email addresses use some variant of the person's name, followed by @ nameofcompany.com:

Firstinitiallastname
Firstname.lastname
Firstname
Firstname_lastname

You can also search the media database Muck Rack (which requires registration) or the email finder RocketReach.

Another way to make contact with editors is to attend conferences or other networking events where they are speaking. Many people come to my pitching panels, conference talks, webinars, and NYU events. Even if you don't get to meet the editor one on one, if you mention the event in a follow-up email, it moves you up the line.

> *Estelle's Edge*: When you start working with an editor, ask them if they can add you to any email lists they use to request pitches for particular assignments. Many editors keep lists, but they won't always remember to add you unless you ask.

Go Straight to the Top

When you have a solid pitch, always submit to your most desired publications first. Wait a week or so, and then, if you don't hear back, move on to your second choices. Many of my students have been surprised when a top publication accepts their piece or pitch.

The Etiquette of Simultaneous Submissions

When you submit your pitch to more than one publication at a time, it's called simultaneous submission. Some editors understand why you are doing it and don't mind; others hate it, especially when your topic is connected to a current news item or announcement, because they are worried about getting scooped by another publication. Whatever you decide to do, if your piece is accepted elsewhere, let the other editor know so they don't waste their time. Hearing this may actually make them more interested in your future pitches.

I believe simultaneous submission generally makes sense unless you know a publication restricts it. Otherwise a writer could spend a year pitching the same piece to one publication at a time and perhaps never hear back from some of them.

For top publications like the *New York Times*, the *Washington Post*, and other news publications, I give the editor a week to review my pitch and then follow up by resending the pitch a week later, before I send it out to other publications.

> *Estelle's Edge*: Here's a trick I've used since my days as a magazine editor. If the editor didn't respond, forward your email and remove the forwarding info and the "FW" in the subject line so it appears that you just sent it. The editor will know, if they saw it before and didn't respond, that you aren't calling them out. Everyone saves face this way, and it's easier than cutting and pasting the information into a new email and adding in the subject line all over again.

The Real Meaning of "Timely"

If you have a piece that needs to get published right away, because it is connected to a breaking news event or current events, put "Timely" in the subject line of your email, or indicate on Submittable that it's timely. As long as you are honest about what you are doing, an editor shouldn't regard this as pushy. I have been known to write, "Since this pitch is timely, please let me know by [DATE], or I will place the story in one of my other outlets," and this has worked well for me.

Editors tell me if you want to connect a story to a new show or movie, that's great, but it doesn't warrant putting "Timely" in your pitch.

Once You Hit Send

Once you have submitted your pitch, fight the urge to keep checking for a response — at least for a week, or two weeks if you are simultaneously submitting and the pitch isn't connected to a newsworthy event. If your piece is related to fast-moving, significant events or breaking news, it's okay to follow up your pitch in the next day or so and to keep "Timely" in the email subject line.

It's hard, but you need to have faith the right match is out there for your piece. When it's accepted, you should alert any other editors you've sent it to by sending them an email or withdrawing your submission on Submittable (even if they never responded to you once). By doing this, you are showing that you value their time.

Don't call an editor or message them on social media unless you know them very well, are currently working with them on an assignment, or are responding to a message from them. Almost all editors hate being called on the phone.

Don't Blog It If You've Pitched It

It's important not to post your work on your blog or a platform like Medium without first trying to place it in several outlets, especially if it's an evergreen piece, which means it can run anytime and isn't connected to breaking news. There is always a way to tweak a piece or a pitch if you are determined to get published.

Impressing Your Editor

Make sure your pitch and submission emails are formatted properly, that you used one space after a period, not two, and checked for correct spelling and grammar. And of course, have good, fresh, timely stories and essays to pitch.

If you work with an editor a lot, it's perfectly appropriate to send them a card around the holidays or the start of the new year. You can also send a little gift, like chocolates, popcorn, jam, or something else tasty.

If you screw up, forgive yourself. You are only human, and editors know that everyone makes mistakes: pitching the wrong editor, misspelling a name, or overlooking a glaring typo. I should know. I once forwarded an email to an editor that I had sent to her competitor and forgot to delete the materials underneath, which showed I had reached out to another editor first. That was a huge mistake, and I believe the editor later mentioned it in a seminar I attended as an example of what not to do (with me cringing in the corner).

The good news is, if you've never worked with the editor before, they are more likely to forget the gaffe, and you as well (just don't use the same email chain for your next pitch); and if you have, they are more likely to forgive you. So forgive yourself first and move on. You have work to do.

Estelle's Edge: If you are pitching to a magazine that has been around a long time, don't assume the audience is the same as it has always been. Do your research.

Editors' Best Etiquette Advice

- We're looking for freelancers who give a clean first draft, answer questions, and turn a piece back in a timely manner.
- Make sure your email address is out there so an editor can find you. Put it on your website or in your bios on social media.
- The editor has the final say. Don't fight your editor. If a line is changed and it isn't true to your experience, you can say, "That wasn't what I was saying," or "That wasn't my experience."
- Some editors see their pubs as a launching pad and love seeing their writers soar. So let the editor know about anything cool that comes out after your piece runs.
- If you file on time and you have clean copy that doesn't require a ton of editing, the editor will want to work with you again, and you will stand out.

CHAPTER SEVENTEEN

Revising and Editing Yourself

Substitute "damn" every time you're inclined to write "very";
your editor will delete it and the writing will be just as it should be.

— MARK TWAIN

Good editing is essential. I don't have many regrets about what I've written, but I do have a few memories of editing mishaps that make me cringe.

One summer, I worked in communications at a company that manufactured shoes, filling in for someone on maternity leave. In the company newsletter, I wrote the lede for the spread featuring the company's newest summer sandals:

> Since time immortal, men and women have been wearing sandals. That seductive Queen-of-the-Nile and legendary femme fatale Cleopatra wore decorative thongs eons before the era of Woodstock.

I thought it was a great lede, accompanied by a photo of the fancy footwear. But after the newsletter was printed, I was so mad at myself that I hadn't caught the glaring error. Of course the opening phrase should have read *time immemorial*. And although I didn't use the cliché "since the dawn of time," I came close. Since then, I've made it a habit to check the spelling and meaning of every unusual word so I'm never embarrassed like that again.

When I look back to some of my earlier work, I've noticed passive constructions, adverb overuse, hyperbole, and clunkier writing than I'd like to admit to. Over the years, I've worked at my craft and improved — and you can work at yours, too.

Think Like an Editor

You may have a lot to say, but for publication, your story has to be tight, and every word has to work. To become a stronger writer, you need to think like an editor.

When you are ready to send a piece of writing out into the world, ask yourself these questions:

Have you eliminated throat-clearing?

A powerful opening brings your reader right into the action or thought of the piece through dialogue, surprising statements, or questions posed to the reader. If any words don't move the story forward, scrap them.

Try eliminating the first few sentences or even the first paragraph. Maybe you have a better start to your story now?

Did you get rid of passive sentences?

Go through your writing and find instances where something happens to the subject (passive) and change them so that the subject is making something happen (active). For example, "This class was taught by me," could be changed to the active "I taught this class." "The cupcakes were eaten by the girls" should become "The girls ate the cupcakes." "The cat was brushed by Joan" becomes "Joan brushed the cat." "I disputed the unfair review I was given" becomes "I disputed my unfair review."

The passive voice can create a feeling of distance and aloofness, which is not a way to engage your reader.

Have you eliminated jargon?

Using words that nobody outside your industry can understand will interrupt the flow of your piece. If technical terms are necessary, make sure you define them, unless you're certain all your readers will understand what they mean.

Did you cut the clichés?

Stay away from well-worn but weak phrases such as "You can take a horse to water, but you can't make him drink," "The chickens have come home to roost," or "Cut to the chase." The reader's eyes will glaze over as they skip those overused phrases, and the editor will see them as amateur moves.

Does each sentence have a point?

Read your piece aloud, line by line, to make sure each sentence has a point or moves the story forward. Make sure the point of the sentence is clear from the beginning. Vary sentence length and construction to retain the reader's interest.

Estelle's Edge: Check how tight your writing is with the websites WritersDiet.com and HemingwayApp.com.

Are you verbing your work?

Strong verbs bring an essay or article to life and can replace cumbersome noun phrases. I refer to this as "verbing" your work. Keep the focus on the action. Here are some examples:

Before: She is blogging.
After: She blogs.

Before: Heroin is the cause of overdoses.
After: Heroin causes overdoses.

Before: Give your post a proofread.
After: Proofread your post.

Before: The plane's approach to the runway was met with the scramble of emergency crews.

After: As the plane approached the runway, emergency crews scrambled.

Did you get active?

Choose the most specific, active verb or metaphor you can find.

Active verbs like *churned, spiraled, collapse, whimpers, stuffed, scorched, whomped, flapping, limps, sped, erased,* and *shuffled* work great in a pitch, piece, or title because they help paint a picture. For example, "She sashayed across the room" is much more expressive than "She walked across the room."

> *Estelle's Edge*: Highlight all the verbs in your piece. Replace any weak verbs with stronger, active verbs. Check out the *Tiny Love Stories* column in the *New York Times* for micro essays using active verbs.

Have you eliminated filler words?

Scan your writing and highlight these expressions: *it will be, there will be, it is, it was, it won't, there are, kind of, stuff, sort of, and so on, there is, a lot,* and *that.* Rewriting to eliminate them will often produce a tighter sentence.

Before: There are many people who take college entrance exams.
After: Many people take college entrance exams.

Before: There is kind of a big brown cat sitting outside my window.
After: A big brown cat is sitting outside my window.

Before: The article, which was written by Sheila, was informative.
After: Sheila's article was informative.

Before: The call that was to her mother was difficult to make.
After: The call to her mother was difficult to make.

Have you minimized the modifiers?

Use adjectives (words that modify nouns or pronouns) like condiments, sprinkled lightly where they will add the most flavor. Ditch weak, overused adjectives such as *terrible, nice, good, bad, amazing,* and *incredible.* Weak adjectival phrases, such as *exact same*, also create sentences with redundant information (e.g., "We had the exact same backpack").

Stephen King says, "The road to hell is paved with adverbs," and I agree.

Adverbs are words or phrases that modify or provide more information about verbs, adjectives, or other adverbs in a sentence. They often answer the questions *how, how much, how many, when, where,* and *why*. Many are formed by adding *-ly* to an adjective.

Remove unneeded adverbs. Scrutinize *-ly* words, like *totally, really, extremely, happily, easily*. They weaken your sentences. Other adverbs that can often be scrapped specify time or frequency (*now, then, late, early, very, just, ever, even, often*).

In each of these sentences, you can delete the adverb.

We *recently* got a puppy.

This is what I need to do *now*.

I haven't been going to the gym *lately*.

You can convey mood and tone through dialogue and strong verbs instead of adverbs. Here is an example:

Before: Impatiently, he told them to hurry up.
After: "Hurry up," he snapped.

You can also add an action:

After: "Hurry up," he snapped, grabbing his son's jacket and pushing him out the door.

Did you write with authority?

Write like you mean what you say and you aren't looking for permission to say it.

Many of my students are hesitant to claim their authority as the writer and constantly undermine it by using words and phrases like *seem, probably, maybe, it seems likely,* or *in most cases.* I tell them to be definitive.

> *Estelle's Edge*: You don't need weak modifiers like *sort of* nice, *pretty* good, *really* happy. Never tell the reader, "I don't know, but..." Write, "I have found" and "I discovered."

Did you include transition sentences that move the piece forward?

Each line of your essay or article should flow into the next, without abrupt topic changes. Strong transitions help readers follow your narrative arc and keep them glued to the page by evoking their curiosity or hinting that something important is about to come, such as:

I was wrong.

She clearly didn't have all the information.

On the other hand...

I didn't see it coming.

The bottom line is...

Sometimes a question can work to take the reader in a new direction, such as:

Was it only me he was thinking of when we kissed?

A line like this allows the writer to introduce the other people "he" might have been thinking of next, such as an ex-girlfriend.
Here's another example:

She heard a screech in front of her house that sounded familiar. Could that be someone she knew?

My former student Mimi O'Connor wrote a hybrid reported piece for Parents.com called "My 8-Year-Old Is Hopping on the Corset

Trend. Should I Be Worried?" after working on the pitch in my NYU class. In her article, framed around her daughter's experience, she used a transitional question after citing an author of a book on the corset who describes it as widely misunderstood and therefore demonized.

Mimi writes:

> So, should parents like me worry about our kids choosing them in virtual games or wearing them in real life? Experts weigh in.

Her question prepares the reader for the new information that is coming.

> *Estelle's Edge*: Think of transition sentences as road signs alerting the reader to pay attention.

Did you begin or end on the most evocative word?

The first and last words or phrases in a sentence should be the strongest because their position makes them stand out for the reader. The last word in the sentence is often a great way to connect to the important next word of the following sentence. For instance, if you are writing about a health situation, you might end on the sickness, and then follow up in the next sentence by saying the person went to the doctor. Here are some examples of this concept in action:

> Before: Because Emily was arrested, she didn't come to work.
> After: Emily didn't come to work because she was arrested.
> Next sentence: The cop booked her into the precinct for shoplifting.

See how the last word of the revised sentence, *arrested*, is naturally connected with the first words of the second sentence, *The cop*? That sentence wouldn't flow as well after a sentence ending with *she didn't come to work*.

In this shorter piece, the end of the first sentence connects with *klutz* at the beginning of the next:

> I was that girl who would stumble, trip, then land on her face.
> "I'm a klutz," I would tell people, laughing, before I learned that it

was not a good idea to label yourself because then people will laugh at you, not with you.

In my piece for the *New York Times* "What to Do When Your Tween is Trash-Talking You," the sports rivalry metaphor flows from one sentence into another:

> "I don't want to hurt your feelings, Mom, but I don't want you picking out my clothes anymore," my very independent 10-year-old daughter announced recently. "We have different taste, and yours isn't good for me."
>
> Her in-your-face delivery has the tone of an athlete taunting someone on a rival sports team. When did I become her opponent?

> *Estelle's Edge*: If you are struggling with a paragraph, let your mind linger on the sentence containing the strongest image. Then move that sentence to the beginning or ending of your piece and add a transition sentence at the end of the previous paragraph or the start of the next.

Did you use specific details?

Giving specific details helps your reader imagine the situation and place themselves in it. Instead of writing, "I loved what you did," write, "I loved the way you sang 'Landslide' to me on our first date." Instead of writing, "He sped toward me in his car," write, "He sped toward me in his vintage Mustang with yellow fenders." Instead of "I write every day," try "I write at my desk in the sunroom for twenty-minute stints, three times a day." As you edit your work, ask yourself, "Is this language as specific as possible?"

Another way to bring detail into your writing is to imagine a person who represents your specific audience and tell them what they need to know. Picture talking with them in a comfortable situation where that person asks you to explain the topic to them, starting with the key issue.

This is particularly helpful advice when you're writing about academic or scientific topics for a general audience. Replace academic jargon with simpler terms. Intersperse long and short sentences to keep from boring the reader. Break up long sentences (more than twenty words) for clarity, or use bullet points.

Do you know the thing about thing?

Overuse of the word *thing* is one of my pet peeves. When my students use it in their work, I cross it out and ask them to find a more specific word. The more sensual the writer's choice of words (language relating to touch, sound, taste, and smell), the more readers can relate to the writing. Think about these examples:

> I enjoyed working on that thing with you.

Instead write:

> I enjoyed working on the new hiring initiative with you.

Compare these sentences:

> When I think about the things we used to do together, it makes me sad.

> When I think of how we used to go out dancing and sip milkshakes from the same straw, it makes me sad.

See the difference? It's a big one.

> *Estelle's Edge*: Use specific nouns and verbs to make a sentence resonate with the reader and stir their emotions. People can relate better to dancing and milkshakes and rain than they can to the word *thing*.

Are you using words (not punctuation) to make your point?

If you want to be taken seriously as a professional writer, stop using exclamation marks sprinkled through your articles and pitches like confetti. It might work for texts, but every editor considers this the mark of an amateur, even if they don't say so to your face.

In his book *10 Rules of Writing*, Elmore Leonard states, "You are allowed no more than two or three exclamation points per 100,000 words of prose."

A stream of exclamations like "The lawnmower went out again!" "My husband forgot to pick up milk!" "The wine tasted terrible!" risks sounding melodramatic.

Estelle's Edge: Convey emotion with your words, not your punctuation.

Did you hit the dek?

Readers and editors love white space on the page, so create it. Keep paragraphs short for an easier read. Subheads and deks (the sentence right below the title of an article) help your reader by creating visual breaks. You can use a variety of other devices to do this, too, such as bullet points, numbers, lists, sidebars, polls, charts, and diagrams.

EDITING CHECKLIST

- ❏ Does your piece have a title that grounds it and evokes action or emotion?
- ❏ Do you have a strong opening that sets the scene and draws the reader in?
- ❏ Have you eliminated most adverbs (*-ly* words)?
- ❏ Have you used strong, active verbs?
- ❏ Have you eliminated passive words and phrases?
- ❏ Have you eliminated jargon and clichés?
- ❏ Have you replaced vague, generic words with vivid, specific words?
- ❏ Do your sentences begin or end on the most powerful word or thought?
- ❏ Are your sentences clear, to the point, and varied in length and structure?
- ❏ Do you use powerful transitional sentences to move from one thought to another?

❏   Does each sentence move the article or essay forward?
❏   Have you organized the copy with subheads and white space?
❏   Have you checked for correct spelling and grammar?
❏   Have you read the piece out loud, and now feel proud?

PART SIX

Protecting Your Psyche

CHAPTER EIGHTEEN

Mastering the Viral Spiral

I would advise anyone who aspires to a writing career that before developing his talent he would be wise to develop a thick hide.

— HARPER LEE

Everybody wants their work to go viral — defined as getting a lot of attention across social media platforms and being shared among readers in a brief space of time. (But do we still want to use that terminology after living through a pandemic?)

If something you wrote has gone viral, you are achieving most writers' dream — getting noticed for your writing. You clearly tapped into a relatable aspect of the human experience. Now you need to figure out how to make the most of this moment and navigate through the emotions you're feeling. That's what this chapter is about.

In a 2012 study, Jonah Berger and Katherine L. Milkman, professors at the Wharton School of the University of Pennsylvania, analyzed over seven thousand articles from the *New York Times* to understand what made a piece go viral. They found that the most widely shared articles elicited high-arousal emotions such as awe, anger, or anxiety, rather than low-arousal, deactivating emotions like sadness.

I don't believe a piece can truly go viral (unless it's an exposé, narrative, or investigative piece) — without you being a part of it. That's why I'm assuming your viral piece is framed around your experience or the experience of someone in your family. You were probably covering a common problem that others are dealing with and can relate to. I believe that is the best way to capture readers' attention. I've learned how to navigate through my own viral moments, so I can help you with yours.

Three of my articles have gone viral. One was an op-ed, the second a personal essay, and the third a hybrid personal essay with reported elements. I always say I'm a late bloomer, but when I bloom, I bloom big. I hope you can learn from my experiences.

My first piece to go viral was called "Why Yahoo Just Became Obsolete," written after I read one Saturday night what Marissa Mayer, the new CEO of Yahoo, had wrought by refusing to allow employees to work remotely (before the pandemic). I wrote the piece in a haze of anger, but it wasn't just a rant. I cited statistics showing that working remotely boosts morale and productivity, along with a new study published by Stanford University researchers showing that workers from home were more productive. I also mentioned the 2012 National Study of Employers, which showed benefits to employees and morale from working at home.

A nascent blogger at the time, I pitched the piece to BlogHer.com (now SheKnows.com). They ran it with minimal edits the following night. It was the most popular feature and most commented-on feature on the site for a week, and it made the evening news nationwide.

When I wrote about my daughter's bad behavior for the *Washington Post*'s parenting section, I added a twist. Instead of just complaining, I examined how my own bad behavior encouraged hers, took my child off the hook, and explained how I intended to do better. The piece ran right before New Year's Eve, with the title "My Child Is Out of Control: Here's What I'll Do in 2015 to Change That."

The essay was shared in all the syndicates that the *Washington Post* has agreements with and even ran in Australia, where my husband's family lives. Later that week it was mentioned on *The View* by Whoopi Goldberg, though she didn't mention my name. I was invited to talk about it on a few radio shows. From there, I started writing parenting pieces regularly for the *Washington Post*.

Bullyproofing and *Good Morning America*

My most recent viral article, "How to Bullyproof Your Child," appeared in the *New York Times* on May 23, 2019. It was a reported piece framed around my daughter's personal experience with bullying.

The story was personally significant for me not only because it concerned my daughter but because I, too, had been bullied as a child. I turned in the article right before Memorial Day and then saw very little reader response to it. I figured, that's the ropes, and went to the beach for the weekend. By Monday, the article had attracted over three hundred comments, not all positive. The following week, it was the paper's most emailed and most popular article, and it held that position for three weeks. *Good Morning America* invited me to appear on the show — the producer later told me they pay attention to anything trending in the *New York Times*. I got a kick out of having my segment wrapped around a clip from the Harry Potter series, showing Harry talking with his friend Luna Lovegood about being bullied. I was also interviewed for the most popular radio program in Canada.

Because of the huge response to my article, I was assigned to work with the *New York Times'* booking department. They vetted every media request and negotiated the terms of interviews, including *Good Morning America*, before I accepted invitations to appear on talk shows and radio programs. I turned down a few shows that I felt might have a "gotcha" aspect to them. Though I had many requests to be interviewed for blogs and other websites, I had to turn them down because of time limitations, and the *New York Times'* focus on mainstream media first.

Making the most of the viral situation, the editor for the *New York Times* made my article the focus of the following week's *Well* newsletter. I shared more about the genesis of the article, my own history of being bullied, and why I rallied to help my young daughter.

My bullyproofing piece attracted 588 comments before the *Times* closed the comments. It was rewarding to hear from the hundreds of readers sharing their experiences and saying they were going to address this issue through role-playing with their kids, as I advocated in the story. But dealing with all the attention from a piece that goes viral can also be emotionally challenging.

Judy Nelson's essay in *HuffPost Personal*, "How Going to a Dead & Company Concert with a Stranger Helped Me Heal after Losing My Son," transformed her life because so many people who had known her son, or had known loss, reached out to Judy after reading her piece. She eventually had to minimize her interactions with readers because they took such an emotional toll.

Making the Most out of Going Viral
Crazy Days Ahead

Going viral is like hopping on a speeding train without knowing where it's headed. You need to make smart decisions, surround yourself with people who will nurture you, and take some time to ground yourself — whether that's through meditation, taking a walk in a garden, talking to a friend or loved one, or going for a bike ride. When you are the center of attention and in the midst of the maelstrom, you have to be centered yourself.

Here are my recommendations based on my experience and others' for what to do now (when the article, op-ed, or essay runs and over the next week or two) and later.

Now

Priority One: Self-Care

- Take care of yourself. Eat right and get enough sleep.
- If you get inundated, feel free to take time off from social media.
- Book a massage or some enjoyable, nurturing activity for the weekend.

Protect Your Privacy

- If your email inbox is swamped, set up a special email address for close family and friends only. Ask someone else to sort

through your regular email for media requests and anything
urgent.

- You can set up an auto-reply email with this message: "I won't
be available for [TIME SPAN] unless it is urgent, to give myself
some breathing room. For media requests, please leave your
information, and someone will get back to you." For casual
friends and well-wishers, you might add something like this:
"I'm receiving hundreds of comments, questions, and requests
about my article. I am taking some time for self-care and will
respond to cordial emails when I am able to. Please, in the
meantime, follow me on social media [share your social media
handles]." You can also offer links to resources or an organization connected to your article, so people can benefit from the
information even if you aren't replying to them directly.
- People from your past may come out of the woodwork. You
don't need to respond to all of them.
- If what you wrote is likely to be controversial, lock down your
social media by making it private, or limiting it to friends and
family. Don't accept any friend or follow requests from people
you don't know well, and make sure your physical address and
other personal information aren't available online.

Estelle's Edge: You can request that the Yellow Pages and
other directories scrub your information by filling out a form.
You can also set up your social media to show only comments
from people you follow, and you can set up email filters to block
messages by content or sender.

Getting Media Savvy

If you have written a widely read piece in a top publication, television,
podcast, and radio producers will come calling. A producer may reach
out to option your story (especially if it's a narrative). Consult a lawyer before signing anything, and never give away movie rights when
writing an article or essay (see chapter 12). If you have written about a

controversial topic and are likely to be cornered in "gotcha" interviews, consider getting media training. I did it years ago through a magazine I worked for and found it very helpful. Whether you do an online search for media training, ask friends and colleagues, or get a recommendation from a professional speakers' or writers' association (check the resources section in this book), make sure you vet the company before spending the money.

> *Estelle's Edge*: The publication's publicity, communications, or booking department can often vet producers of television and radio shows and podcasts who invite you to appear.

For interviews on TV, podcasts, or radio, or for other publications, formulate three to five talking points to focus on. This helps you stay on track, reduces the risk of saying something you didn't mean, and ensures your message is consistent across all media. For my *New York Times* article, I wrote my talking points out on a note card and reviewed it before giving any interviews. They were:

- I wrote this piece for the *New York Times* because of my daughter's experience being bullied when she was six years old. I was seeking ways to empower my child.
- When I saw a column in *Psychology Today* focused on role-playing, it made me remember a guidance counselor at my elementary school who suggested role-playing to help me when I was being bullied. It changed my perception of being a victim.
- Role-playing made my daughter feel that she had some power, that I wasn't just commiserating with her.
- I empowered her by teaching her how to address the teasing, not swoop in and solve her problem.
- My daughter knows I love her, and she knows I support her. What she needed from me was the right words and the ability to make them work.

> *Estelle's Edge*: Stick to your talking points, even if the interviewer tries to take you in a different direction.

Social Media and Your Own Promotions

This is a great time to attract more followers for your website, blog, Substack (if you have one), and social media posts, which expand your influence. Here are some ways to build on your media exposure:

- Write a blog post about the experience of going viral.
- Create a freebie for new sign-ups to your website, newsletter, or blog.
- Post about your experience on social media, sharing your emotions and photos so people can follow along.
- Create a TikTok or Instagram reel pointing to your viral article.
- If you have your own podcast, do an episode on your article.

> *Estelle's Edge*: It's not only published articles that go viral. If one of your social media posts or tweets attracts a lot of views and comments, consider making it into an article, an essay, or a micro memoir (see chapter 5).

Publications

You can expand your reach through the publication your viral article ran in, as well as other sites and magazines.

- Your editor might ask you for a follow-up article.
- The publication might run a profile of you or feature you in another section.
- You can email your viral clip to magazine or online publication editors with pitches for other articles.
- If a dream editor gives you an assignment related to your viral article, go for it, but ask for at least a week to write it, since you will be busy.

Books

- If you've been wanting to get an agent or write a book, now is a good time to try.
- Reach out to your dream agent, the one you most would like to sign with because of their high-caliber clientele and reputation.

- If a dream agent or publisher approaches you for a book project, go for it.

Speaking Engagements

- If you like the idea of speaking engagements, this is the time to sign up with a speakers bureau. Harry Walker Agency and Lyceum Agency are two of the most prominent, but you can find others by Googling.

Later

Priority One: Self-Care

- Keep following the self-care routine described above.
- Do some guided meditations or guided imagery. You can find them in apps or online, and I offer a helpful one in chapter 19.
- Exercise, if you find it a helpful way to blow off steam and mitigate the effects of stress eating.
- Affirmations can be helpful, such as "I can handle the deluge of emotions I'm feeling and getting from others," or "I give myself permission to enjoy this moment." You can also record your affirmations and play them in the morning or before bedtime.

Interviews

You may still get invitations to appear on TV, but not as many. But if you interview well, you may become a valued guest on talk shows and podcasts.

Social Media and Your Own Promotions

- Place your viral clip and other work on a free online portfolio on a site like Contently, Muck Rack, Journo Portfolio, or Clippings.me. It will keep all your work together and make it easy to refer to your pieces for emails, follow-up pitches, or publicity. It is another way to highlight your writing, especially when you can share the link. All you need to do is sign up for the site and start posting.

- Write follow-up blog posts on your experience of being in the spotlight.
- Start a Substack.
- Keep writing about your experience on social media, so people can follow along.
- Place yourself on websites such as HARO (Help a Reporter Out) or Profnet as a subject-matter expert.
- If you have your own podcast, do follow-up episodes and connect with other people in your area of expertise.
- If you've retained the rights to your piece or they revert back to you (see chapter 12), you can try to sell a reprint of the article or essay.

Publications

- Take advantage of opportunities to be interviewed as an expert for other writers' stories.
- Branch out. If your viral piece was a personal essay, try writing a reported piece, an interview, a profile, or another kind of story, or find a new element of your viral story to write about.
- Pitch a column on the subject that went viral.
- Keep pitching magazine or online publication editors you want to write for, including a clip of your viral article.
- If other editors offer you assignments, take the opportunities.
- Interview experts for another article on your topic.
- Write about writing about your topic for industry publications like *Publishers Weekly*, *Writer's Digest*, and *Poets & Writers*.

Books

- If you want to write a book, this is the time. Choose a genre for a book based on your topic (such as a children's book, self-help book, or memoir).
- Study up on how to write a book proposal, and draft one for your book.

- Interview experts for a book on your topic.
- If you haven't signed with one yet, keep reaching out to agents.
- Write a collection of essays.
- Submit an essay to an anthology.

> *Estelle's Edge*: I have been included in seven anthologies. It is always good to give your work a second life (if you kept the rights). If the anthology is prestigious, or a project you strongly support, then write an original piece for it.

Speaking Engagements

- Create a media kit to showcase yourself as a speaker. It can include clips of your TV, radio, or podcast appearances, a bio, and a photo.
- Craft a talk for conferences, speaking engagements, and industry events.
- Contact local universities, schools, organizations, associations, clubs, religious groups, and libraries that use speakers and ask to be considered. Any organization you are connected to in your daily life can be a place where you can reach out and ask to speak to the members.
- You can also find book clubs that focus on the topic of your book or talk, and see if you can speak to the members either in person or online, through Zoom or video. Your librarian might be able to help you identify those clubs.

Teaching and Education

- Teach a class or webinar based on the topic of your viral article. Search online for how to formulate a syllabus. Online teaching platforms like Teachable, Udemy, and Outschool are good options for setting up teaching because they provide the structure for class sessions, materials, assignments, and feedback. See if you can dip your toe in the water with short one-night or one-day sessions. Market your class to local universities, associations, religious organizations, and community groups.

- Create your own webinar on your website and offer tickets via an event management system like Eventbrite.com.

Tips for Going on TV and Being Interviewed in Any Media

Many writers who are invited to appear on TV don't have the faintest clue what to do. Here's some advice from my own experience appearing on TV, both from interviews about my viral article and from my career as a magazine editor.

1. Wear solid-colored clothing that isn't black or white. I wore cobalt blue for my appearance on *Good Morning America*, and I have worn hot pink and burgundy clothing for other appearances. Those colors look good in close-up. Avoid busy patterns.

2. Avoid wearing long necklaces that could hit the lavalier microphone and jewelry that reflects light.

3. Ask whether the show's professional makeup artist and hair stylists can do your hair and makeup. When I appeared on morning shows as a magazine editor, they always managed to fit me in if I asked in advance.

4. Ask if they can send a car to pick you up, and bring you home, if you don't live nearby or it's an early-morning show. Most producers anticipate this request and will agree to it.

5. If you have written a book, ask if the host can mention it, or if you can display it on camera.

6. Prepare for adversarial questions by anticipating them and coming up with answers. It can be helpful to practice with a friend, relative, or mentor.

7. During the interview, if the host goes off topic, bring the conversation back to your talking points. Use expressions like "But what I'm really here to talk about is," "That reminds me," "Let me add," or "This is what is most important." Use the words *but* and *and* to shift the topic back to what you want to discuss.

8. For difficult topics, if the host says something that is not accurate, firmly disagree by saying, "That is not correct," in a positive way and then correct the statement.

9. If the host is trying to get you to speculate on a hypothetical question, say, "I'd rather stick to the facts and not speculate," then bring the discussion back to your topic.

10. If the host is sharing a secondhand comment, do not respond, since the remark may be taken out of context. Say, "That's news to me," and get back to your topic.

11. Ask for a clip right after the program airs. I always record the shows, but if you can get a clip from the producer, that is ideal.

When You're Threatened by Trolls

If you have written anything controversial — and let's face it, controversy is what often takes the spotlight — the trolls will come for you. In fact, even if what you've written seems innocuous, they'll come anyway. Some people act viciously when they are anonymous. So you have to be ready.

After I wrote "My Child Is Out of Control" for the *Washington Post*, I had trolls telling me that child protective services should come and take my daughter away. After I wrote about fighting with my husband for *Redbook*, trolls said I shouldn't be married. You just have to expect strong reactions because your writing is getting noticed.

My number one rule for dealing with trolls is, Don't engage. If the trolls are on social media, block them whenever possible.

As I wrote in a piece for *Wired*:

> I have a tenet that I follow when it comes to social media conflagrations: "Don't add your air to someone else's fire."

If the trolls show up in the comments section, never reply. You might even choose not to read the comments. I actually do read them, but I don't take them personally. I have developed a thick skin after years in publishing (on both sides of the wall). Bottom line: I don't let anyone dictate my value but me.

Your mantra should be "They don't know me."

Don't fight back. You will lose. If you engage with trolls, you will only trigger their adrenaline (as well as raising your own blood pressure), and you won't change their minds, but you *will* waste your time and potentially make yourself even more of a target.

As I said in the *Wired* piece:

> I feel fairly safe on my FB page, although I've been known to make liberal use of the mute buttons when people annoy me or make snarky comments, but in public places (despite the false feeling of intimacy), it is the same as sharing your deepest or even most casual thoughts with the thousands of people who used to walk through Times Square. You wouldn't do that, so why would you do it online?

You may have friends and family who disagree with what you wrote. They aren't trolls. In that case, you may want to have a phone call or one-on-one conversation, hearing them out, letting them know how you feel, and agreeing to disagree if necessary. If you're not up for that conversation, let it go. Sometimes just saying, "I hear where you're coming from" can help. If a relationship is important to you, and you would feel bad letting this disagreement wreck it, then try to talk it through.

If you can ignore the naysayers and trolls (and I hope you can), this is your time to shine and go for what you want. The news cycle moves quickly. It's a good idea to strike while you are hot — and right now you are.

CHECKLIST FOR PREPARING WHEN YOU GO VIRAL

- ❏ Have you made time for self-care?
- ❏ Have you made your social media private or limited who can contact you through it?
- ❏ Have you scrubbed your personal information from the internet?
- ❏ Have you set up a way for people to reach you?
- ❏ Have you set up an auto-reply email addressing the situation and asking for patience, while encouraging media requests and other opportunities, sending people to other resources, and building your following?

❑ Are you sorting through your email to get to the important asks — media requests, speaking opportunities, requests for articles and book proposals?

❑ Have you thought about how you will make the most of your perceived expertise on the topic or the experience?

❑ Are you focused on what is important now, and aware of what will be important to focus on later?

❑ Are you proud of what you've achieved? Take a moment to acknowledge that your hard work has paid off and you deserve the accolades you are receiving.

CHAPTER NINETEEN

Rejection Projection

All you need is the plan, the road map,
and the courage to press on to your destination.

— Earl Nightingale

Being rejected feels awful — and not just in publishing. But we all need to learn how to power through it. When I was editing women's magazines, I went to beauty events where the editors at top publications (called the Seven Sisters) would come in wearing black suits with miniskirts, like they were in a Robert Palmer video, totally owning the place. They didn't bother to give the time of day to me or other editors who worked for "lesser" publications. But decades later, most of these entitled editors have dropped off the publishing map. I'm still here.

Hanging in there has meant dealing with a lot of rejection. In the beginning, it was because of my writing. I made many of the mistakes and craft errors I cover in this book, especially when starting out. I have improved over the years by employing the tools and techniques I'm teaching you. As I continued to work at my craft, my acceptance rate climbed. The same has been true for the students I work with.

A big part of what I do as a teacher is teach my students not to lose faith when the odds seem stacked against them. How you handle a rejection can make a difference in how the editor perceives you when it is time for the next pitch — and just as in baseball, there is always a next pitch.

The Five Forms of Rejection – and How to Craft Your Response

So your pitch or piece was rejected? We've all been there. No matter how well you target your submissions and how persistent you are, you will face rejection. You must realize it's not *you* who is being rejected. It is this one particular submission to this one specific market, and there can be many reasons for that rejection.

Once you've acknowledged the emotional impact of rejection, you have choices about how to move forward: you can revise the piece, change the focus, shorten it, use it for an anthology submission, put it up on Medium (or another platform) or your website, use it in a podcast, make it into a TikTok, or run it as a Facebook post.

Here are some common forms of rejection and ways to learn from them.

1. **"Thanks, it's not a fit."** This feels dismissive, but sometimes it just means you didn't follow the submission guidelines. Or maybe your pitch was too long and rambling, or your writing was filled with changing tenses. This is where you need to be a sleuth and read the publication carefully.

   It's useful to cut and paste a story you admire from the publication, and then compare your story with it. Examine its introduction and narrative arc, how the piece flows, and what resonates about it (perhaps a powerful opening or a universal takeaway). Revise so your story meets those criteria before your next submission.

   Deviations from submission guidelines probably won't cause an editor to reject a brilliant story, but they could tip the balance if an editor is undecided or having a bad day. Pay attention to word counts, formatting specifications, required file formats, and instructions for emailing pitches.

2. **"We just ran a story or essay similar to yours. But please do submit again."** Don't make the same mistake twice. Search the publication's website for pieces similar to yours before sending it in. Find a good fit for your piece by researching different publications. To give yourself a refresher in brainstorming and coming up with ideas, take another look at chapter 1.

3. **"I really love your writing, and this is a fantastic story, but we aren't covering [TOPIC] at the moment. Please submit again, because I would love to work with you."** This is a gift. Any time an editor uses superlative words (*fantastic, love it, fabulous voice*), it is a sign you are connecting with them, so make the most of that connection. Email the editor right away to thank them for the feedback, and as soon as you can, send something else that might be a fit. Editors are looking for writers whose work excites them, so why not yours?

4. **"I would love to work with you on something, but this piece isn't it, because ..."** Sometimes writers get rejections with very specific feedback about what is wrong with a piece. For example, when I was working as a guest editor for Narratively, I was looking for original fresh, offbeat, immersive narrative stories that weren't covered in other major publications, and which would surprise, delight, and captivate readers. Stories on frequently covered topics, like the aches and pains of aging, didn't make the cut.

   If you get a response that gives clear directions or instructions, that's gold, because you can apply that information to your next pitch or submission. For example, the editor may say they are already covering that topic in one way, but they might be interested in a different angle, if you can come up with one. When I was the editor of W.I.T. (Women in Touch), someone pitched me an article on entrepreneurs. I said, "This feels too general, but if you can focus on women who have had one year of business success, then I would be interested." A student of mine pitched an essay about fraught family relationships. The editor asked her to send a pitch on a different but related story, focusing on estranged siblings, and accepted the revised essay.

Estelle's Edge: Don't wait too long to send another pitch to the editor. They have already invested in you by giving personal and constructive feedback. Show that you have taken it to heart.

5. **No response.** No response is still, well, a response, even if it means someone never opened your email. Here's what to do: when the piece is published somewhere else, send a link or PDF to the editor with a note reminding them you initially submitted this piece to them.

   I once submitted a pitch to Quartz that the editor responded to three months later, saying it wasn't a fit. I replied, sharing the piece based on the same pitch that ran in the *Washington Post*, which also became a cover story in the print version of the *Post*'s Local Living section.

   This is what I wrote:

   Thanks so much for getting back to me. The *Washington Post* ran it and also made it the print cover story of the local living section. Here is the link.

   I do have another pitch, though. I have a piece that I would like to write based on the death of Debbie Reynolds and other childhood icons, titled "Identifying with the Dying of Our Icons."

   I have been feeling a great deal of anxiety since the recent deaths of celebrities, and it culminated in a panic attack after Debbie Reynolds, former Hollywood star, passed away yesterday, a day after Carrie Fisher died.

   Her pivotal role in *The Unsinkable Molly Brown*, made in the decade I was born, was very much the soundtrack to my life. My husband always says that where other people see boundaries, I don't, and that's what Molly had, too.

   Now, on the precipice of a new year, with a fraught political, economic and cultural climate, the hands of time are ticking for everyone, whether it is the ones who identify with George Michael's sexual identity and drug struggles, the people relating to Carrie Fisher's struggle with mental health, or the ones like me who grew up watching Old

Hollywood even years later and identifying with movies. We feel, no matter what generation we are in, that we are at the end of a point in time. We feel vulnerable, and that is scary.

Thanks for your consideration for this piece. I could turn it in very quickly if you want it.

The result was a piece on the psychological impact of the deaths of celebrities that ran in Quartz, and a relationship with that editor. So be bold. Taking that extra step might just get you noticed. And it will feel so good.

Repurpose Rejected Pitches and Essays

When my students get rejected, I remind them the perfect home for their piece is out there; they just have to keep trying. I once submitted a story I loved to over thirty publications before I got a yes. I don't do that these days because I don't have the time, but I know how to be persistent and teach my students how to keep going with it. If you learn how to believe in your work, others will believe in it, too. And that doesn't mean posting on social media ten times a day about how hard it is. It means doing the work.

I like to write detailed pitches and then boil them down to a shorter version. However, I keep the longer version and save the content to use in other pieces: I call it longpitch(TOPIC) in my files. Once in a while I review my rejected pitches to see if I can match them with trending topics to find a different angle. For example, an essay on being adopted could become a reported piece on the newest trends in adoption. A rejected essay on your problems with migraines could become a reported piece on the newest therapies for migraine sufferers. If a piece has been rejected by national publications, you can also pitch local and regional publications, which are often looking for fresh material and don't have as many writers to rely on as national publications do. They usually pay less, but if you've already done the reporting, it will take less of your time. Most of them also purchase reprints, so you may find a new market for the work you've already published.

EXERCISE: THE REJECT FILES

Take a rejected pitch and see if you can tweak it for a different publication. Can you make it fit a literary magazine, trade publication, beauty magazine, fitness magazine, or alumni magazine?

Release Your Residual Fear of Rejection

Writing, creating, and getting published — or rejected — can be stressful. When I feel pressured, I look at myself in the mirror and repeat the mantra "Remember who you are." Who I am is a wife, a mother, a teacher, a journalist, someone who has love and friends in her life. I am grateful and I am worthy. That usually keeps me calm when I am about to embark on a new project or speak in front of a crowd. Why don't you try it for yourself?

Another stress reliever is this guided-imagery trip suggested by the hypnotherapist Tara Sutphen, host of the podcast *Transformations by Tara*, in an article I wrote for *Forbes*.

1. Find a comfortable spot and close your eyes. Breathe deeply and imagine yourself at the beach. Visualize walking in the sand.
2. Breathe deeply. Lie in the sand. Feel the sun. Smell the salt air. Scoop up the sand on your fingers and toes. Listen to the seagulls.
3. Feel the sand grains run gently off your body. As you feel the sand, tell yourself that you can feel the stress melting off.
4. See the stress leave. Breathe deeply and relax completely.

This visualization releases stress; as your breath slows, your heart rate and blood pressure drop. Research shows controlled breathing not only relaxes muscles, it also helps the immune system and provides an emotional release.

I learned another stress-reduction tactic from the book *Timeshifting* years ago. I tell myself either first thing in the morning or at night while lying in bed, "Right here, right now, during this minute of time, you are fine. You are okay." It's a way to support and nurture myself while staying present.

Rejection Reasons You Can Address

- Did you familiarize yourself with the publication? If you are submitting to a print-only magazine, did you buy and read a few issues? If the publication is online, did you read as many pieces as necessary to ensure your topic and style are a good fit?
- Was your voice right? Every publication has its own voice and style. If your voice was too different, the editors may have thought it would be too much effort to edit or work with you. Write for that publication's readers.
- Did you follow submission guidelines? If the publication wants 700 words, and you sent 1,500, that could be a reason you were rejected.
- Did your lede hook the editor? Was your opening paragraph strong (with a startling statement or amusing anecdote)? Did your article contain enough information to fulfill the promise of the lede?
- Has it been done before? This is where you need to read and keep up with trends. Always make sure your pitch has a fresh angle or an unusual twist.
- Have you made your case? See if you can sum up your pitch in a single question the reader can ask. Then ask what you are teaching the reader and what they will take away from your article.
- Have you done your research?
- Do you have credible experts?
- Does your data work to support your point? Make sure your statistics, poll results, research studies, and surveys are up to date.
- Were you too wordy? Concise writing uses strong nouns and verbs. Including too many adjectives and adverbs, or writing with rambling, confusing syntax, is a sure way to get rejected. Revise your piece until every word works.

- Is your material original? Editors want to be the first to publish. If you are submitting a story that you have already featured on your blog or elsewhere online, they will immediately reject it.
- Do you know if a similar piece is in the works? If the magazine has just assigned a piece similar to your pitch, there isn't much you can do about it. But if this is the only reason your work is rejected, the editor will tell you that and invite you to submit again.

Throw a Pity Party for One

You are only human. Sometimes you need to comfort yourself. I'm a believer in consoling myself with hours of reality television (*Real Housewives* is a favorite), along with chocolate and going down a gossip-site rabbit hole online. I also reach out to sympathetic writer friends who will buoy me by saying, "It's their loss," or "You'll get there," or "What were they thinking?" That works even better than chocolate to soothe myself — even the gourmet kind.

Getting published is a marathon and not a sprint. The race isn't over until it's over. As Thomas Edison said, "Genius is 1 percent inspiration and 99 percent perspiration." It's about consistently showing up after everyone else has given up.

CHAPTER TWENTY

If You Build a Platform, Will They Come?

A candle loses nothing
by lighting another candle.

— JAMES KELLER

*P*latform is a buzzy, often misunderstood word. Having a platform simply means a way to market or promote your work, using your visibility to reach an audience. It also means there is an audience out there. Your platform is important, but it has no value without purpose — a belief that what you are doing matters because it is connected to helping others. During the height of the pandemic, I took a course on discovering your purpose, and it confirmed that mine is to write and tell my stories, to edit and to teach, and to find joy in doing that.

Words have always been my playground. I collect them, use them, edit them, love them, and make up rhymes with them. Having a platform that makes my teaching and writing accessible to many people gives me pleasure, and that is why I wrote this book.

Plan on a Platform

Before Facebook, Twitter, Instagram, TikTok, and LinkedIn, the only ways writers could build a platform or increase their public visibility were by appearing on television and radio shows, speaking at conferences, and sharing clips. More recently, writers have created an online presence by curating content on Twitter, blogging, publishing articles online, and joining Facebook and other social media groups.

A platform is not the only way to get your ideas and writing noticed, but it's an effective one. A platform will evolve out of your body of work and give you visibility. If you have a platform, share it with your editor to show that many people see your work, and that you are part of communities that are engaged with you and your writing. Your platform becomes even more helpful if you are interested in writing a nonfiction book, which requires a base of people who are already interested in what you have to say.

A platform can include:

- Publishing your best work in highly regarded, widely read publications.
- Your well-read blog, Substack, email newsletter, or website showing your connection to communities of people who care about what you have to say.
- Credible websites that link to your site or blog (such as top journalism organizations, magazines, and medical websites such as WebMD). This makes search engines rate your site as more important, which means it will rank higher and be more visible in search results.
- A respected organization or news story mentioning you in connection to the topic you are writing about.
- A verified Facebook, Twitter, or Instagram page (or all three). Keep in mind that endlessly posting on social media won't build your platform. You have to start with your body of work.
- A presence on TikTok connected to the subjects you write about.
- Any awards connected to writing or to a cause, health issue, or organization you are writing about.

- Partnering with influential people on projects that will increase your visibility.
- Articles that quote you as an expert.
- Columns you write regularly.
- Books you have written.
- Speaking at events and attending events or conferences where you can expand your network.

So How Do You Start Building a Platform?

Building a platform is a multifaceted process, but here are some first steps.

- Choose your niche: Are you writing about midlife? Aging? Humor? Parenting? Publishing? What do you most want to write about? Do a Google search for websites and publications in your niche, including regional ones.
- It's okay if you have one main specialty in writing, but you can branch out to do other projects, too.
- Join writers' organizations. Networking and making connections can help you move forward in your career.
- Be on social media. Many publications favor writers who have an active following and a wide audience for their work.
- Share links to your articles on social media to make sure your followers always see them and to increase the audience for your publications and books. Share other people's work as well, so that your platform is not just about you. Being generous on social media helps build your reputation as a helpful colleague in the writing community.
- Consider creating a regular email blast to update followers.
- Speak at conferences. If you are in demand as a speaker, you will usually interest people in your writing. You can research conferences that tie in with your area of expertise and see when they put out requests for speakers' proposals.
- Develop your audience through events and other promotions.
- Create your own network by launching a podcast in the area

you write about, writing a newsletter or Substack, or starting a YouTube channel. (Make podcasts and videos only if they're appropriate for your specialty. And keep in mind that every writer doesn't present well on video, so be sure a video enhances your brand before you release it.)

I present myself as a widely published journalist and essayist, podcaster for *Freelance Writing Direct*, former editor in chief of five glossy magazines, and adjunct writing instructor at New York University. My students consider me their literary fairy godmother because I help them get published in top publications. I differentiate myself from other journalists and essayists with my background as a magazine editor and the publishing success rate of my students.

Estelle's Edge: Try to use the same social media handle on every platform. For example, I'm @EstelleSErasmus. Have a good photo of yourself available for social media, your website, and publications. If you like certain colors, you may want to incorporate them into your website design as part of your brand.

EXERCISE: MAPPING YOUR PLATFORM

Here is a simple exercise to help you reach your goals.

1. Go back to your mapping template (see chapter 1).
2. Find the section about you. Draw a line and write down everything you are doing to build and promote your work.
3. Draw another line and write down your goals, such as getting into bigger publications, writing more essays, appearing on podcasts, starting a newsletter, or writing a book.
4. Circle any actions from step 2 that you can do quickly to promote your work: posting on social media, sharing the content of someone else who has a lot of followers, writing a quick blog post.
5. Put a square around any actions that will take more planning: starting a newsletter or a Substack, teaching a class, putting together a webinar, building a website.

6. Break the squared actions into smaller steps and circle those steps, too. For teaching a class, they might include researching how to write a syllabus, viewing class structures online, putting together an outline of what you would say in a class session, and researching places to teach.

Put a date in your calendar for each baby step, and each week do one of the items you circled. Each time you look at your list, you will remember who you are and what you want to achieve.

In incremental steps, you will reach your goals, and it will be an organic process.

Stand Out from the Crowd

Your brand — your professional and public persona — helps you get your writing noticed. Here are some ways to promote your brand and build your platform:

- Add voice to your short pieces, giving a personal slant to the introduction and conclusion.
- If you have been writing personal essays, start adding journalistic touches to all your pieces (research, quotes from experts or associations or authors with books coming out).
- Try to focus your new pieces only in the area (e.g., health, fitness, beauty, tech) you are interested in writing about.
- Once you have experience writing about a specific subject, such as parenting or health, see if you can get a column on that subject in a small publication, which will help you get recognition from larger publications.
- Consider trying to get a column on an international website.

Estelle's Edge: Ask yourself these questions:

Who are you?

What do you do better than anyone else?

Your skill set plus your personality equals your brand.

Rules for Posting on Social Media

I am a huge advocate of social media for enhancing community, resources, and networking. But I follow certain social media rules:

- Never post rants, because the vents of today are the regrets of tomorrow.
- Never share fake news.
- Share other people's content as much as you share your own.
- Take social media breaks occasionally.
- Always ask family members for permission before writing about them online. That keeps everyone safe.

Having a platform and building a bigger one is always great. But for me family comes first.

PLATFORM BUILDING CHECKLIST

❏ Do you know who you are and why you stand out?
❏ Have you decided on your goals and started taking steps toward them?
❏ Are you building community in some way?
❏ Are you adding your experiences into your writing?
❏ Are you helping people with what you offer?
❏ Do you speak at conferences?
❏ Do you have an email list?
❏ Do you share other people's content?

PART SEVEN

Words

of Wisdom

CHAPTER TWENTY-ONE

Find Your Inspiration

Imagination is more important than knowledge.

— Albert Einstein

Publishing is a long game. Sure, you can get quick viral hits if you are lucky and the timing is right, but those do not make a career. Sure, you can become a social media star (whatever that means), but again, that doesn't make you a writer.

What makes a career is persistence, resilience, learning how to package and position yourself to break through the noise, an ability to pivot, a sense of humor — and more than a dash of inspiration.

Creative Visualization Is the Key to a Life of Purpose

While I was working in one of my first jobs at an advertising agency, I saw the book *Creative Visualization* by Shakti Gawain in the window of a New Age bookstore.

I was hooked from the first sentence: "Creative visualization is the technique of using your imagination to create what you want in your life." Reading about the power of the mind and the imagination introduced me to my inner world. It taught me that the key to change in any area of your life is to change your thinking, because your thoughts can create your reality.

That bookstore became my lunchtime destination. It was my new school, though I'd recently graduated from college, and the contents of its shelves became my new textbooks.

I learned how to ask the universe for what I wanted while taking steps toward achieving it. With this added power, I started moving from a life of frustration and waiting into a life of purpose and excitement.

How fitting that years later, my publisher for this book would be New World Library, the publishing company started by Shakti Gawain and Marc Allen.

Shakti Gawain also said, "What we create within us is always mirrored outside of us." Taking those words to heart, I developed a philosophy of living encompassing these tenets:

Visualize Your Goals into Being

Picture yourself the way you want to be — in a new job or opportunity, feeling more fulfilled. Then try to feel the emotions you will experience when you achieve your goal. For example, before I met my husband, I imagined a mystery man's arms lovingly wrapped around me every night, and feeling adored by someone wonderful. I visualized having a fabulous publisher putting out my book. Visualizing helps manifest your aspirations.

Tell people what you want. The universe does not reward people who hide their light or keep their dreams and goals a secret. Molly Brown was the first movie character I saw who showed me that there is no shame in ambition — seeking love, money, or success — no matter what the world tells you. In *The Unsinkable Molly Brown* she says, as an illiterate young girl, "I mean more to me than I mean to anybody else. And nobody wants to see me down like I wants to see me up." Sound selfish? Maybe. But I've learned that there is no shame in true self-love that demands respect from others. In fact, it is the foundation of a healthy life and healthy relationships.

You Never Know When Your Bad Luck's Your Good Luck

Think about it: maybe you overslept, but because that happened, you avoided a highway accident. Or you didn't get the job you wanted, but that's why you were available when your dream job opened up. So don't rail at your bad luck, because it might be a rabbit's foot in disguise. For example, I never worked for the biggest magazines, and while I thought that was a liability, it ended up being an asset. After three years at *American Woman*, I became editor in chief of *Woman's Own*. Because it was a small publication (our circulation was about two hundred thousand) and had a small staff, I learned much more about the nuts and bolts of producing a magazine than I would have as editor of a larger publication. It turned out to be superb training for the shift to digital, where editors do it all.

Catapult Yourself outside Your Comfort Zone

I wrote about reinventing yourself for a piece for *Next Avenue*. As I said in the article, "Learning a new skill keeps your mind smart and facile as you get older."

Recently I started podcasting and began taking tennis lessons. Other people take up mah-jongg or pickleball. I remember when I interviewed a former Tibetan monk for one of the magazines I worked for, he taught me self-healing energy work (a form of Reiki), which I now use any time I have an ache or get a sunburn. I also used it to comfort my daughter when she was little and got a boo-boo.

Live in the Present Moment

This is the hardest rule of all for me, but it's essential. Even when I'm caught up in my writing, laser-focused on my computer or my thoughts, I try to make time for my daughter when she gets home from school. We talk and share the best parts of our day. That connection with her and my husband keeps me grounded.

Get Help to Light Your Way

As you start to advance in your career, you can make huge leaps forward with help and motivation from professional instructors. You can take classes on how to pitch and on how to write personal essays, like the ones I teach.

Writing coaches can be your guide through the often rocky terrain of publishing. They can help develop story structure, teach craft, polish prose, keep you accountable, and, yes, offer inspiration.

Many, like me, offer line editing as well as developmental editing. The best coaches come with bona fide credentials and are experienced in the areas of writing you are interested in.

To protect yourself when hiring a professional, always vet them first. Look for testimonials on their website. The ones to trust are those who use students' and editors' full names for credibility. They should be widely published and have a good track record of helping their students get published. I also advise against paying huge amounts up front. Try to find people who have been involved in the writing and publishing industry for years and are connected to organizations and associations in a deep way that will help you.

Practice Gratitude

I'm a big believer in rituals focused on gratitude and goals. I blow out a birthday candle every year before midnight as an annual gratitude ritual, and it starts my birthday off with a special spark. I recommend you do the same for an inspiring start to your latest age or stage.

Step 1: I usually use a long, white, tapered candle (to represent purity of thought), but this year I chose a green candle to represent growth. You can chose the color that best suits you.

Step 2: Visualize a protective shield around you. I always imagine a column of white light surrounding me.

Step 3: As you light the candle, loudly tell the universe (or if you believe in them, your angels) what you are grateful for in your life.

Step 4: Ask the universe for what you want in the coming year. This part can include anything from a new car to world peace, better bylines, less combative relationships, or new love. Really, you can ask for whatever, um, lights your fire.

Step 5: Right when the clock strikes midnight, or a few minutes before, focus your intention on the flame of the candle, verbally summarize your asks, and repeat your gratitude for everything you already have.

Step 6: I always end the ritual by saying out loud, "Thank you so much. So shall it be, and so it is … Amen." Then I blow out the candle.

Trust me, it works.

Shakti Gawain once said, "The more light you allow within you, the brighter the world you live in will be."

I'm very grateful that I now have the power, through this book and my teaching, to change people's lives for the better. That is the true power of creative visualization.

CHAPTER TWENTY-TWO

Your Words Matter

Your life is a story. Write the one you want to read.
— A. D. POSEY

We have covered a lot together in this book. If you follow the advice in each chapter, you will have a toolkit for becoming a better writer and storyteller, finding your voice, getting your name out there, and building your platform and career, one fabulous article or essay at a time. But please have patience with yourself while going through the process. Like Rome, a writer is not built in a day.

It's difficult, if not impossible, to build a career as a writer when you're working without a support system. While you navigate your path, buoy yourself by finding your networks, online or offline, through like-minded people you meet, or via the camaraderie and sharing in organizations. I'm grateful for the friends and colleagues I have found — and continue to find — through publishing, social media, and attending writers' conferences over the years. So find your people. Take a class. Attend a conference. Explore groups on social media. I've met some of my best friends that way, who have shared opportunities and helped me grow as a writer. You can, too.

I am interested in helping you on your journey, even beyond the lessons in this book. I love sharing advice on publishing to help you grow as a writer and a creative. To learn more, listen to the *Freelance Writing Direct* podcast.

Sign up for my newsletter "Writing That Gets Noticed" on Substack at estelleserasmus.substack.com, and check out my classes at EstelleSErasmus.com.

I also like to hang out on social media, sharing advice and curating good content. Find me on all forms of social media at @EstelleSErasmus.

Follow #Writinggetsnoticed and #freelancewritingdirect on all my platforms.

Never give up. Follow my advice, believe in yourself, and you will get your writing noticed.

Acknowledgments

This book began as a labor of love when I started taking notes about everything I'd been teaching my students as a writing coach and for my classes at New York University and *Writer's Digest*.

I'm a big believer in dreams and following them, but you have to take the first step. My first step toward making this book a reality was going to the Atlanta Writers Conference, helmed by George Weinstein, and signing up for a manuscript consultation with Georgia Hughes of New World Library.

Thank you to my agent, Rita Rosenkranz, who made my day at the ASJA conference when she told me, "I like books about writing," and to everyone at New World Library, especially Georgia Hughes and Kristen Cashman. From the beginning, Georgia and the whole team at NWL — from design to sales to copyediting to publicity — have been a pleasure to work with. Most important, her savvy edits have made the book better. She gets me.

Thanks to my current and former students, people I've edited, and all those who have allowed me to share their work: Heidi Borst, Nicolette Branch, Emily Brisse, Jennie Burke, Connie Chang, Tess Clarkson, Jocelyn Cox, Mary Derbish, Ivy Eisenberg, Emily P. G. Erickson, Nir Eyal, Jessica Wozinsky Fleming, Suzie Glassman, Salina Jivani, Allison Kenien, Linda Lowen, Angela Lundberg, Cheryl Maguire, Jenn McKee,

Kimberly Nagy, Judy Nelson, Rochelle Newman-Carrasco, Mimi O'Connor, Susan M. Sparks, Lauren Stevens, and Tara Sutphen.

A huge thanks to Jenny McPhee at New York University's School of Professional Studies/PALA. I so appreciate your support of me and my endeavors, and I adore working with you and your team: Andrea Chambers, Miguel A. Ortiz-Crane, Afua Preston, Ken French, Anne Wolff, and everyone at NYU.

Thank you to Amy Jones at *Writer's Digest* for believing in my column for the past two years and your encouraging words. It has been a wonderful ride. Thank you to Robert Lee Brewer, Sarah Hall, Sue Johnson, Tara Johnson, Moriah Richard, and Taylor Sferra, and to Phil Sexton for connecting me with the team.

William Dameron, Vishavjit Singh, and Juli Fraga: thank you for allowing me to analyze your glorious essays, and for your immense talent. Thank you to news anchor Ernie Anastos for making my interview with you on *Fox 5 News* so easy, informative, and pleasant.

A special thank-you to the generous colleagues, editors, authors, and friends who have given me leads on jobs and gigs, conference opportunities, and advice about publishing, publishing a book, and running a podcast, and who inspire me: Wendi Aarons, Sherry Amatenstein, Michele Borba, James Brannigan, Janice Eidus, Bernice Elting, Ken Fakler, Irina Harris, Vanessa Hua, Jeanette Hurt, Amy Klein, Holly Koenig, Laura Laing, Jen Malia, Courtney Maum, Ava McDonald, Allison Hong Merrill, Sherry Beck Paprocki, Ronit Plank, Dawn Raffel, Bobbi Rebell, Ashleigh Renard, NJ Rongner, Art Swift, Linda K. Wertheimer, Michael Zam, and my fellow New World Library author Minda Zetlin.

I'm grateful to the great editors who I've worked with over the years or who have spoken to me for this book, conference panels, classes, events, and columns: Charanna Alexander, Anjuman Ali, Holly Baxter, Susan Borison, Kim Brooks, Melissa Bykofsky, Julia Calderone, Elizabeth Chang, Julia Dennison, Joanna Douglas, Beth Dreher, Amelia Edelman, Richard Eisenberg, Shelley Emling, Alexandra Finkel, Hattie Fletcher, Margaret Guroff, Anna Halkidis, Angela Haupt, Lisa Heffernan, Alan Henry, Sharon Holbrook, Jenny Hollander, Carrie Horn, Jessica Hullinger, Amy Joyce, Erin Kahr, Erin

Keane, Allison Klein, Iris Krasnow, Anna Lane, Marisa LaScala, Miya Lee, Janet Manley, George Mannes, Dinty W. Moore, Emily McCombs, Noah Michelson, Evan Miller, Farah Miller, Amy Newmark, Meaghan O'Connell, Katie O'Reilly, Shannon Palus, Tara Parker-Pope, Conz Preti, Jeannie Ralston, Teri Rizvi, Susan Segrest, Paul Smalera, Marcelle Soviero, Brendan Spiegel, Donna Talarico, James Taranto, Mia Taylor, Lindsey Underwood, Shelby Vittek, Alison K. Williams, Mari-Jane Williams, Kristina Wright, Roberta Zeff, and Andrea Zimmerman.

A great big thank you to the organization I have been a part of since 1997, the American Society of Journalists and Authors (ASJA). Almost every move forward in my career can be attributed to an opportunity that came about from a connection through ASJA. I have also been a longtime member of the American Society of Magazine Editors. I'm a newer member of the Women's Media Group, and I am enjoying the camaraderie.

Thank you to my friends who support me, commiserate with me, and love me even when I'm having a tough day, and to my mom and dad, Miriam and Jerry.

Thank you to my muse, my inspiration, my precious daughter, Crystal, who takes my breath away every day with her sense of self, intelligence, and beauty.

And finally, thanks always to my husband, Werner, the best man I've ever met, who provides encouragement, support, and love. He always has my back and protects me from publishing anything that could blow up my life for a byline.

Resources for Writers

A professional writer is an amateur who didn't quit.
— RICHARD BACH

Associations and Websites

American Medical Writers Association (AMWA), AMWA.org.

American Society of Journalists and Authors (ASJA), ASJA.org. The largest professional association focused on independent writers.

American Society of Magazine Editors, Asme.media. The principal organization for the editorial leaders of magazines and websites published in the United States.

Association of Health Care Journalists (AHCJ), HealthJournalism .org. Focuses on excellence in health care and medical reporting.

Association of Writers & Writing Programs (AWP), AWPWriter.org. Provides support, advocacy, resources, and community to writers, college and university creative writing programs, and writers' conferences and centers.

Authors Guild, AuthorsGuild.org. The collective voice of American authors.

Authors Guild Resources for Latinx Writers, AuthorsGuild.org/whats
-new/seminars-member-events/business-bootcamps-for-writers
/community-resources/latinx-writers.

Editorial Freelancers Association (EFA), The-EFA.org. A professional resource for editorial specialists and those who hire them.

Education Writers Association (EWA), EWA.org. Aims to strengthen
the community of education writers and improve the quality of
education coverage to better inform the public.

Girls Write Now, GirlsWriteNow.org. A nonprofit with the mission to
break down barriers of gender, race, age, and poverty to mentor
the next generation of writers and leaders.

Investigative Reporters and Editors, IRE.org. A grassroots nonprofit
organization dedicated to improving the quality of journalism.

National Association of Science Writers (NASW), NASW.org. Supports good science writing.

National Society of Newspaper Columnists, Columnists.com. An
organization for writers of serial essays, including columnists and
bloggers, of any medium.

National Writers Union, NWU.org. A union for all genres of writers.
Offers connections to other writers and contract advice.

Op-Ed Project, TheOpEdProject.org. Offers advice on writing op-eds
and a list of newspapers all over the country accepting op-eds.

Pen America, Pen.org. Organization with a focus on literary writing.

Society of American Travel Writers, SATW.org. A professional organization focused on travel writing.

Society of Professional Journalists (SPJ), SPJ.org. Dedicated to encouraging the free practice of journalism and stimulating high
standards of ethical behavior.

Women's Media Group, WomensMediaGroup.org. A New York City–
based nonprofit association of women who have achieved promi-
nence in the many fields of media.

Books about Writing and Getting Published

There are many books out there about writing and publishing, but
these are the ones I refer to most.

Lisa Cron. *Story Genius: How to Use Brain Science to Go beyond Outlining and Write a Riveting Novel.* New York: Ten Speed Press, 2016.

Beth Ann Fennelly. *Heating & Cooling: 52 Micro-Memoirs.* New York: Norton, 2018.

Jane Friedman. *The Business of Being a Writer.* Chicago: University of Chicago Press, 2018.

Julia Goldberg. *Inside Story: Everyone's Guide to Reporting and Writing Creative Nonfiction.* Santa Fe, NM: Leaf Storm Press, 2017.

Natalie Goldberg. *Writing Down the Bones: Freeing the Writer Within.* Boulder, CO: Shambhala, 2016.

Vivian Gornick. *The Situation and the Story.* New York: Farrar, Straus and Giroux, 2002.

Stephen King. *On Writing: A Memoir of the Craft.* New York: Scribner, 2020.

Anne Lamott. *Bird by Bird: Some Instructions on Writing and Life.* New York: Knopf Doubleday, 1995.

Adair Lara. *Naked, Drunk, and Writing: Shed Your Inhibitions and Craft a Compelling Memoir or Personal Essay.* Berkeley, CA: Ten Speed Press, 2010.

Courtney Maum. *Before and After the Book Deal: A Writer's Guide to Finishing, Publishing, Promoting, and Surviving Your First Book.* New York: Catapult, 2020.

Brenda Miller. *A Braided Heart: Essays on Writing and Form.* Ann Arbor: University of Michigan Press, 2021.

Brenda Miller and Suzanne Paola. *Tell It Slant.* New York: McGraw-Hill, 2019.

Allison K. Williams. *Seven Drafts: Self-Edit Like a Pro from Blank Page to Book.* Norwalk, CT: Woodhall, 2021.

Journalists' Resources

American Press Institute, AmericanPressInstitute.org. Helps news organizations and journalists improve public-service journalism.

ChatGPT, Chat.openAI.com The artificial intelligence chatbot is helpful for idea generation and research, but it should not replace your own writing.

Merriam-Webster Dictionary, Merriam-Webster.com. Free online dictionary and thesaurus.

Neiman Storyboard, NiemanStoryboard.org. A publication of the Neiman Foundation for Journalism at Harvard University that showcases exceptional narrative journalism and explores the future of nonfiction storytelling.

Open Notebook, TheOpenNotebook.com. A nonprofit that offers tools for science, environmental, and health journalists, such as examples of science-focused pitches.

Poynter, Poynter.org. A nonprofit media institute and newsroom that provides fact-checking, media literacy, and journalism ethics training to citizens and journalists.

Who Pays Writers?, WhoPaysWriters.com. Shows what publications are paying for articles.

Your Dictionary, YourDictionary.com. Free online dictionary and thesaurus.

Glossary of Publishing Terms

article: A nonfiction piece of writing that aims to serve the reader or report information.

byline: A line under the title of an article, essay, or op-ed naming the writer of the piece.

clip: A published article a writer offers to an editor as proof of their ability and experience.

content editing: The big picture of editing. Checking that all the necessary elements, quotes, and information are included in a story and that it is logically constructed. At magazines this is usually the responsibility of a senior level editor.

copyediting: Editing a piece with a focus on grammar, punctuation, and phrasing.

dek: The often-italicized text underneath an article's headline that provides a bit more information on the content.

editor: A person who selects content, works with writers, edits articles, and writes headlines.

editorial director: Plans, coordinates, and top edits all written content for a publication or a website, and establishes the company's vision for the publication. They supervise and allocate work to editors in chief and editorial managers.

editor in chief: The most senior editor at a publication, aside from the editorial director, responsible for the content, the overall look of the publication, and the top hires. When it comes to day-to-day decisions, the buck stops here.

evergreen: A term referring to an article that is not time-sensitive, so it can be run at any time.

front of book (FOB): A section at the front of a magazine that includes short articles and columns and a letter from the editor.

hook: The part of a piece or pitch that shows what is special and timely about the piece.

kill fee: A fee paid to the writer when an article accepted for publication is withdrawn by the editor, typically 10–20 percent of the stipulated fee for the article.

lede: The first paragraph of a piece, which tells you what it's about.

line editing: Part of copyediting: editing an article line by line, fixing grammar, punctuation, usage, and spelling errors.

listicle: An article presented in the form of a list, often displayed online as a series of web pages with links to the previous and next items.

masthead: A listing of the staff of a publication, including editors, production staff, and sales and advertising managers. It typically appears near the front of a print magazine and in the "About" section of a digital publication.

op-ed: A short, timely piece that offers a personal take or opinion on a topic in the cultural zeitgeist or the news.

peg: A way of linking an article or pitch to a holiday, book, movie, cultural moment, television show, or meme to make the piece timely.

personal essay: An essay featuring one person's point of view; also known as a first-person essay.

pitch: A succinct proposal for an article, and sometimes an essay, that a writer sends to an editor.

proofreading: The final stage of checking a publication for typographic and other errors before its release.

pull quote: A quote taken from the text of an article that is used as a design element.

service article: An article offering advice and information to assist readers.

subheads: Headlines for different parts of an article that guide the reader and offer visual breaks in the copy.

writing coach: An instructor who works with writers on an individual or group basis to help them develop their skills, voice, and style.

writing on spec (speculation): Writing an essay or article with no promise of publication or payment.

Notes

Earlier versions of some chapters or parts of chapters were published in *Brevity*, *Forbes*, *Hippocampus Magazine*, and *Writer's Digest*.

Introduction

p. xii   *an essay I'd written about Crystal*: "Estelle Sobel Erasmus Reading 'And She Danced,'" video from *Listen to Your Mother: NYC 2012 at the Goldman-Sonnenfeldt Auditorium*, www.youtube.com/watch?v=CmV4abTKy8Q; Editors of BlogHer, eds., *The BlogHer '12 Voices of the Year* (New York: Open Road Integrated Media, 2012); Estelle Erasmus, "The Secret of My Daughter's Dance," *Huffington Post*, March 17, 2014, https://www.huffpost.com/entry/and-she-danced_b_4978967.

p. xiii   *a personal essay in* Marie Claire: Estelle Erasmus, "Quite Possibly the Creepiest Roommate Story Ever," *Marie Claire*, July 17, 2014, https://www.marieclaire.com/culture/a10150/creepy-roommate-story.

p. xiii   *"My Child Is Out of Control"*: Estelle Erasmus, "My Child Is Out of Control," *Washington Post*, December 30, 2014, https://www.washingtonpost.com/news/parenting/wp/2014/12/30/my-child-is-out-of-control-heres-what-ill-do-in-2015-to-change-that.

p. xiii   *"My Child Is Still Out of Control"*: Estelle Erasmus, "My Child Is Still Out of Control," *Washington Post*, February 11, 2016, https://www.washingtonpost.com/news/parenting/wp/2016/02/11/my-child-is-still-out-of-control.

p. xiii   *the new rules for babysitting*: Estelle Erasmus, "Add Social Media to the List of

Things You Tell a New Babysitter," *Washington Post*, December 6, 2016, https://www.washingtonpost.com/lifestyle/on-parenting/add-social-media -expectations-to-the-list-of-things-you-tell-a-new-babysitter/2016/12/05 /60181b98-b595-11e6-b8df-600bd9d38a02_story.html.

p. xiii   *why it was positive for our marriage*: Estelle Erasmus, "6 Reasons We Don't Let Our Daughter Sleep in Our Bed," *Washington Post*, November 12, 2015, https://www.washingtonpost.com/news/parenting/wp/2015/11/12/why-we-dont -let-our-daughter-sleep-in-our-bed.

p. xiii   *powerful phrases every parent needs*: Estelle Erasmus, "6 Powerful Phrases Every Parent Should Use," *The Week*, December 17, 2019, https://theweek.com/articles /880354/6-powerful-phrases-every-parent-should-use.

p. xiii   *the scientific benefits of getting a pet*: Estelle Erasmus, "5 Scientific Reasons You Should Get a Pet For Your Teen," *Your Teen*, July 25, 2019, https://yourteenmag .com/health/teenager-mental-health/why-you-should-get-a-pet; *How Pet Therapy is Beneficial For Teens*, video, Fox 5 New York, July 26, 2019, https://www.fox5 ny.com/news/how-pet-therapy-is-beneficial-for-teens.

p. xiii   *"How to Bullyproof Your Child"*: Estelle Erasmus, "How to Bullyproof Your Child," *New York Times*, May 23, 2019, https://www.nytimes.com/2019/05/23 /well/family/how-to-bullyproof-your-child.html; Estelle Erasmus, "How to Teach Your Kids to Address Teasing," *Good Morning America*, May 30, 2019, https:// www.goodmorningamerica.com/family/video/teach-kids-address-teasing -63367176; Roberta Zeff, *Well Family Newsletter*, *New York Times*, May 30, 2019, https://static.nytimes.com/email-content/ML_13815.html?fbclid=IwAR18lPR 2vN8uQeffO8DdYK6kBAhZRF2ho3rzKAL8C_-VZhN9cKknU8oVPkc.

p. xiv   *the* Freelance Writing Direct *podcast*: *Freelance Writing Direct* podcast, https:// podcasts.apple.com/us/podcast/freelance-writing-direct/id1647429472 ?i=1000584885494.

p. xiv   *the brain understands and remembers best*: L. S. Vygotsky, *Mind in Society* (Cambridge, MA: Harvard University Press, 1978).

p. xiv   *how to keep kids engaged in school*: Estelle Erasmus, "How to Keep Kids Engaged in School — with Games," *Wired*, February 9, 2021, https://www.wired.com /story/how-to-keep-kids-engaged-in-school-with-games.

Chapter 1: Creative Alchemy

p. 4   *rote activity allows the mind to wander*: Kalina Christoff, Alan M. Gordon, Jonathan Smallwood, Rachelle Smith, and Jonathan W. Schooler, "Experience Sampling during fMRI Reveals Default Network and Executive System Contributions to Mind Wandering," *Proceedings of the National Academy of Sciences* 106, no. 21 (May 2009): 8719–24, https://doi.org/10.1073/pnas.0900234106.

p. 4   *aerobic exercise allows the growth of new cells*: D. L. Schacter, D. R. Addis, and P. L. Buckner, "Remembering the Past to Imagine the Future: The Prospective Brain," *Nature Reviews Neuroscience* 9 (September 2007): 657–61, https://doi .org/10.1038/nrn2213.

p. 4   *being around people working on their own creative projects*: K. Desender, S. Beurms, and E. Van den Bussche, "Is Mental Effort Exertion Contagious?" *Psychonomic Bulletin and Review* 23 (2016): 624–31, https://doi.org/10.3758 /s13423-015-0923-3.

p. 5   *walking increases a person's creative output*: M. Oppezzo and D. L. Schwartz, "Give Your Ideas Some Legs: The Positive Effect of Walking on Creative Thinking," *Journal of Experimental Psychology: Learning, Memory, and Cognition* 40, no. 4 (2014): 1142–52.

p. 5   *Our brains process familiar information quickly*: Schacter, Addis, and Buckner, "Remembering the Past."

p. 6   *even when we take a break*: S. Ritter and A. Dijksterhuis, "Creativity: The Unconscious Foundations of the Incubation Period," *Frontiers in Human Neuroscience* 8 (April 2014): 215, https://doi.org.10.3389/fnhum.2014.00215.

p. 6   *"Write shitty first drafts"*: Anne Lamott, *Bird by Bird: Some Instructions on Writing and Life* (New York: Knopf Doubleday, 1995).

Chapter 2: Incubating Ideas

p. 12   *come up with a tantalizing or provocative title*: Erasmus, "How to Bullyproof Your Child"; Estelle Erasmus, "The Doula Who Saved My Life," *Washington Post*, May 2, 2016, https://www.washingtonpost.com/news/parenting/wp/2016/05/02/the -doula-who-saved-my-life.

p. 13   *"For sale, baby shoes, never worn"*: The quote probably did not originate with Hemingway. According to a post on the website Quote Investigator, "For Sale, Baby Carriage, Never Used," was published in a newspaper feature called *Terse Tales of the Town*. See also Nikola Budanovic, "For Sale, Baby Shoes, Never Worn": Tracing the History of the Shortest Story Ever Told," *Vintage News*, September 24, 2017, https://www.thevintagenews.com/2017/09/24.

p. 13   *the regions of the brain associated with learning and creativity*: Audrey L. H. van der Meer and F. R. Rudd van der Weel, "Only Three Fingers Write, but the Whole Brain Works: A High-Density EEG Study Showing Advantages of Drawing over Typing for Learning," *Frontiers in Psychology* 8 (May 2017): 706, https://doi.org .10.3389/fpsyg.2017.00706.

p. 14   *As Vivian Gornick points out*: Vivian Gornick, *The Situation and the Story* (New York: Farrar, Straus and Giroux, 2002).

p. 14   *Then the night terrors started*: Erasmus, "The Doula Who Saved My Life."

Chapter 3: Finding and Honing Your Voice

p. 17 *Everyone in the show was a mother*: "Estelle Sobel Erasmus Reading 'And She Danced'," https://www.youtube.com/watch?v=CmV4abTKy8Q.

p. 19 *Amy, who's missed all of her work deliverables*: Ivy Eisenberg, "I Quit My Job at 50 to Reinvent Myself. Pro Tip: Don't Do This," Narratively, January 1, 2020, https://narratively.com/i-quit-my-job-at-50-to-reinvent-myself-pro-tip-dont-do-this.

p. 21 *I looked at the license plate*: Estelle Erasmus, "A Fake Uber Driver Tried to Pick Up Me and My Daughter," Romper, September 3, 2019, https://www.romper.com/p/a-fake-uber-driver-tried-to-pick-up-me-my-daughter-18718520.

p. 21 *As the doctor checked her vitals*: Estelle Erasmus, "Becoming a Mom Has Totally Transformed Me," Parenting.com, February 2016.

p. 22 *I watched as my parents methodically divested themselves*: Estelle Erasmus, "I Was Determined to Be a Great Mother and a Loving Daughter: This Was Easier Said Than Done," *Salon*, November 8, 2015, https://www.salon.com/2015/11/08/i_was_determined_to_be_a_great_mother_and_a_loving_daughter_this_was_easier_said_then_done.

p. 22 *On our last call*: Estelle Erasmus, "Singing My Dad Back to Me," *New York Times*, November 16, 2020, https://www.nytimes.com/2020/11/13/well/family/singing-my-dad-back-to-me.html.

p. 22 *I joke to my friends*: Estelle Erasmus, "I Constantly Fight with My Husband — and That's OK," *Good Housekeeping*, August 12, 2015, https://www.goodhousekeeping.com/life/relationships/a33883/i-constantly-fight-with-my-husband.

p. 23 *"So, are you treating my boy right?"*: Estelle Erasmus, "The Benefits of Meeting My Mother-in-Law at My Lowest Point," Yahoo!Life, July 30, 2015, https://www.yahoo.com/lifestyle/the-benefits-of-meeting-my-mother-in-law-at-my-125432731993.html.

p. 23 *At first, they didn't want to accept*: Salina Jivani, "My Family Moved to America and into a Real Haunted House," *HuffPost Personal*, October 22, 2021, https://www.huffpost.com/entry/haunted-house-pennsylvania-ghost-immigration_n_616d7c65e4b065735730c5ef.

p. 24 *"I luff you, because you're sveet"*: Estelle Erasmus, "The Healing Words of My Holocaust-Surviving Grandmother," *Brain, Child*, September 13, 2018, https://brainchildmag.com/2018/09/the-gift-of-grandma-genia.

p. 25 *Nothing about my pregnancy*: Estelle Erasmus, "The Savage Song of My Birthright Blues," in *Mothering through the Darkness: Women Open Up about the Postpartum Experience*, ed. Jessica Smock and Stephanie Sprenger (Berkeley, CA: She Writes, 2015).

p. 27 *My future husband sat beside me*: Tess Clarkson, "The One Thing Fear Pushed Me to Do," *AARP: The Girlfriend*, February 22, 2022, https://www.thegirlfriend.com/parenting/the-one-thing-fear-pushed-me-to-do.

p. 27   *Rays of pride beamed from my 7-year-old's cherubic face*: Heidi Borst, "How to Build a Child's Self-Esteem. Hint: It Doesn't Involve Praise," *Washington Post*, July 26, 2021, https://www.washingtonpost.com/lifestyle/2021/07/26/child -self-esteem-confidence.

p. 28   *"Do you think of me when you masturbate?"*: Estelle Erasmus, "The Sex-Talking-Therapist I Went to As a Teen," *Salon*, October 16, 2016, https://www.salon.com /2016/10/16/the-sex-talking-therapist-i-went-to-as-a-teen-do-you-want-to -learn-how-to-be-a-woman-not-a-scared-little-girl. This essay appeared earlier as "Therapy Undercover: Satin Shirts and Sex Talk," in Sherry Amatenstein, ed., *How Does That Make You Feel? True Confessions from Both Sides of the Therapy Couch* (Berkeley, CA: Seal Press, 2016), 135–45.

p. 29   *My 14-year-old daughter constantly abandons her coat*: Cheryl Maguire, "How to Stop Thinking Your Teen Is Pushing Your Buttons," *New York Times*, April 10, 2019, https://www.nytimes.com/2019/04/10/well/family/parenting-teenager -pushing-buttons.html.

Chapter 4: At Your Readers' Service

p. 34   *Every parent with a tween or teen child*: Estelle Erasmus, "5 Scientific Reasons You Should Get a Pet for Your Teen," *Your Teen*, July 25, 2019, https://yourteenmag .com/health/teenager-mental-health/why-you-should-get-a-pet.

p. 34   *A group of medical school friends*: Cheryl Maguire, "Building Social Capital Is Critical for Strong Relationships," *Washington Post*, February 3, 2022, https:// www.washingtonpost.com/wellness/2022/02/03/adhd-relationships-social -capital-tips.

p. 35   *When my 10-year-old daughter was shunned by her friends*: Erasmus, "How to Bullyproof Your Child."

p. 35   *Parents of LGBTQ teens*: Estelle Erasmus, "LGBTQ Sex Education: What Parents Need to Know," *Your Teen*, June 21, 2018, https://yourteenmag.com/health/teen -sexuality/safe-sex-education.

p. 35   *It was the third night*: Kimberly Nagy, "The Importance of Doing What You Love — a Space for Theater," *Your Teen*, May 14, 2019, https://yourteenmag.com /health/teenager-mental-health/importance-of-doing-what-you-love.

p. 35   *My 5-year-old launches himself*: Jessica Wozinsky Fleming, "Why Roughhousing Is Good for Kids, and How to Keep It Safe," *Washington Post*, December 27, 2021, https://www.washingtonpost.com/parenting/2021/12/27/roughhousing-benefits -kids.

p. 36   *Many editors like how-to stories*: Estelle Erasmus, "Can Honey Cure Rosacea? One Beauty Editor Says Yes," Yahoo, September 23, 2015, https://www.yahoo.com /lifestyle/can-honey-cure-rosacea-one-beauty-editor-says-yes-129597962188

.html; Estelle Erasmus, "How I Fell In Love with Growing Older," *Redbook*, June 30, 2015, https://www.redbookmag.com/life/charity/a38875/how-i-fell-in-love -with-growing-older; Salina Jivani, "These Apps Saved My Sanity (and Probably My Marriage)," *Wired*, September 11, 2021, https://www.wired.com/story/family -organization-apps-saved-my-marriage.

p. 37   *Although I still stew when getting cut-off at drop-off*: Erasmus, "My Child Is Still Out of Control."

p. 38   *Friend Type 1: If You Have Nothing Nice to Say*: Estelle Erasmus, "What Should I Do about My Tween's Toxic Friend?" *Good Housekeeping*, May 10, 2021, https:// www.goodhousekeeping.com/life/parenting/a36356220/tween-toxic-friend.

p. 39   *We Wash Our Hands*: Estelle Erasmus, "Elijah the Prophet Will Toast You on Zoom: Ways to Get through a Socially Distanced Passover," *Independent*, April 9, 2020, https://www.independent.co.uk/voices/passover-coronavirus-pandemic -zoom-a9458596.html.

p. 40   *"Lend Perspective without a Lecture"*: Estelle Erasmus, "When Your Tween Is Bored," *New York Times*, July 2, 2020, https://www.nytimes.com/2020/07/02 /well/family/tweens-boredom-summer.html.

p. 40   *"Take Your E's"*: Estelle Erasmus, "When Your Tween Acts Up in Lockdown," *New York Times*, May 6, 2020, https://www.nytimes.com/2020/05/06/well/family /coronavirus-tween-conflict-lockdown-parenting.html.

Chapter 5: Essay Formats

p. 48   *My parents lived together their whole lives*: Estelle Erasmus, "How to Prevent Falls and Find Comfort in a New Home for Seniors," *Washington Post*, January 25, 2022, https://www.washingtonpost.com/home/2022/01/25/seniors-home-safety -fall-prevention.

p. 48   *When I get paper cuts*: Jocelyn Cox, "I was a Competitive Figure Skater for 11 Years," *Insider*, February 2, 2022, https://www.insider.com/professional-figure -skater-on-how-pain-altered-her-life-2022-2.

p. 49   *In a piece I wrote for* Wired: Estelle Erasmus, "Friends, Fleetwood Mac, and the Viral Comfort of Nostalgia," *Wired*, December 8, 2020, https://www.wired.com /story/fleetwood-mac-dreams-friends-nostalgia.

p. 51   *"Why can't you find someone?"*: Estelle Erasmus, "Tiny Love Stories: Maybe More Than Slightly," *New York Times*, April 27, 2021, https://www.nytimes.com /2021/04/27/style/tiny-modern-love-stories-why-cant-you-find-someone.html.

p. 51   *My joyful, bright, freckle-faced younger brother*: Jennie Burke, "Tiny Love Stories: My Bright, Freckle-Faced Little Brother," *New York Times*, May 17, 2022, https://www.nytimes.com/2022/05/17/style/tiny-modern-love-stories-i-begged -him-for-a-sign.html.

p. 52   *In the dance recital photograph*: Linda Lowen, "Pat the Bunny," *The Writer*, December 2017.

p. 53   *two literary essay formats*: Brenda Miller and Suzanne Paola, *Tell It Slant* (New York: McGraw-Hill, 2019); Brenda Miller, *A Braided Heart: Essays on Writing and Form* (Ann Arbor: University of Michigan Press, 2021).

p. 54   *unfairbnb*: Linda Lowen, "Unfairbnb," NOW: The Publication for the Hobart Festival of Women Writers, 2022, https://hfwwnow.squarespace.com/blog2 /z6tvtoyr8de5vcle28s3hm7ovrflnv.

p. 54   *First position: Your feet behind your mother's waist*: Emily Brisse, "How It Slips Away," *Two Hawks Quarterly*, May 31, 2016, https://twohawksquarterly.com /2016/05/31/slips-away-emily-brisse.

p. 55   *"All these stories weave and intersect"*: Miller and Paola, *Tell It Slant*.

Chapter 6: The Art (and Arc) of Writing a Personal Essay

p. 58   *It was a balmy summer Friday evening*: Estelle Erasmus, "The Gas Goes Out and the Train Goes In," *New York Times*, August 20, 2016, https://www.nytimes .com/2016/08/20/nyregion/metropolitan-diary-the-train-must-go-in.html.

p. 59   *"Giving Up the Ghost Baby"*: Estelle Erasmus, "Giving Up the Ghost Baby," Purple Clover, October 26, 2016.

p. 59   *a creepy roommate from years ago*: Erasmus, "Quite Possibly the Creepiest Roommate Story Ever."

p. 59   *how people constantly wanted to touch my pregnant belly*: Estelle Erasmus, "You're Pregnant. Why Does That Make Everyone So Determined to Touch You?" *Washington Post*, October 12, 2015, https://www.washingtonpost.com/national /health-science/youre-pregnant-why-does-that-make-people-so-determined-to -touch-you/2015/10/12/0e0a6118-5bc2-11e5-b38e-06883aacba64_story.html.

p. 60   *Earlier this year, just days shy of my daughter's 12th birthday*: Jenn McKee, "We're in a New Era of Period Positivity, and It's Empowering for Young Girls," *Good Housekeeping*, September 28, 2020, https://www.goodhousekeeping.com/life /parenting/a34045000/first-period-positivity.

p. 60   *"I hope my dog fucking bites you"*: Angela Lundberg, "My Secret Life Tracking Down Debtors," Narratively, March 2, 2020, https://narratively.com/my-secret -life-tracking-down-medical-debtors.

p. 61   *"Patrick" popped up as a match*: Susan M. Sparks, "I Fell for a Catfish Who Scammed Me Out of Thousands of Dollars," *HuffPost Personal*, October 8, 2021, https://www.huffpost.com/entry/romance-dating-online-scam-nigeria _n_6159ac29e4b099230d24868e.

p. 61   *In the silence that came*: Suzie Glassman, "What My Best Friend's Death Taught Me about Life," *AARP: The Girlfriend*, May 31, 2022, https:// www.thegirlfriend .com/relationships/what-my-best-friends-death-taught-me-about-life.

p. 62 *It's 2003 and I am stuck*: Eisenberg, "I Quit My Job at 50 to Reinvent Myself. Pro Tip: Don't Do This."

p. 62 *Standing in a Missouri funeral parlor*: Tess Clarkson, "After My Parents Died, I Cut My Siblings out of My Life for Good," *Independent*, July 22, 2021, https://www.independent.co.uk/voices/parents-died-cut-out-siblings-covid -b1888972.html.

p. 63 *As a child, my first brush with a ghost*: Salina Jivani, "My Family Moved to America and into a Real Haunted House," *HuffPost Personal*, October 22, 2021, https://www.huffpost.com/entry/haunted-house-pennsylvania-ghost-immigration _n_616d7c65e4b065735730c5ef.

p. 63 *I ask my family*: Jennie Burke, "The First Christmas without Him: Finding Joy in 2020 after the Loss of My Brother," *Independent*, December 22, 2020, https://www.independent.co.uk/voices/christmas-grief-brother-death-overdose-peace -tree-b1777888.html.

p. 64 *I grabbed my phone*: Tess Clarkson, "I Helped a Stranger at the End of His Life," *Washington Post*, December 24, 2021, https://www.washingtonpost.com/life style/2021/12/24/hospice-volunteer-christmas-life-lesson.

p. 64 *I "popped" six months into my pregnancy*: Erasmus, "You're Pregnant."

p. 68 *readers' brains are stimulated by reading sensory language*: S. Lacey, R. Stilla, and K. Sathian, "Metaphorically Feeling: Comprehending Textural Metaphors Activates Somatosensory Cortex," *Brain and Language* 120, no. 3 (March 2012): 416–21, https://www.sciencedirect.com/science/article/abs/pii/S0093934X12000028.

p. 69 *inspired by Joe Brainard's memoir* I Remember: Joe Brainard, *I Remember* (1975; repr., New York: Granary Books, 2001).

p. 73 *I froze when I saw the subject line*: Judy Nelson, "How Going to a Dead & Company Concert with a Stranger Helped Me Heal after Losing My Son," *HuffPost Personal*, February 28, 2020, https://www.huffpost.com/entry/grateful-dead -parenting-grief_n_5e554901c5b63b9c9ce41e4a.

p. 73 *Roughly two hours south of Atlanta*: Excerpts from unpublished draft and published version of Lauren Stevens, "Georgia on My Mind," in *Proud to Be: Writing by American Warriors, Volume 7*, ed. James Brubaker (Cape Girardeau, MO: Southeast Missouri State University Press, 2018).

p. 75 *what is the situation?*: Vivian Gornick, *The Situation and the Story* (New York: Farrar, Straus and Giroux, 2002).

p. 76 *my story about an inappropriate therapist*: Erasmus, "The Sex-Talking-Therapist I Went to As a Teen."

p. 77 *The morning I woke up from a night-terror-free sleep*: Estelle Erasmus, "Postpartum Rage: One Mom's Uncontrollable Anger after Giving Birth," Parents.com, July 9, 2021, https://www.parents.com/baby/health/postpartum-depression /i-was-uncontrollably-angry-after-giving-birth.

p. 78   *I discovered that our brains perceive time*: Allison Kenien, "Time Was Flying as I Watched My Kids Grow Up in Front of Me," *Insider*, March 10, 2022, https://www.insider.com/how-i-slowed-down-time-to-enjoy-my-kids-more-2022-3.

p. 78   *It's been nearly ten months*: Tess Clarkson, "The Time I Met My Husband's Ex at Their Kid's Football Game," Scary Mommy, June 14, 2022, https://www.scary mommy.com/lifestyle/the-time-i-met-my-husbands-ex-at-their-kids-football -game.

p. 79   *We all chant "Hey now!"*: Nelson, "How Going to a Dead & Company Concert with a Stranger Helped Me Heal."

p. 79   *As we drive away from the flight line*: Excerpts from unpublished draft and published version of Stevens, "Georgia on My Mind."

p. 81   *Instead there is an invisible, silent enemy*: Estelle Erasmus, "Quarantine Has Done the Impossible — Allowed Me to Hold onto My Tween," Romper, May 4, 2020, https://www.romper.com/p/my-tween-is-frozen-in-place-i-am-momentarily -able-to-relax-22870711.

p. 81   *Lined up in neat rows*: Mary Widdicks, "My Father's Fanatical Feud with the Bullies Next Door Became an All-Out War," Narratively, June 15, 2020, https://narratively.com/my-fathers-fanatical-feud-with-the-bullies-next-door-became -an-all-out-war.

p. 84   *So, as I face the finality*: Erasmus, "Singing My Dad Back to Me."

p. 84   *My doula came back for a final visit*: Erasmus, "The Doula Who Saved My Life."

p. 84   *Joy and wonder alighted on my father's face*: Connie Chang, "Connecting My Children to Their Heritage in Mandarin," *New York Times*, February 12, 2021, https://www.nytimes.com/2021/02/12/well/family/chinese-heritage-mandarin .html.

p. 85   *Georgia was part goddess*: Nicolette Branch, "Remembering Georgia," in *Chicken Soup for the Soul: I'm Speaking Now*, ed. Amy Newmark and Breena Clarke (Cos Cob, CT: Chicken Soup for the Soul, 2021).

p. 87   *So, I will not yell at the cable company*: Erasmus, "My Child Is Out of Control."

p. 87   *an essay for* Salon *in which the words* my daughter *appeared*: Erasmus, "I Was Determined to Be a Great Mother."

p. 87   *This is the same kid*: Estelle Erasmus, "What to Do When Your Tween Is Trash-Talking You," *New York Times*, September 18, 2019, https://www.nytimes.com /2019/09/18/well/family/parenting-tween-conflict.html.

p. 88   *I couldn't tell my husband what was happening*: Erasmus, "Giving Up the Ghost Baby."

p. 90   *"You own everything that happened to you"*: Anne Lamott (@ANNELAMOTT), Twitter, April 23, 2012, 5:16 p.m., https://twitter.com/ANNELAMOTT/status /194580559962439681.

p. 93   *the haircut is an objective correlative*: William Dameron, "After 264 Haircuts, a

Marriage Ends," *New York Times*, February 10, 2017, https://www.nytimes.com /2017/02/10/style/modern-love-conversion-therapy-gay-husband-haircuts.html.

p. 94   *And what you will find is*: Alyssa Newcomb, "Read Savannah Guthrie's Heartfelt Commencement Speech at George Washington University," *Today*, May 19, 2019.

Chapter 7: Analyzing Essays

p. 97   *I settled on a rock in Central Park*: Vishavjit Singh, "Captain America in a Turban," *Salon*, September 10, 2013, https://www.salon.com/2013/09/10/captain _america_in_a_turban.

p. 102   *Like many Midwesterners*: Juli Fraga, "Seoul Searching in San Francisco," CityLab/Bloomberg, October 14, 2016, https:/ www.bloomberg.com/news /articles/2016-10-14/reconnecting-with-korea-in-san-francisco.

p. 106   *Elizabeth lofted the black cape*: William Dameron, "After 264 Haircuts, a Marriage Ends," *New York Times*, February 10, 2017, https://www.nytimes.com/2017/02/10 /style/modern-love-conversion-therapy-gay-husband-haircuts.html.

Chapter 8: Writing Op-Eds and Timely Cultural Pieces

p. 113   *When Charlize Theron was in the news*: Estelle Erasmus, "If I Were Charlize Theron When a Bystander Called the Police for Disciplining Her Tantruming Son," Mamapedia, November 17, 2014, https://www.mamapedia.com/voices/if-i -were-charlize-theron-when-a-bystander-called-the-police-for-disciplining-her -tantruming-son.

p. 113   *I wrote about why my husband does the laundry*: Estelle Erasmus, "My Husband Does the Laundry. And He Should," *Washington Post*, May 4, 2015, https://www .washingtonpost.com/news/parenting/wp/2015/05/04/my-husband-does-the -laundry-and-he-should.

p. 114   *how sheltering in place during the pandemic*: Estelle Erasmus, "Quarantine Has Done the Impossible — Allowed Me to Hold onto My Tween," Romper, May 4, 2020, https://www.romper.com/p/my-tween-is-frozen-in-place-i-am-momentarily -able-to-relax-22870711.

p. 115   *my distress that Dressbarn was shutting down*: Estelle Erasmus, "Dressbarn Was My Favorite Fashion Secret," *AARP: The Girlfriend*, June 4, 2018, https://www .thegirlfriend.com/lifestyle/dressbarn-was-my-favorite-fashion-secret-but-then -they-ruined-a-good-thing.

p. 115   *music helps Alzheimer's patients*: Estelle Erasmus, "Singing My Dad Back to Me," *New York Times*, November 16, 2020, https://www.nytimes.com/2020/11/13/well /family/singing-my-dad-back-to-me.html.

p. 115   *My student Jennie Burke wrote her* New York Times *piece*: Jennie Burke, "Defying the Family Cycle of Addiction," *New York Times*, September 18, 2020, https://www.nytimes.com/2020/09/18/well/family/addiction-opiates-surgery-pain-management.html.

p. 116   *an op-ed I wrote for the* Independent: Estelle Erasmus, "Britney's Army," *Independent*, August 4, 2021, https://www.independent.co.uk/voices/britneys-army-freebritney-detectives-investigation-b1896686.html.

Chapter 9: How to Pitch to Publications So You Don't Get Ghosted

p. 122   *a foster parent over the age of fifty*: Estelle Erasmus, "Found Family," *AARP: The Magazine*, February–March 2021, https://s3.amazonaws.com/external_clips/3698797/AARP.MyKids.RandyBender.FosterCare.FebMar2021.pdf?1612809369.

p. 131   *think ahead about national holidays*: Estelle Erasmus, "I Never Let My Daughter Sit on Santa's Lap. Now She's Old Enough to Tell Me I Made the Right Choice," *Insider*, December 24, 2019, https://www.insider.com/why-never-let-child-sit-santas-lap-2019-12; Estelle Erasmus, "How We Celebrate Both Hanukkah and Christmas," Kveller, December 7, 2012, www.kveller.com/how-we-celebrate-both-hanukkah-christmas.

p. 131   *essays with connections to recently deceased celebrities*: Estelle Erasmus, "Why Do People Take the Public, Social-Media Spectacle of Celebrity Death So Personally?" Quartz, January 9, 2017, https://qz.com/879857/why-do-people-take-the-public-social-media-spectacle-of-celebrity-death-so-personally; Estelle Erasmus, "Why Penny Marshall's 'Laverne' Was the Role Model That Saved Me," *AARP: The Ethel*, December 5, 2022.

Chapter 11: Analyzing Pitches

p. 141   *Among the many regular columns*: All About the Pitch announcement, *Writer's Digest*, March 6, 2021. https://www.writersdigest.com/be-inspired/writers-digest-march-april-2021-issue-reveal.

p. 142   *Where Have All the School Nurses Gone?*: Pitch for Gina Rich, "Why Are Our School Nurses Disappearing?" *Good Housekeeping*, January 24, 2020, https://www.goodhousekeeping.com/life/parenting/a30520693/school-nurse-shortage.

p. 143   *Why Doesn't Anyone Want to be Called Grandma (or Grandpa) Anymore?*: Pitch for Laurie Yarnell, "Grandparents Don't Want to Be Called 'Grandma' and 'Grandpa' Anymore," *Good Housekeeping*, October 27, 2020, https://www.goodhousekeeping.com/life/parenting/a34437946/alternative-names-grandma-grandpa.

p. 144   *I've been watching a lot of Twitch lately*: Pitch for John Alexander, "If You Can

Learn Twitch, You Can Learn Mandarin," *Wired*, February 12, 2021, https://www
.wired.com/story/twitch-chat-language-learning-mandarin-chinese.

p. 145   *I am a gamer and a freelance writer*: Pitch for Reece Rogers, "The Queer Appeal
of 'Dead by Daylight,'" *Wired*, October 27, 2020, https://www.wired.com/story
/queer-appeal-dead-by-daylight-lgbtq-community.

p. 146   *I never imagined I'd be telling my two children*: Pitch for Jamie Beth Cohen, "We
Decided to Tell Our Kids When We're Having Sex," *HuffPost Personal*, December
22, 2020, https://www.huffpost.com/entry/parents-sex-positive-kids_n_5fdba7e
4c5b610200988c105.

p. 146   *The topic of my piece is the film* Promising Young Woman: Pitch for Karen
Lewis, "I Took Revenge on My Rapist," *HuffPost Personal*, February 9, 2021,
https://www.huffpost.com/entry/promising-young-woman-rape-revenge
_n_601ff75cc5b689330e3033dd.

p. 147   *In the first year of Covid-19, I learned to fish*: Pitch for Kate Morgan, "The Year of
the Fish," *Sierra*, March 16, 2021, https://www.sierraclub.org/sierra/year-fish.

p. 149   *Luke "Strider" Jordan*: Pitch for Jacqueline Kehoe, "The Great Plains Trail Is a Work
in Progress," *Sierra*, January 5, 2023, https://www.sierraclub.org/sierra/4-november
-december/field-trip/great-plains-trail-work-progress.

p. 150   *I would like to pitch something on the pros and cons of older motherhood*: Pitch for
Linda K. Wertheimer, "Like Naomi Campbell, I'm an Older Mother," *Independent*, May 18, 2021, https://www.independent.co.uk/voices/naomi-campbell
-baby-older-mother-b1849778.html.

p. 151   *An Argument for Humor in the Addiction Memoir*: Pitch for Sarah Shotland,
"A Priest Walks into a Bar," *Creative Nonfiction*, Winter 2019, https://creative
nonfiction.org/writing/a-priest-walks-into-a-bar.

p. 152   *I Learned the Hard Way*: Pitch for Jill Reid, "I Learned the Hard Way That My
Marriage Was on the Edge of Collapse — Again," Your Tango, August 26, 2022,
https://www.yourtango.com/love/learned-hard-way-marriage-edge-collapse.

p. 153   *The Bitter Truths I Learned*: Pitch for Lara Zibarras, "Getting Pregnant Spiraled
Me into an Eating Disorder," Your Tango, September 6, 2022, https://www.your
tango.com/health-wellness/getting-pregnant-spiraled-me-into-eating-disorder.

p. 154   *With the help of our family*: Pitch for Jennie Burke, "Defying the Family Cycle of
Addiction," *New York Times*, September 18, 2020, https://www.nytimes.com
/2020/09/18/well/family/addiction-opiates-surgery-pain-management.html.

p. 155   *Sometimes the Best Thing to Do*: Pitch for Estelle Erasmus, "When to Reply on
Social Media — and When to Not," *Wired*, May 26, 2021, https://www.wired.com
/story/when-to-reply-on-social-media-and-when-to-not.

p. 155   *I loved your piece this summer*: Pitch for Emily P. G. Erickson, "What to Expect
When You're Expecting the Worst," *New York Times*, January 14, 2021, https://
www.nytimes.com/2021/01/14/parenting/pregnancy-loss-emotional-cushioning
.html.

p. 157　*I have a pitch for Narratively*: *"Music Saved My Life"*: Pitch for Juli Fraga, "Music Saved Her Life. Now She Wants to Save Yours," Narratively, March 26, 2020, https://narratively.com/music-saved-her-life-now-she-wants-to-save-yours.

Chapter 12: Your Pitch Landed

p. 163　*The negotiating experts Roger Fisher and William Ury*: Roger Fisher and William Ury, *Getting to Yes: Negotiating Agreement without Giving In* (New York: Penguin, 2011).

Chapter 14: Interviewing Experts

p. 204　*Nir Eyal, the author of* Indistractable: Nir Eyal, "Home-Schooling Tweens and Teens during Coronavirus Closings," *New York Times*, March 12, 2020, https://www.nytimes.com/2020/03/12/well/family/coronavirus-school-closings-home schooling-tweens-teens.html.

Chapter 15: Data Rush

p. 216　*When Grammy-winning singer Carrie Underwood opens her mouth*: Estelle Erasmus, "PSA: Science Says It's Totally Fine to Have Babies after 35," Parents .com, updated January 23, 2023, https://www.parents.com/getting-pregnant/age /pregnancy-after-35/psa-its-totally-fine-to-have-babies-after-35-science-backs.

Chapter 16: Researching Publications and Editor Etiquette

p. 226　*Although I unfortunately never took him up*: Estelle Erasmus, "Blowing the Best Invite of My Life," Ozy, July 28, 2017, https://web.archive.org/web/2020102 4064149/https://www.ozy.com/true-and-stories/blowing-the-best-invite-of-my -life/79797.

Chapter 17: Revising and Editing Yourself

p. 240　*"The road to hell is paved with adverbs"*: Stephen King, *On Writing: A Memoir of the Craft* (New York: Scribner, 2020), 125.

p. 241　*My former student Mimi O'Connor*: Mimi O'Connor, "My 8-Year-Old is Hopping on the Corset Trend. Should I Be Worried?" Parents.com, August 12, 2021, https://www.parents.com/kids/development/corset-trend-dangers.

p. 242　*I was that girl who would stumble*: Estelle Erasmus, "Having a Child in Midlife Cured Me of My Klutziness," Scary Mommy, December 20, 2015.

p. 243   *"I don't want to hurt your feelings, Mom"*: Estelle Erasmus, "What to Do When Your Tween Is Trash-Talking You."

p. 245   *"You are allowed no more than two or three exclamation points"*: Elmore Leonard, *10 Rules of Writing* (New York: William Morrow, 2007).

Chapter 18: Mastering the Viral Spiral

p. 249   *In a 2012 study*: J. Berger and K. L. Milkman, "What Makes Online Content Viral?" *Journal of Marketing Research* 49, no. 2 (2021): 192–205, https://doi.org/10.1509/jmr.10.0353.

p. 250   *My first piece to go viral*: Estelle Erasmus, "Why Yahoo Just Became Obsolete," BlogHer, February 24, 2013, available at https://web.archive.org/web/20130228023136/www.blogher.com/why-yahoo-just-became-obsolete.

p. 250   *When I wrote about my daughter's bad behavior*: Estelle Erasmus, "My Child Is Out of Control."

p. 251   *My most recent viral article*: Erasmus, "How to Bullyproof Your Child."

p. 252   *Judy Nelson's essay in HuffPost Personal*: Nelson, "How Going to a Dead & Company Concert with a Stranger."

p. 260   *I have a tenet that I follow*: Estelle Erasmus, "When to Reply on Social Media — and When to Not," *Wired*, May 26, 2021, https://www.wired.com/story/when-to-reply-on-social-media-and-when-to-not.

Chapter 19: Rejection Projection

p. 266   *Thanks so much for getting back to me*: Pitch for Estelle Erasmus, "Why Do People Take the Public, Social-Media Spectacle of Celebrity Death So Personally?" *Quartz*, January 9, 2017, https://qz.com/879857/why-do-people-take-the-public-social-media-spectacle-of-celebrity-death-so-personally.

p. 268   *this guided-imagery trip*: Estelle Erasmus, "Ways to De-stress This Holiday Season while Minding Your Business," *Forbes*, November 27, 2020, https://www.forbes.com/sites/estelleerasmus/2020/11/27/ways-to-destress-this-holiday-season-while-minding-your-business/?sh=34e084336a77.

p. 268   *controlled breathing not only relaxes muscles*: Waleed O. Twal, Amy E. Wahlquist, and Sundaravadivel Balasubramanian, "Yogic Breathing When Compared to Attention Control Reduces the Levels of Pro-inflammatory Biomarkers in Saliva: A Pilot Randomized Controlled Trial," *BMC Complementary Medicine and Therapies* 16 (August 2016): 294, https://doi.org/10.1186/s12906-016-1286-7.

p. 268   *another stress-reduction tactic*: Stephan Rechtschaffen, *Timeshifting: Creating More Time to Enjoy Your Life* (New York: Doubleday, 1996).

Chapter 21: Find Your Inspiration

p. 279   *"Creative visualization is the technique of using your imagination"*: Shakti Gawain, *Creative Visualization: Use the Power of Your Imagination to Create What You Want in Your Life* (Novato, CA: New World Library, 2016), 4.

p. 280   *"What we create within us is always mirrored outside of us"*: Shakti Gawain, *Living in the Light: Follow Your Inner Guidance to Create a New Life and a New World* (Novato, CA: New World Library, 2011), 102.

p. 281   *"Learning a new skill keeps your mind smart"*: Estelle Erasmus, "6 Steps to Reinvent Yourself after a Major Life Change," *Next Avenue*, September 12, 2016, https://www.nextavenue.org/6-steps-to-reinvent-yourself. See also Shirley Leanos, Esra Kürüm, Carla M. Strickland-Hughes, Annie S. Ditta, Gianhu Nguyen, Miranda Felix, Hara Yum, George W. Rebok, and Rachel Wu, "The Impact of Learning Multiple Real-World Skills on Cognitive Abilities and Functional Independence in Healthy Older Adults," *Journals of Gerontology Series B* 75, no. 6 (June 2020): 1155–69, https://doi.org.10.1093/geronb/gbz084.

Index

About the Author

Estelle Erasmus, an award-winning journalist, writing coach, and in-demand speaker, has written for over 150 publications, including the *New York Times,* the *Washington Post, AARP: The Magazine, AARP: The Girlfriend, AARP: The Ethel, Next Avenue, Newsweek,* the *New York Daily News,* the *Independent, HuffPost Personal, Good Housekeeping, Insider, Marie Claire, Wired, Vox, Salon,* and more. She has been editor in chief of five national glossy magazines, with a combined reach of over ten million readers, and a former guest editor for Narratively. She hosts the *Freelance Writing Direct* podcast, covering tips, tricks, and strategies on writing, craft, and creativity. She is an adjunct instructor teaching writing courses for NYU's School of Professional Studies/Center for Publishing and Applied Liberal Arts, wrote the *All About the Pitch* column for *Writer's Digest,* teaches for Writer's Digest University, and is a judge for the magazine's personal essay contest. She has appeared on *Good Morning America* and *Fox 5 News with Ernie Anastos* and has had her articles mentioned on *The View.*

Estelle is a member of the American Society of Magazine Editors, the American Society of Journalists and Authors, the Authors Guild, and Women's Media Group. She lives with her husband, daughter, and Havanese dog, Rose, in northern New Jersey.

You can follow her writing advice on Twitter, Instagram,
Substack, and TikTok: **@EstelleSErasmus.**
For more information, visit **EstelleSErasmus.com.**